Letts study aids

Revise Commerce

A complete revision course for O level and CSE

Bill Jones B Com, M Phil

Head of Business Studies, Churchfields High School, West Bromwich

Charles Letts & Co Ltd
London, Edinburgh & New York

First published 1985
by Charles Letts & Co Ltd
Diary House, Borough Road, London SE1 1DW

Editor: Karen Sparrock
Design: Anne Davison
Illustrations: Tek-Art

ISBN 0 85097 633 2

Printed by Charles Letts (Scotland) Limited

Acknowledgments

The author and publishers are grateful to the following organizations for permission to use artwork and other items in the following figures:

Banking Information Service for Figs. 9.2, 9.9, 9.11
Barclays Bank for Figs. 9.8, 9.13
BEAB for Fig. 13.1
British Standards Institution for Fig. 13.1
The Design Council for Fig. 13.2
Midland Bank plc for Fig. 9.10
National Girobank for Figs. 10.1, 10.2
National Westminister Bank plc for Fig. 9.7

Preface

This book has been designed to help students prepare for GCE O-Level, 16+ and CSE examinations in Commerce. It should also prove useful to those taking similar examinations such as those set by the Pitman Examinations Institute and the Royal Society of Arts.

Revise Commerce is based on a thorough analysis of all the syllabuses set by the different examination boards (a table of analysis appears on p. viii), and the major part of the book consists of a detailed study of those topics on which examination questions are likely to be set. Most benefit can be gained from *Revise Commerce* if it is used as the basis of a one- or two-year course of study and not simply for the purposes of last minute revision. The core material is followed by a self-test unit and examination questions taken from previous years. In most cases, answers are given so that you can check your progress.

I am grateful for the help which many people have given me in writing this book. In particular I must thank Clive Bentley, John Loveridge, John Luckhurst and the staff of Charles Letts and Co Ltd for their advice and support. I must also record my thanks to the following examination boards who gave permission for examination questions to be reproduced.

The Associated Examining Board (AEB)
University of Cambridge Local Examinations Syndicate (UCLES)
Joint Matriculation Board (JMB)
University of London University Entrance and School
Examinations Council (London)
Northern Ireland General Certificate of Education Examinations Board (NIEC (GCE) & (CSE))
University of Oxford Delegacy of Local Examinations (OLE)
Southern Universities' Joint Board (SUJB)
Welsh Joint Education Committee (WJEC (GCE) & (CSE))
Associated Lancashire Schools Examinations Board (ALSEB)
East Midland Regional Examinations Board (EMREB)
London Regional Examining Board (LREB)
North West Regional Examinations Board (NWREB)
The South-East Regional Examinations Board (SEREB)
South Western Examinations Board (SWEB)
The West Midlands Examinations Board (WMEB)
Yorkshire and Humberside Regional Examinations Board (YHREB)

WHJ

Contents

Part I

Introduction and guide to using this book

Revise Commerce will help you to pass your examination in Commerce providing you use the book properly. The purpose of this introduction is to guide you so that you gain most benefit from using the book.

1 Look at the syllabus analysis which appears on p. viii. You may find that there are some topics covered in the book which you do not need for the examination which you are taking. Remember, however, that the syllabus analysis gives only a general guide to syllabus requirements and you should obtain more detailed information. For advice on this look at Part IV on p. 132.

2 The topics which are usually tested in Commerce examinations form the basis of the core units of Part II. The more important points in each unit are shown in **heavy type.**

3 Read each unit carefully and then test your understanding of a unit with the corresponding self-test unit in Part III. If you get a number of answers wrong go back to the core unit and read it again.

4 In Part IV there are hints on examination technique. Make sure that you read this section. You may understand the work covered in Part II but you have to demonstrate your understanding of the work by writing good answers to examination questions.

5 In Part V there is a wide range of past questions from CSE, 16+ and GCE O-level examinations. They have been arranged so that there is a set of questions testing each of the core units. Answers to these questions are also given in Part V. Use these answers sensibly! Attempt a question first and then see how your answer compares with the one given. Remember that in some cases there are a number of correct answers possible.

Table of analysis of examination syllabuses

● Unit required for a syllabus

● Unit where only a simplified treatment is required

Unit		AEB	Cambridge	JMB	London	NIEC	OLE	SUJB	WJEC
	Level	O	O	O	O	O	O	O	O
	Syllabus	015	7100	Govn., Econs. and Commerce	100		7886	7101	0106
	Number of papers	2	1	1	1	1	1	1	1
	Multiple choice/short-answer questions	30%		30% (common core)					
	Extended-answer questions	70%	100%	20% (common core) 50% (commerce)	100%	100%	100%	100%	100%
	Coursework								
	Title								
1	Production	●	●	●	●	●	●	●	●
2	Retailing	●	●	●	●	●	●	●	●
3	Wholesaling	●	●	●	●	●	●	●	●
4	Channels of distribution	●	●	●	●	●	●	●	●
5	The middlemen of trade	●	●	●	●	●	●	●	●
6	Foreign trade	●	●	●	●	●	●	●	●
7	Business documents used in home trade	●	●	●	●	●	●	●	●
8	Business documents used in foreign trade	●	●	●	●	●	●	●	●
9	Banking: the commercial banks	●	●	●	●	●	●	●	●
10	Other kinds of bank and methods of payment	●	●	●	●	●	●	●	●
11	Buying and selling on credit	●	●	●	●	●	●	●	●
12	Advertising and marketing	●	●	●	●	●	●	●	●
13	Consumer protection	●	●	●	●	●	●	●	●
14	Insurance	●	●	●	●	●	●	●	●
15	Transport	●	●	●	●	●	●	●	●
16	Communications		●	●	●	●	●	●	●
17	Business accounts	●	●		●	●	●	●	●
18	Private sector firms	●	●	●	●	●	●	●	●
19	The issue of shares and the Stock Exchange	●	●	●	●	●	●	●	●
20	Public enterprise	●	●	●	●	●	●	●	●
21	Income and saving	●	●	●	●	●	●	●	●
22	Government spending and income	●		●			●	●	●

Cambridge/WMEB	**ALSEB**	**EAEB**	**EMREB**		**LREB**		**NIEC**	**NREB**	**NWREB**	**SEREB**	**SREB**	**SWEB**	**WJEC**	**WMEB**	**YHREB**		
16+ (O/GCE)	CSE	CSE	CSE	CSE	CSE	CSE	CSE	CSE	CSE	CSE	CSE	CSE	CSE	CSE	CSE	CSE	
					A	B			12A	05A	R	1710	0207		A	B	
1	1	1	1	2	1	1	2	1	1	2	1	2	1	1	1	1	
30%	15%	25%	20%	20%	30%	20%	40%	35%	20%	20%	30%	50%	40%	20%	80%	40%	
50%	60%	55%	50%	80%	70%	60%	40%	40%	55%	30%	70%	50%	60%	60%		60%	
20%	25%	20%	30%			20%	20%	25%	25%	50%			Optional	20%	20%		*Unit*
•	•	•	•	•	•	•	•	•	•	•	•	•	•	•	•	•	**1**
•	•	•	•	•	•	•	•	•	•	•	•	•	•	•	•	•	**2**
•	•	•	•	•	•	•	•	•	•	•	•	•	•	•	•	•	**3**
•		•	•	•	•		•	•	•	•	•	•	•			•	**4**
•	•	•	•	•	•		•	•	•	•	•	•	•	•	•	•	**5**
•	•	•	•	•	•		•	•	•	•	•	•	•	•	•	•	**6**
•	•	•	•	•	•	•	•	•	•	•	•	•	•	•	•	•	**7**
										•							**8**
•	•	•	•	•	•	•	•	•	•	•	•	•	•	•	•	•	**9**
•	•	•	•	•	•	•	•	•	•	•	•	•	•	•	•	•	**10**
•	•	•	•	•	•	•	•	•	•	•	•	•	•	•	•	•	**11**
•	•	•	•	•	•	•	•	•	•	•	•	•	•	•	•	•	**12**
•	•	•	•	•	•	•	•	•	•	•	•	•	•	•	•	•	**13**
•	•	•	•	•	•	•	•	•	•	•	•	•	•	•	•	•	**14**
•	•	•	•	•	•	•	•	•	•	•	•	•	•	•	•	•	**15**
•	•	•	•	•	•	•	•	•	•	•	•	•	•	•	•	•	**16**
•		•	•	•	•			•	•	•		•	•	•	•		**17**
•		•	•	•	•	•	•	•	•	•	•	•	•	•	•	•	**18**
•		•	•	•	•	•	•	•	•	•	•	•	•	•	•	•	**19**
•		•	•	•	•	•	•	•	•	•	•	•	•	•	•	•	**20**
•	•	•	•	•	•	•	•	•	•	•	•	•	•	•	•	•	**21**
•			•	•		•	•	•	•		•	•	•	•	•		**22**

Examining boards

GCE Boards

AEB	Associated Examining Board Wellington House, Aldershot, Hampshire GU11 1BQ from 1 Jan 1986: Stag Hill House, Guildford, Surrey GU2 5XJ
Cambridge	University of Cambridge Local Examinations Syndicate Syndicate Buildings, 1 Hills Road, Cambridge CB1 2EU
JMB	Joint Matriculation Board Manchester M15 6EU
London	University Entrance and School Examinations Council University of London, Stewart House, 32 Russell Square, London WC1B 5DN
NIEC	Northern Ireland Schools GCE Examinations Council Beechill House, 42 Beechill Road, Belfast BT8 4RS
Oxford	Oxford Local Examinations Delegacy of Local Examinations, Ewert Place, Summertown, Oxford OX2 7BX
SUJB	Southern Universities' Joint Board for School Examinations Cotham Road, Bristol BS6 6DD
WJEC	Welsh Joint Education Committee 245 Western Avenue, Cardiff CF5 2YX

16+ Boards

Cambridge/WMEB	See Cambridge or WMEB address

CSE Boards

ALSEB	Associated Lancashire Schools Examining Board 12 Harter Street, Manchester M1 6HL
EAEB	East Anglian Examinations Board The Lindens Lexden Road, Colchester, Essex CO3 3RL
EMREB	East Midland Regional Examinations Board Robins Wood House, Robins Wood Road, Apsley, Nottingham NG8 3NH
LREB	London Regional Examinations Board Lyon House, 104 Wandsworth High Street, London SW18 4LF
NIEC	Northern Ireland Schools CSE Examinations Council Beechill House, 42 Beechill Road, Belfast BT8 4RS
NREB	North Regional Examinations Board Wheatfield Road, Westerhope, Newcastle upon Tyne NE5 5JZ
NWREB	North West Regional Examinations Board Orbit House, Albert Street, Eccles, Manchester M30 0WL
SEREB	South East Regional Examinations Board Beloe House, 2/4 Mount Ephraim Road, Royal Tunbridge Wells, Kent TN1 1EU
SREB	Southern Regional Examinations Board 53 London Road, Southampton SO9 4YL
SWEB	South Western Examinations Board 23-29 Marsh Street, Bristol BS1 4BP
WJEC	Welsh Joint Education Committee 245 Western Avenue, Cardiff CF5 2YX
WMEB	West Midlands Examination Board Norfolk House, Smallbrook Queensway, Birmingham B5 4NJ
YHREB	Yorkshire and Humberside Regional Examinations Board 31-33 Springfield Avenue, Harrogate, North Yorkshire HG1 2HW

Part II Core Units

1 Production

1.1 Producers and Consumers

Anyone involved, at any stage, in the provision of **goods** *or* **services** is a **producer.** Thus a typist providing a service in a steelworks is just as much a part of production as those directly involved in making steel.

In contrast, **consumers** are members of the public who use goods and services. Part of consumer spending is on **necessities** (food and drink, clothing and shelter) which are essential for survival. The rest is spent on **luxuries** (televisions, cameras etc).

1.2 Branches of Production

Production can be divided into:

1 **Industry**
2 **Commerce**
3 **Direct services**

1 **Industrial** workers can be divided into (a) extractive, (b) manufacturing, and (c) constructive.

Extractive workers obtain raw materials and food from the land and the sea. Examples of such workers are farmers, fishermen, coalminers and workers on oil rigs.

Manufacturing workers take the raw materials from extractive industry and convert (or change) the raw materials into semi-finished or finished products. Thus sand and other raw materials will be used to make glass windscreens for cars.

Constructive workers take the products from manufacturing industry and build, for example, roads and houses. Those who **assemble,** for example, cars are also part of the constructive industry.

2 **Commerce** is concerned with the means by which raw materials and finished products are distributed to those who wish to buy them. The activities which make up commerce are shown in Fig. 1.1.

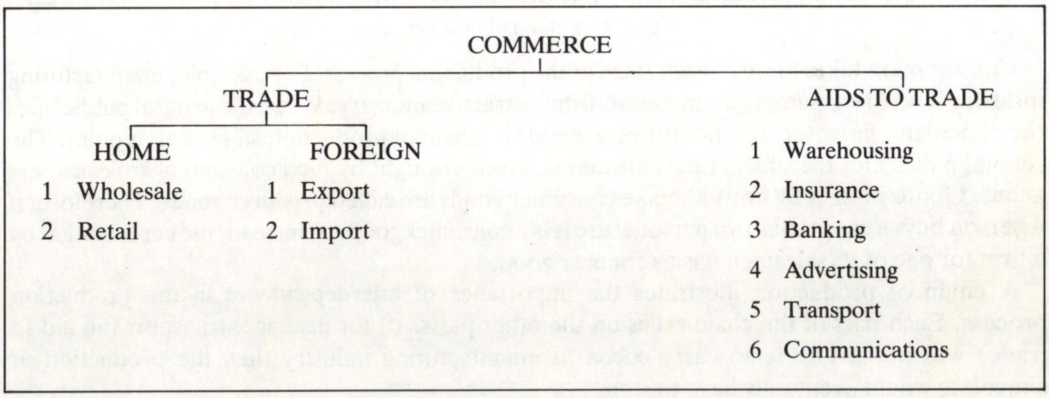

Fig. 1.1 The divisions of commerce

The basic commercial activity is **trade** which is the **buying and selling of goods.** Thus in home trade **wholesalers** buy goods from manufacturers and sell them to **retailers** who, in turn, sell goods to the general public. In foreign trade goods are sold to **(exports)** and bought from **(imports)** other countries.

So that trade can easily take place the **aids** (or **ancillaries**) to trade are necessary. Thus, for example, warehousing is needed to store goods. Insurance provides compensation if goods are stolen and banking allows payments to be made by cheque and borrowing using loans and overdrafts. Advertising makes goods known to the public. Transport enables goods to be delivered by sea to other countries and communications allows firms to make contact by telephone.

The activities just described are only a few examples of trade and aids to trade. More detail of each division of commerce will be found in later units.

3 Those involved in **direct services** are not concerned with the provision of goods but, instead, provide personal services to the public. Examples of such workers are doctors, dentists, the police, teachers and entertainers.

It is true that those working, for example, in banks and shops also provide a service to the public. Such workers have already been classified as commercial workers and do not, therefore, belong to direct services. Direct service workers are an important part of production because (a) an educated and healthy work force allows the output of goods and services to be increased and (b) the demand by individuals for direct services rises with the improvement in a country's standard of living.

1.3 Primary, Secondary and Tertiary Industry

Another classification of industry which is sometimes used is that of:

1 Primary industry, which is another name for extractive industry.
2 Secondary industry, which includes the manufacturing and constructive industries.
3 Tertiary industry, which includes commerce and direct services.

1.4 Chains of Production

A **chain of production** shows the different stages of production necessary so that a good can eventually reach the final consumer. Fig. 1.2 shows a simplified chain of production for chocolate.

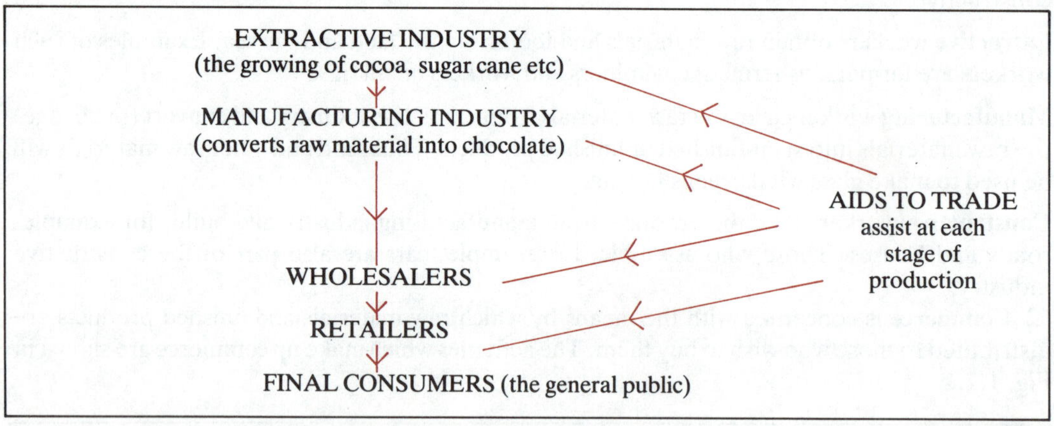

Fig. 1.2 A chain of production

Consumption takes place at each stage of the production process. For example, manufacturing industry buys or consumes raw materials from extractive industry. When the general public buys the chocolate, however, it is not for resale and the chain of production stops at that point. The general public are, therefore, **final** consumers. Goods bought by final consumers are **consumer goods.** Goods bought by firms to make consumer goods are called **producer goods.** Therefore, if a person buys a car for his own personal use it is a consumer good. If, instead, the car is bought by a firm for one of its salesmen it is a producer good.

A chain of production illustrates the importance of **interdependence** in the production process. Each part of the chain **relies** on the other parts. If, for instance, transport (an aid to trade) was not available to carry cocoa to manufacturing industry then the production of chocolate would eventually have to stop.

1.5 Mass Production and Economies of Scale

A feature of modern production is that it often takes place on a very large scale (**mass production**) which results in lower average costs of production (**economies of scale**). Thus, in Fig. 1.3 as the output of television sets increases the cost of producing each television set falls.

Output of television sets	*Average costs of production* £
10 000	260
20 000	250
30 000	230

Fig. 1.3 Economies of scale

Economies of scale result from:

1 buying economies — because large firms can buy in large quantities (in bulk) they can obtain supplies at low prices.

2 financial economies — larger firms can obtain finance more cheaply than small firms e.g. through the issue of shares.

3 risk bearing economies — large firms can spread their risks through being involved in the production of a number of quite different products. A small firm may only be able to produce one type of product and, if sales of that product fall, the small firm will be badly hit.

4 managerial economies — large firms are able to employ specialists such as accountants and personnel officers which a smaller firm would not be able to do. This is an application of the **division of labour** (see Unit 1.7).

5 technical economies — larger firms can afford to buy more specialized and efficient machinery such as computer systems.

Although there are advantages to most firms in becoming larger there could be a loss in efficiency as firms become too large to manage. If this happens average costs of production can rise as output increases and **diseconomies of scale** can occur.

1.6 Horizontal Growth, Vertical Growth and Diversification

There is an incentive for firms to become larger in order to achieve economies of scale. Such a growth in the size of a firm can occur **internally,** or, more easily, by **taking-over** other firms. Whichever method is used a number of types of growth can be identified.

1 Horizontal growth: this occurs when one firm expands in the same line as its existing activities, e.g. a supermarket chain opening another branch.

2 Vertical growth (a) **forward:** this occurs when a firm moves forward along the chain of production into the activities of its customers, e.g. a manufacturer of shoes opening up its own shoe shops; (b) **backward:** this occurs when a firm moves back along the chain of production into the activities of its suppliers, e.g. a butcher taking over a meat wholesaler.

3 Diversification: this occurs when one firm moves into quite a different area, e.g. a manufacturer of cigarettes taking over a manufacturer of potato crisps.

1.7 Specialization by Individuals

Specialization or the **division of labour** occurs when individuals concentrate on producing those things at which they are most efficient. The production process is, therefore, divided into a large number of small tasks to allow specialization to take place. Thus in a car assembly plant one group of employees will spend all their time putting in windscreens while a different group will put on tyres.

Advantages of specialization

1 Firms can select workers with aptitudes for specific tasks.

2 An employee will find it easier and quicker to learn a job if it is a small task.

3 By continually performing a small task employees become more skilled and output increases.

4 No time is lost because employees do not have to switch from job to job.

5 Because the production process is divided into a series of small tasks, specialized machinery can be used for these tasks, e.g. equipment to tighten the wheels on a car.

6 As a result of the division of labour firms become more efficient and are able to produce more goods at lower cost which, in turn, benefits consumers.

There are, however, a number of possible disadvantages of specialization.

Disadvantages of specialization

1 Because workers only perform one task they may get bored and output will fall.

2 When there is specialization interdependence increases and if one group of employees goes on strike then other parts of the chain of production will be affected.

3 As machines are developed to carry out small tasks labour might be replaced by machines and unemployment created.

4 If more machinery is used individual craftsmanship is lost and standardized goods result. Thus when the consumer buys a washing machine there is little difference in the machines produced by the different manufacturers.

1.8 Other Examples of Specialization

As well as individuals specializing in the production process, **firms, regions within countries** and **countries** also specialize. Fig. 1.4 gives examples of such specialization.

	Specialization by	*Area of production*
Firms	British Leyland	cars
	The Prudential	insurance
Regions within countries	The City of London	financial services
	Worcestershire	fruit
Countries	France	wine
	Japan	electronic goods

Fig. 1.4 Examples of specialization

1.9 Exchange

To show the importance of exchange it is necessary to identify three types of economy.

1 Subsistence (or peasant or primitive) economy

2 Barter economy

3 Money economy

1 In a **subsistence** economy there is little specialization and exchange. People grow and make everything they need for themselves. This is sometimes called **direct production** because people obtain goods without help from others. **Indirect production,** in contrast, is where others help to produce part of a person's needs as in the case of the barter and money economies.

2 In a **barter** economy there is more specialization. **Surpluses** result and **exchange** is necessary. For example, a farmer may concentrate on growing wheat. Some of the wheat will be consumed by the farmer but some will be left over (the surplus). This surplus of wheat will then have to be exchanged for the surpluses produced by others. In a barter economy, however, only goods are exchanged and **no money** is involved. This can lead to difficulties such as:

(a) the double coincidence of wants— a farmer with a surplus of wheat wishes to obtain clothes. The farmer, therefore, has to find a person with a surplus of clothes who needs wheat!

(b) the problem of valuing goods— since money is not used in a barter economy a price system does not operate. It is, therefore, difficult to fix an 'exchange rate' between different goods.

(c) the indivisibility of goods— some goods, e.g. live animals, cannot be split into smaller parts and this makes exchange for smaller items impossible.

(d) the storage of some goods— a surplus of perishable goods cannot be stored for exchange at a later date.

3 Because of the problems associated with a barter economy a **money** economy was developed in which money is used as a **medium of exchange** and a **price system** is able to operate. In a money economy there is considerable specialization and exchange. Surpluses are created and sold for money and this money is then used to buy goods and services.

1.10 Money

Forms of money

Money is anything which is **acceptable** in the **payment of a debt.** In the past shells, cattle, grain and beads have all been used as forms of money, but in modern economies the main forms of money include notes, coins, current account balances, credit cards, and postal orders.

Of these, current account balances are the most important because most payments are made using cheques.

Characteristics of money

Although acceptability is the most important characteristic of money other desirable features include:

1 portability — easily carried;
2 durability — will last a long time;
3 divisibility — can be divided into smaller amounts;
4 easily recognized — notes do not have to be closely examined before they are accepted;
5 uniform in quality — all 50 pence coins are of the same quality;
6 scarcity — if notes and coins are too freely available prices will rise and the public will be reluctant to hold on to money for very long.

Functions of money

A form of money is important because money fulfils a number of important functions. Money is a:

1 **measure of value** which allows a price system to operate.
2 **means of exchange** which allows goods and services to be more easily bought and sold.
3 **store of wealth.** A person's savings (or wealth) can be measured using money.
4 **means of deferred payment.** When consumers buy on credit, for example, the amount they owe is measured using money.

Money and legal tender

Legal tender is money which **must** be accepted in payment of a debt. Notes are legal tender up to any amount but coins are only legal tender up to certain amounts. For example, 50 pence coins are legal tender up to £10, other 'silver' up to £5 and 2 pence and 1 pence coins up to 20 pence. **Cheques** are **not** legal tender because creditors can legally refuse to accept them if they are offered in payment of debts.

2 Retailing

2.1 The Position of Retailers in the Chain of Production

Retailers are the final link in the chain of production. They are part of trade and **sell goods to the general public.** Larger retailers usually buy goods in bulk directly from manufacturers but the smaller retailer often has to buy in smaller bulk from wholesalers (see Fig. 2.1).

Manufacturers ⟶ Larger retailers
Manufacturers ⟶ Wholesalers ⟶ Smaller retailers

Fig. 2.1 How retailers are supplied

2.2 Services Provided by Retailers

The services that a retailer provides for the public will vary from retailer to retailer. However, there are three main services which are performed by **all** retailers. These are:

1 **to provide the goods that customers want.** A clothes shop in a poor neighbourhood would not stock expensive goods because such clothes would probably not sell.

2 to provide the goods **when** customers want them. Some retailers stay open late for those who are unable to shop during the day.

3 to provide goods **in suitable quantity** for customers. Large and small retailers buy in bulk and then have to split up this bulk into smaller quantities which are more suitable for the needs of customers. The word 'retail' does, in fact, mean to split into smaller quantities.

In addition to these three main functions a retailer could provide any of the following services:

4 delivery to homes;
5 ordering goods not in stock;
6 giving advice, particularly for technical goods;
7 repairing goods;
8 providing credit.

2.3 Types of Retailer

2.3.1 Small shops

Small shops are sometimes called **unit** shops when there is only one branch, although a small shop, by definition, can have up to nine branches. They are often run by families operating as sole traders or partnerships (see Units 18.3 and 18.4) and, for this reason, they are also called **independent retailers.** They usually specialize in a narrow range of goods, e.g. butchers, tailors, greengrocers, grocers, and are usually located in the suburbs where they are near people's homes. They normally buy their goods from wholesalers.

Advantages to the customer

1 There is a friendly atmosphere and the shopkeeper often knows the customer by name.

2 The shop is near the customer's home and the expense of travelling to a shop is therefore reduced or eliminated.

3 The shop may open at times which suit the customer e.g. on a Sunday morning.

4 The customer may be able to pay for goods at the end of the week (informal credit).

5 The shopkeeper may take orders and then deliver to the customer's home.

6 The shopkeeper may work hard to provide an efficient service because he owns the shop and will benefit from increased trade.

7 The owners of small shops are able to give specialist advice to customers because they have concentrated on selling a narrow range of goods, e.g. advice on hi-fi equipment.

Disadvantages to the customer

1 The major disadvantage is that prices are often higher in small shops. Small shops cannot afford to buy in very large quantities and the prices at which they buy goods are therefore higher than those paid by the larger retailers who can buy in greater bulk directly from manufacturers.

2 The small shop may not have a very wide range of goods because the shop cannot afford to buy or stock a large selection of goods.

3 Some of the goods sold by small shops may not sell quickly and therefore may not be in good condition when bought by the customer.

The declining importance of small shops is shown by the fact that their share of the retail trade has fallen significantly in the last twenty years and a large number of small shops have had to close. The major cause of this decline has been the competition from chain (or multiple) stores which have been able to charge much lower prices. To try to halt this decline many small shops now belong to **voluntary chains** or **groups** or buy from **cash and carry wholesalers** (see Unit 3.4.) The increasing importance of large multiples is shown in Fig. 2.2.

	percentage share of the retail trade 1978	1980	1982
Single outlet retailers (with one branch)	32	30	28
Small retailers (with between two and nine branches)	15	14	15
Large multiple retailers (with ten or more branches)	28	31	33
Co-operative societies	7	7	6
Large mixed businesses (department stores, variety chain etc)	14	14	14
Mail order	4	4	4
	100	100	100

Source: Retail Trade in the United Kingdom 1983, Euromonitor Publications Ltd.

Fig. 2.2 Retail sales by form of organization

2.3.2 Chain (or multiple) stores

Chain (or multiple) stores must have at least **ten** branches and are usually owned by public limited companies (see Unit 18.6). Some chain stores are **specialist** chain stores because they concentrate on selling a narrow range of goods, e.g. Currys (electrical goods), Burton's (men's clothing), H. Samuel (jewellery). **Variety** chain stores, in contrast, sell a wide range of goods e.g. Marks & Spencer, Boots. (A number of variety chain stores were originally specialist chain stores which have diversified e.g. 'Boots the Chemist'.) Chain stores are often located in town centres but some, particularly those selling groceries, are also found in the suburbs.

An important feature of the organization of a chain store is the control by the head office—this is called **centralization.** Head office will make all the important decisions concerning the chain e.g. what goods to buy, the quantities to be bought, from which manufacturers to buy, what advertising to use. It is then the responsibility of each branch manager to follow closely the instructions from head office although there may be some 'local' decisions which the branch manager will have to make, e.g. head office may tell a branch manager how many staff can be employed, but it will be up to the manager to select such staff.

Effects and benefits of centralization

1 Head office is able to buy in bulk from manufacturers on behalf of the chain, and can obtain goods at lower prices.

2 The chain becomes more efficient because head office can employ such specialists as buyers, advertisers and accountants to run the chain.

3 All the branches within one chain are identical e.g. in store layout, in outside appearance, in the goods sold and prices charged. Such **standardization** allows national advertising to take place.

4 If goods are not selling in one branch they can be transferred to a different branch. Also, if losses are made by one branch then these can be covered by the profits of more successful branches. These are examples of chain stores being able to **spread their risks.**

Advantages to the customer

1 The major advantage is that prices are usually lower because of bulk buying.
2 Many chain stores have their **own brands** e.g. Winfield (Woolworth), St. Michael (Marks & Spencer) which are sold more cheaply than goods carrying the manufacturer's brand name.
3 Goods will be of identical quality and price at all branches within one chain store.
4 If a customer is dissatisfied with goods bought these can usually be exchanged at any branch of that chain store.
5 Many of the chain stores sell goods using self-service which many customers prefer (see Unit 2.4).

Disadvantages to the customer

1 The journey to a chain store may be inconvenient if only a few items are needed.
2 It is often difficult to get advice particularly where there is self-service.
3 Shopping is impersonal because the customer's name is not known.
4 As a chain store gets larger it may be difficult to manage effectively and the customer may suffer, e.g. an order may get lost.

2.3.3 Department stores

A department store sells a very wide range of goods e.g. food, electrical goods, carpets, clothing, furniture. It is, therefore, sometimes described as **a collection of shops under one roof** but under the control of one firm which is usually a public limited company.

Department stores often occupy very large buildings in expensive city centre sites where they are able to attract a large number of customers. Each store is divided into a number of departments and each of these departments specializes in a particular type of good or service. In some stores each department is controlled by a **buyer** who is responsible for the activities of that department. The buyer has to decide what goods to buy for his department and what prices to charge, although the buyers employed by one store will, in turn, be responsible to the general manager of that store for the profitability of their departments. A high standard of service is given in department stores; there are many assistants to give advice, credit is relatively easy to obtain, and restaurants and cloakrooms are provided.

It is possible for a firm to own only one or a small chain of department stores but the trend, increasingly, has been towards mergers between department stores to form larger **multiple department stores.** For example, House of Fraser and Debenhams now own a large number of department stores throughout the United Kingdom. Unlike the smaller department stores which still rely on the buyer acting for his own department, the larger multiple department stores buy centrally and the responsibilities of the buyer are reduced becoming more like those of a branch manager of a chain store (see Unit 2.3). In addition to the advantages of bulk buying the multiple department store can also enjoy other economies of scale including national advertising and management expertise.

Advantages to the customer

1 The customer can choose from a wide selection of goods and can buy all that is needed without leaving the store.
2 There are many assistants to serve and give advice.
3 Shopping is more comfortable because restaurants, lifts and cloakrooms are provided.
4 Goods can be ordered by telephone.
5 Delivery and credit are usually available.

Disadvantages to the customer

1 The major disadvantage is that prices are high because of the many services provided and because the department store is often located in city centres where rent and rates are high.
2 A customer has to travel to the city centre to shop at such a store.
3 Some customers dislike shopping at department stores because such stores are regarded as exclusive and for the rich only. Such a view is changing, however, as department stores have had to alter their image to attract as many customers as possible.

2.3.4 Mail order

Mail order firms, which are usually public limited companies, sell by:

1 using **part-time agents,** who are often housewives, operating on a **commission** basis. Customers choose goods from catalogues and place orders with the agents. The goods are then delivered directly to the customer or sent to the agent who will pass them on to the customer.

2 directly contacting the public by, for example, sending catalogues to potential customers, placing advertisements in newspapers and on television or by delivering pamphlets to homes. Goods ordered are then sent directly to the customer and no selling agent is involved at any stage.

There are a number of ways in which payment can be made for goods bought from mail order firms.

1 Cash can be sent or a credit card number can be quoted when the order is placed i.e. **cash with order** (CWO).

2 Cash can be paid when the goods are delivered i.e. **cash on delivery** (COD).

3 Goods can be bought on **credit** and the payment spread over, say, twelve or twenty-four months. Weekly or monthly payments would then have to be made to the mail order firm. Such credit is usually of the deferred payment type (see Unit 11.2).

4 Transcash (see Unit 10.3.6).

Advantages to the customer

1 Credit can be easily obtained.

2 Goods can be chosen at leisure in the comfort of the customer's home which is particularly helpful for those who are at work all day.

3 Mail order is useful for those who live far away from shops or who cannot easily get to shops e.g. the disabled.

4 Certain goods can be obtained through mail order which are not available in local shops or for those living in rural areas where the choice of goods may be limited.

Disadvantages to the customer

1 Prices are often higher than in chain stores. Although the mail order firm benefits from being able to buy goods in bulk and not having to use expensive sites for shops, such benefits can be outweighed by the high costs of running a mail order operation e.g. postage, packing, catalogues, advertising, bad debts.

2 It takes time for goods to arrive.

3 Advertisements can be misleading and the goods may not be of the quality expected by the customer.

4 Advice cannot be easily obtained because the buyer and seller do not meet.

5 Perishable goods (such as fresh vegetables) cannot be bought on mail order.

6 It is more difficult to exchange items bought on mail order.

2.3.5 Retail co-operative societies

Retail co-operative societies are different from other forms of retailing because of the principle of co-operation which affects the way in which they are organized. The main features of a retail co-operative society are:

1 open membership — anyone over the age of 16 years can become a member (shareholder) of a co-operative society by buying shares for any amount between £1 and £10 000.

2 democratic control — each member of a society is allowed only one vote no matter how many shares that member has purchased. Thus, when electing a management committee to run the society, a shareholder who has paid in the maximum of £10 000 has the same voting rights (one vote) as the shareholder who has paid in the minimum of £1.

3 payment of interest on shares — a limited amount of interest is paid on the sums shareholders have contributed to the society.

4 distribution of the surplus (profit) of the society — the profits of many retail co-operative societies are given to customers in the form of **dividend stamps** although some societies distribute profits by lowering prices. The number of stamps given to a customer is based on the value of goods that customer has bought. The stamps are collected in special books and full books can be:

(a) exchanged for **cash,**

(b) exchanged for **goods,** *or*

(c) added to the share capital of the customer, provided, of course, that he/she is a shareholder in the society.

In Fig. 2.3, the book of stamps has the lowest value when it is exchanged for cash.

Value of one book of dividend stamps when:	
exchanged for cash	40p
exchanged for goods	50p
added to share capital	50p

Fig. 2.3 The value of dividend stamps

Goods and services sold by co-operatives

Retail co-operative societies are involved in a number of activities which, together, cover most kinds of retailing. There are some societies which:

1 own shops that specialize in a narrow range of goods e.g. selling groceries or shoes or operating freezer centres.

2 own variety chain stores or department stores.

3 provide services directly to the public e.g. milk and bread deliveries to homes, laundries and funeral services.

In addition, the Co-operative Bank Ltd and the Co-operative Insurance Society which are owned by the Co-operative Wholesale Society (CWS) (see Unit 3.6) provide banking and insurance services.

Advantages to the customer

1 The customer knows that he can become a member of the society and can influence the way in which it is run.

2 The customer can benefit from the educational, social and welfare benefits which co-operatives provide for members.

Disadvantages to the customer

1 Prices in smaller co-operatives are high because they cannot buy in the same bulk as, for example, multiple stores.

2 Many possible customers believe that the image of the retail co-operative is too old-fashioned.

Problems faced by retail co-operative societies

The disadvantages of shopping at co-operatives have clearly outweighed the advantages because the co-operatives' share of the retail trade has fallen significantly in the last thirty years. This has been due to:

1 the existence of far **too many small retail societies.** Although 'the co-op' is a familiar name throughout the country each town or district used to have its own co-operative society which was quite separate from and independent of other co-operative societies. Such small, local societies were unable to achieve the economies of scale especially bulk-buying gained by their major competitors which were the large multiples.

2 **poor management.** Many of the smaller societies, in particular, did not have sufficiently experienced managers, and the running of such societies was hampered by the inexperience of the management committees whose members were drawn from the shareholders of the co-operative.

3 **insufficient capital** to finance the development of new stores and the renovation of existing ones.

To improve their trading position societies have merged (many of the smaller societies have been taken over by the larger ones), and unprofitable branches have been closed. A particular feature has been the expansion of Co-operative Retail Services Ltd (CRS) which is now the largest retail co-operative in the United Kingdom. CRS is different from other retail societies because it is a national organization with branches throughout the country. The other societies, although they have increased in size, are still regional.

Economies of scale have been achieved. As societies merged and became larger more experienced managers could be recruited and bulk buying became easier to achieve. (The role of the Co-operative Wholesale Society is particularly important in the purchase of goods for retail co-operative societies.)

Advertising has been increased and shops have been modernized to try to improve the 'old-fashioned' image of the co-operative shop.

2.3.6 Hypermarkets

A hypermarket, e.g. Carrefour, is very large and must, by definition, have a selling area of **at least 4650m²**. It is often situated on the edge of a town where there is enough reasonably priced land available. Its location is also close to main roads and motorways because it needs to attract customers from a wide geographical area who will drive to the store. For this reason large car parks are available and other services for motorists are provided like cheap petrol or tyre fitting. To attract the whole family to the store restaurants and play areas are often provided.

The hypermarket is mostly self-service and sells a wide range of mostly cut-price goods including groceries, clothing, gardening equipment and televisions. The range of goods is therefore greater than a grocery chain store but not as great as a department store.

Advantages to the customer

1 Prices are low because the hypermarket can buy in bulk.
2 A large variety of items can be bought at one shop.
3 Parking is easier when compared with shopping in city centres.

Disadvantages to the customer

1 The cost of petrol may make it uneconomic for a customer to travel a long distance to a hypermarket.
2 If a product is not available at a hypermarket an alternative shop at which to purchase that product could be many miles away.

The development of hypermarkets in the United Kingdom has been slow. Many local authorities have been unwilling to give planning permission for such stores because developments on the outskirts of a town could result in a loss of green belt areas. If a hypermarket becomes very successful then a loss of trade could result for town centre shops which might close and cause a loss in rates for the local authority. It would also involve the building of more roads near the hypermarket in order to ease traffic congestion.

2.3.7 Discount stores

Discount stores are sometimes called discount warehouses but they are **retailers** and not wholesalers. They specialize in selling, for example, electrical goods, furnishings or wines and spirits, e.g., Comet, Trident. They are able to sell at low prices because they can buy in bulk, self-service is often employed, a minimum standard of display is used in shops, and charges are made for services such as delivery to customers' homes. They are usually located on the edges of city centres but near main roads so that there is access for customers. They rely heavily on advertising and detailed price lists are often displayed in press advertisements.

Advantages to the customer

1 Prices are low.
2 Detailed price lists help the customer to compare different goods.

Disadvantages to the customer

1 Little advice is available.
2 A wide range of goods may not be available because the store will concentrate on selling the more popular brands.

2.3.8 Doorstep selling, mobile shops and party selling

Traders go from door-to-door selling cleaning products, encyclopaedias (**doorstep selling**), greengroceries, groceries, ice-cream (**mobile shops**). Housewives arrange parties where goods such as household items, jewellery or clothes are sold e.g. Tupperware (**party selling**).

Advantages to the customer

1 The customer does not have to travel to shops.
2 Goods can be demonstrated at home.

Disadvantages to the customer

1 Prices are usually high.
2 Competitors' goods cannot be seen or compared.

2.3.9 Local markets

A local market is usually held on the same days each week and consists of a number of stalls which cover a wide range of products. The market trader rents his selling area from the organizer of the market which is often a local authority.

Advantages to the customer

1 Prices are low because the market trader has few expenses.
2 Bargaining can take place.
3 Goods are sometimes 'sold off' at cheaper prices at the end of a day.

Disadvantages to the customer

1 It may be difficult to exchange goods.
2 In bad weather shopping can be uncomfortable in open markets (although a number of markets are covered).

2.3.10 Automatic vending

Coin-operated vending machines are used to sell products such as cigarettes, confectionery or soft drinks. The machines are located outside shops, in railway stations and in hotels.

Advantages to the customer

1 Goods are available twenty-four hours a day.

Disadvantages to the customer

1 Prices are high.
2 Machines are sometimes jammed and it is often difficult to find anyone that can help or to get a refund.

2.4 Self-service and Self-selection

Self-service occurs when goods, which are clearly priced, are set out on shelves within easy reach of customers. Customers select the goods they want and place them in a basket or trolley which is taken towards the exit where one or more check-outs are placed. All the goods are paid for at once and taken from the premises by the customer. There is no delivery service provided (but there might be a 'carry-out' service to the car). A store rarely has 100% self-service, however, and there could be a **counter service** for items like cigarettes, wine or fresh meat. Self-service is used extensively by supermarkets, superstores and hypermarkets (Fig. 2.4 gives one possible classification of these types of retailer). A number of small shops have also introduced self-service.

	Minimum selling area	*Number of checkouts*	*Self-service and selling*
Supermarkets	2000 ft^2 (186m^2)	at least 3	mainly food
Superstores	25 000 ft^2 (2325m^2)	10—20	food plus a wide to very wide range of non-food
Hypermarkets	50 000 ft^2 (4650m^2)	at least 15	food plus a limited to wide range of non-food

Fig. 2.4 Classification of supermarkets, superstores and hypermarkets

In contrast, **self-selection** employs the same ideas as self-service except that cash points are dotted throughout the store. A customer can therefore pay for an item at one cash point and then move to another part of the shop, select a second item and pay for it at a different cash point. Self-selection is used by variety chain stores and department stores. The growth of self-service and self-selection has been helped by the development of **branding** and **packaging** (see Unit 12.8) and by the need for shops to reduce their wage costs by cutting the numbers of sales staff.

Advantages to the retailer

1 Sales increase because many customers prefer self-service and they can inspect goods before purchase.
2 Prices are reduced because of lower wage costs.
3 **Impulse buying** occurs because of attractive displays, i.e. customers will buy goods they did not originally intend to buy.

Disadvantages to the retailer

1 Converting shops to self-service can be expensive e.g. the costs of shelving or installation of security devices.
2 Some custom may be lost from those who prefer counter service.
3 Pilfering may occur which will reduce the retailer's profit.

Advantages to the customer

1 Selection of goods is easy.
2 Prices are clearly marked.
3 Shopping is often quicker.
4 Prices are low particularly if **loss-leaders** are used.
(A loss-leader is an item which a shop sells at below cost price. The intention is to attract the customer into the shop to buy the loss-leader which is usually a basic foodstuff e.g. bread or sugar. While in the shop the customer will buy other items thus allowing the shop to make a profit overall. Loss-leaders work best for self-service shops where they can be placed in such a position that the customer has to pass many other products to reach them.)

Disadvantages to the customer

1 Advice or assistance is often difficult to obtain.
2 Impulse buying could result in over-spending.
3 There could be delays at check-outs.

2.5 Recent Developments in Retailing

2.5.1 Shopping precincts

A shopping precinct (or centre) is an area **exclusively** devoted to shops e.g. Bull Ring (Birmingham), Victoria Centre (Nottingham), Brent Cross Centre (London). Such a precinct consists of a whole range of shops including department stores, variety and specialist chain stores and small shops. A number of precincts have been purpose-built, often on a number of floors, with escalators, lifts, car parks, information desks for shoppers, security patrols and special access for vehicles delivering to precinct shops. Where towns have not been able to have purpose-built precincts a similar effect has been achieved by banning traffic from shopping areas, a process known as **pedestrianization.**

2.5.2 Franchising

Franchising occurs when a person or firm (the **franchisee**) rents the name, product and method of selling from the owner of the franchise (the **franchisor**). The franchisee is also given the **exclusive** right to operate the franchise in a given geographical area. The franchisee pays an initial franchise fee and further payments linked to turnover and/or profits are also made to the franchisor. The franchisor helps the franchisee by:

1 **advising** on the location of the franchise,
2 giving **training** in running the franchise,
3 **supplying** materials and equipment at competitive prices,
4 **advertising** on behalf of all the franchisees within one chain.

Franchising is found in catering (Wimpy, Kentucky Fried Chicken), car maintenance, printing and a wide range of other trades suitable for small businesses. A number of franchisors belong to the **British Franchise Association** which is a trade association (see Unit 13.6) responsible for standards within this form of retailing.

2.5.3 Use of technology

A feature of the retail trade has been the increasing use made of electronic equipment. Examples are:

1 electronic checkouts. Many grocery items already have, on their labels, **bar codes** (Fig. 2.5)

5 010003 003118

Fig. 2.5 A bar code

which contain information about an item such as the manufacturer's name or the brand name of the product. At the check-out these labels can be passed through a laser beam which reads the information and transmits it to the electronic cash register. The register then produces for each customer an accurate and detailed list of the items bought. With this type of cash register the cashier does not have to key in any information about the items purchased.

2 light pens. Light pens can be used to scan the bar codes of those products on the shelves of a store. This allows the firm to know precisely what goods are in stock.

The effects of the **increased use** of electronic equipment in shops include: fewer mistakes at check-outs; customers can move through check-outs more quickly and shops can have more precise information about what goods are in stock. There will then be less likelihood of stock shortages and surpluses.

3 Wholesaling

3.1 The Functions of Wholesalers

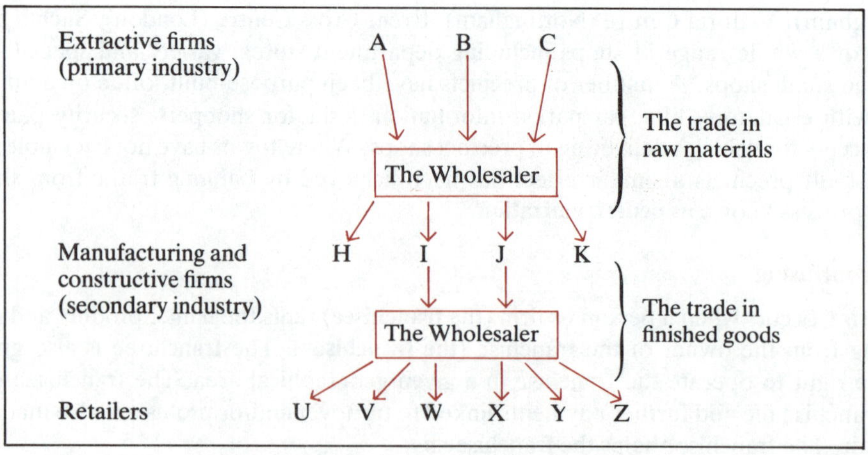

Fig. 3.1 The importance of the wholesaler

The wholesaler can be important at two stages in the chain of production (Fig. 3.1). In the early stages of the chain the wholesaler buys **raw materials** (primary products) from primary industry and then sells the material to secondary industry. When raw materials have been converted into manufactured goods (**finished goods**) the goods are bought by wholesalers for resale to retailers. The wholesaler, therefore, provides important services to both manufacturers and retailers although in some chains of production the wholesaler is not used (see Unit 3.2).

Services provided by wholesalers to manufacturers

The wholesaler:

1 sells raw materials obtained from home and abroad to manufacturers.

2 buys finished products in **bulk** from home and foreign manufacturers. The selling costs of manufacturers are reduced because they only deal with large orders.

3 stores raw materials and finished products which reduces the need for manufacturers to have warehousing.

4 can make advance or immediate payments to manufacturers.

5 provides information for manufacturers; by talking to retailers the wholesaler can discover which of a manufacturer's products are liked by the public.

6 evens out price fluctuations. When the price of a raw material is **increasing** a wholesaler, already storing large quantities of this raw material, can release some on to the market preventing the price from rising as much. When the price of a raw material is **falling** the wholesaler releases less of it on to the market.

7 finds a market for the goods of manufacturers by persuading retailers to buy them.

8 takes over some of the risks of manufacturers. There is always the risk that the price of a finished product may fall or the product may go out of fashion and not sell. If the wholesaler buys goods immediately they have been manufactured then the risks will no longer be borne by the manufacturer but by the wholesaler.

9 can collect goods from manufacturers thus reducing the need for manufacturers to obtain transport.

Services provided by wholesalers to retailers

The wholesaler:

1 sells finished goods to retailers.

2 breaks bulk for retailers. The wholesaler buys finished goods in very large quantities from the manufacturer but sells to retailers in much smaller quantities.

3 stores goods so that retailers can quickly obtain supplies.

4 stocks a wide range of goods from many manufacturers.

5 can give credit to retailers thus reducing the need for retailers to borrow from other sources.

6 provides information for retailers by giving details of new products about to be introduced by manufacturers.

7 evens out price fluctuations (see also point 6 — services to manufacturers).

8 takes over some of the risks of retailers by storing goods.

9 delivers to retailers.

10 can grade, pack and blend products for retailers e.g. wine can be bottled, tea can be graded and then blended.

3.2 THE DECREASING IMPORTANCE OF THE WHOLESALER

The importance of the wholesaler in the distribution of finished goods from manufacturers to retailers has declined because of other ways in which this distribution can be achieved (Fig. 3.2). In Fig. 3.2 a distinction should, however, be made between those methods of distribution where:

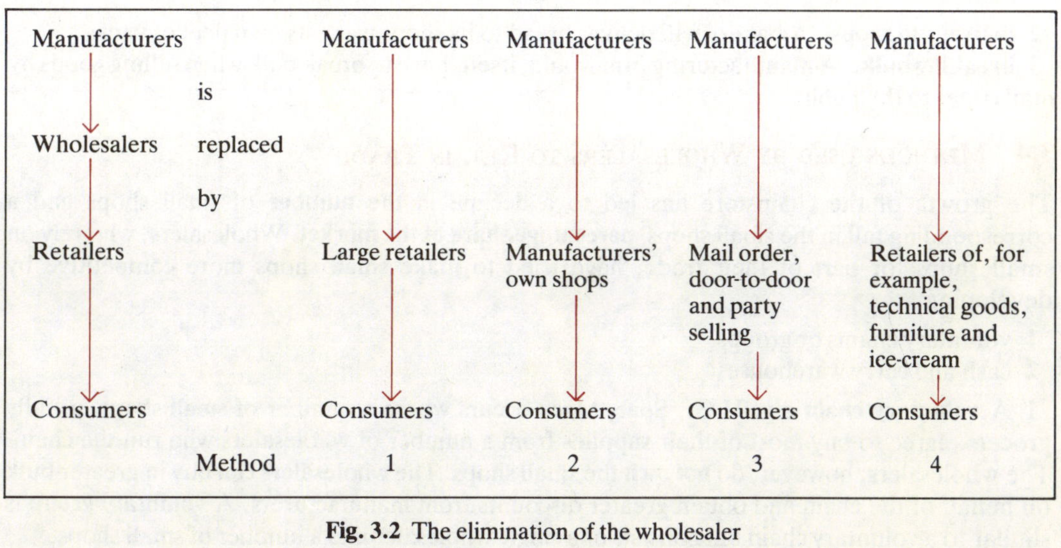

Fig. 3.2 The elimination of the wholesaler

1 the wholesaler has played a rôle but **that rôle has become less important** and has been replaced by other methods of distribution (Methods 1, 2 and 3 in Fig. 3.2). For example, the increasing importance of chain stores, which are able to buy in bulk from manufacturers, has reduced the need for wholesalers.

2 the wholesaler has **never played a significant rôle** (Method 4 in Fig. 3.2). For example, because furniture is a high cost/high bulk product which is sold in relatively large retail outlets, there is no advantage to be gained from distribution through wholesalers.

Method 1 Large retailers are able to buy in extremely great bulk from manufacturers, and the growth of packaging and branding (see Unit 12.8) has also helped to make this method of distribution much more important.

Method 2 A number of manufacturers have taken over the rôles of both wholesaler and retailer by opening their own shops in order to achieve greater control over the sales of their own products to the public e.g. in the sale of shoes and beer. This method can also result where retailers set up factories to manufacture products to be sold in their shops e.g. Boots has integrated backwards.

Method 3 The wholesaler is also eliminated when manufacturers sell to the public using mail order, door-to-door and party selling (see Unit 2).

Method 4 A number of goods has always been directly sold by manufacturers to retailers, e.g. technical goods like computers and cars, goods with a low rate of turnover (see Unit 17.3) like furniture, or perishables like bread and ice-cream.

Methods 2 and 3 are often referred to as **direct selling** or **direct dealing** because manufacturers sell directly to consumers through their own retail operations.

3.3 The Functions of Wholesalers which are not Eliminated

Unit 3.2 has dealt with the methods of distribution where the wholesaler is not required. However, **not all** of the wholesale functions are eliminated and several **still need to be performed.** For example, the functions of:

1 warehousing. A large chain store might have a number of regional depots to store goods bought from manufacturers (Fig. 3.3).

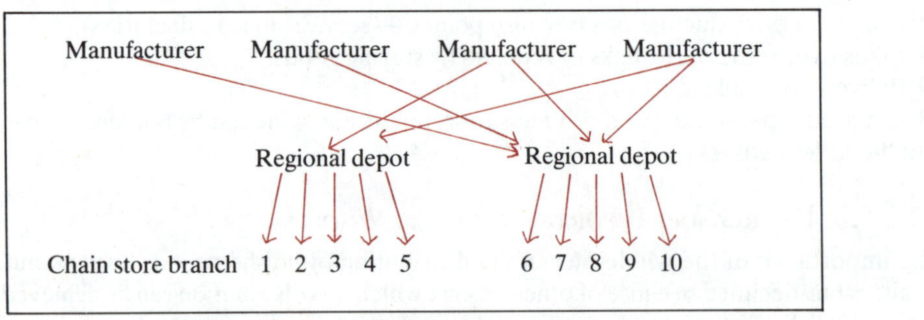

Fig. 3.3 The regional depots of a chain store

2 delivery to shops. A bakery will deliver bread to its shops using its own fleet of vans.

3 breaking bulk. A manufacturing firm would, itself, have to break bulk when selling goods by mail order to the public.

3.4 Methods used by Wholesalers to Retain Trade

The growth of the chainstore has led to a decline in the **number** of small shops and a corresponding fall in the small shops' **percentage share of the market.** Wholesalers, who rely on small shops for part of their trade, have tried to make small shops more competitive by developing:

1 voluntary chains or groups
2 cash and carry warehouses

1 A **voluntary chain** e.g. V.G., Spar, Mace occurs where a number of **small shops,** usually grocers, agree to buy most of their supplies from a number of wholesalers who run the chain. The wholesalers, however, do **not own** the small shops. The wholesalers can buy in greater bulk on behalf of the chain and obtain greater discounts from manufacturers. A voluntary **group** is similar to a voluntary chain but consists of a **single** wholesaler and a number of small shops.

Advantages to the small retailer of belonging to a voluntary chain (group)

(a) Cheaper supplies can be obtained which are passed on to the public in the form of lower prices.
(b) The shop has access to the chain's own brands which would not otherwise be available.
(c) The chain advertises nationally and provides display materials for use in shops e.g. posters for shop windows.
(d) Loans can be obtained from the chain for refitting a shop.

Disadvantages to the small retailer of belonging to a voluntary chain (group)

(a) The small shop will be less independent and decisions about products stocked and advertising will be made by the chain itself and not by the small shop.
(b) The success of the small shop will be closely linked to the success of the chain.

2 To reduce expenses, a cash and carry wholesaler **does not offer credit** or **delivery** and the warehouse is operated like a supermarket with self-service and check-outs.

Advantages to the small retailer of buying from a cash and carry wholesaler

(a) Prices are cheaper because the wholesaler's expenses are lower.
(b) The small shop has immediate access to the warehouse and does not have to wait for delivery.

Disadvantages to the small retailer of buying from a cash and carry wholesaler

(a) There is no delivery and therefore the shopkeeper needs both to use his own vehicle and to find time to visit the wholesaler.
(b) Credit is not available.

3.5 The Location and Organization of Wholesale Warehouses

Location of a wholesale warehouse

When deciding the location of a warehouse the wholesaler has to bear in mind:
1 the nearness of the warehouse to customers viz. retailers.
2 the nearness of the warehouse to suppliers viz. manufacturers.
3 the availability of good transport facilities e.g. nearness to a motorway.
4 other factors such as the cost and availability of labour and land and whether there are any planning restrictions.

If a wholesaler has to distribute over a wide area he may decide, like a chain store (see Fig. 3.3), to have a number of smaller regional warehouses spread across this wide area instead of having just one major warehouse.

Organization of a wholesale warehouse

The organization of a wholesale warehouse will vary from warehouse to warehouse and will depend upon such considerations as the size of the wholesaling operation and the range and type of products being handled. One possible structure is shown in Fig. 3.4.

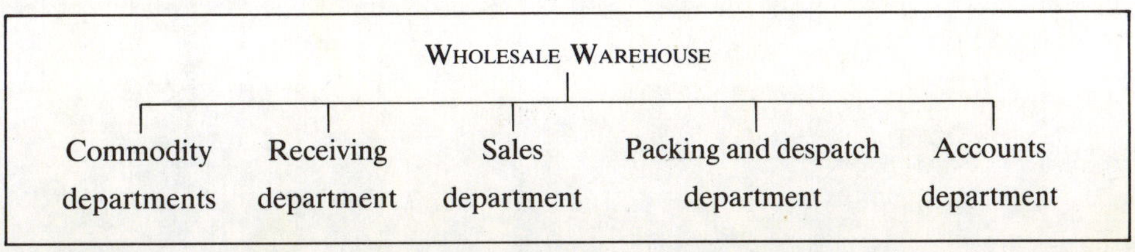

Fig. 3.4 The departments of a wholesale warehouse

Commodity departments The warehouse may have a number of commodity departments each of which specializes in a particular product. A **buyer** will be in charge of each of these departments and, as in a department store, will be responsible for buying goods for his department.

Receiving department It is the function of the receiving department to check and store goods delivered to the warehouse.

Sales department The sales department is responsible for dealing with orders placed by customers. These orders can be received by telephone, through the post, through the warehouse's own representatives calling on shops or through visits by retailers to the wholesaler's showrooms.

Packing and despatch department The packing and despatch department is responsible for ensuring that the correct goods are delivered to customers. Where a wholesaler still packs and blends commodities then these functions may be performed by this department.

Accounts department The accounts department deals with payments to suppliers, from customers, to employees and so on. Where goods are sold on credit this department will also ensure that the credit limit of a customer has not been exceeded.

3.6 Types of Wholesaler

There are many types of wholesaler, or middlemen of trade (see Unit 5), involved in commercial activity and these include:

1 **specialist** wholesalers dealing in a **narrow** range of goods e.g. petroleum products

2 **general** wholesalers dealing in a **wide** range of goods e.g. by stocking groceries, electrical goods and hardware

3 **cash and carry** wholesalers (see Unit 3.4)

4 the **Co-operative Wholesale Society** (CWS) The CWS supplies the retail co-operative societies with many of their products. Some of these products are made by the CWS, e.g. those using the Co-op brand name, while other products are bought from different manufacturers. It is also involved in extractive industry e.g. by owning tea plantations and has additional interests including ownership of the Co-operative Insurance Society and the Co-operative Bank.

The CWS is controlled by representatives drawn from individual retail co-operative societies who elect a board of directors to run the CWS. The number of votes which representatives can cast is related to the volume of trade of each retail society. Retail societies receive a dividend on purchases from the CWS.

4 Channels of distribution

4.1 Introduction

Channels of distribution refer to the different ways in which goods can move from **producers to consumers.** Thus, in the case of **manufactured goods,** one channel is from manufacturer to wholesaler to retailer to consumer (see Fig. 3.2). To enable goods to reach consumers a number of activities are usually present in each channel. These are:

1 **buying and selling,** e.g. wholesalers selling to retailers
2 **storage,** e.g. chain stores storing goods in regional depots
3 **transport,** e.g. goods moving from regional depots to chain store branches
4 **advertising,** e.g. retailers informing customers of the goods available in shops

The channels of distribution for manufactured goods have been dealt with in Unit 3. The purpose of Unit 4 is to deal with the channels of distribution for: **foodstuffs** and **raw materials.**

4.2 The Distribution of Foodstuffs

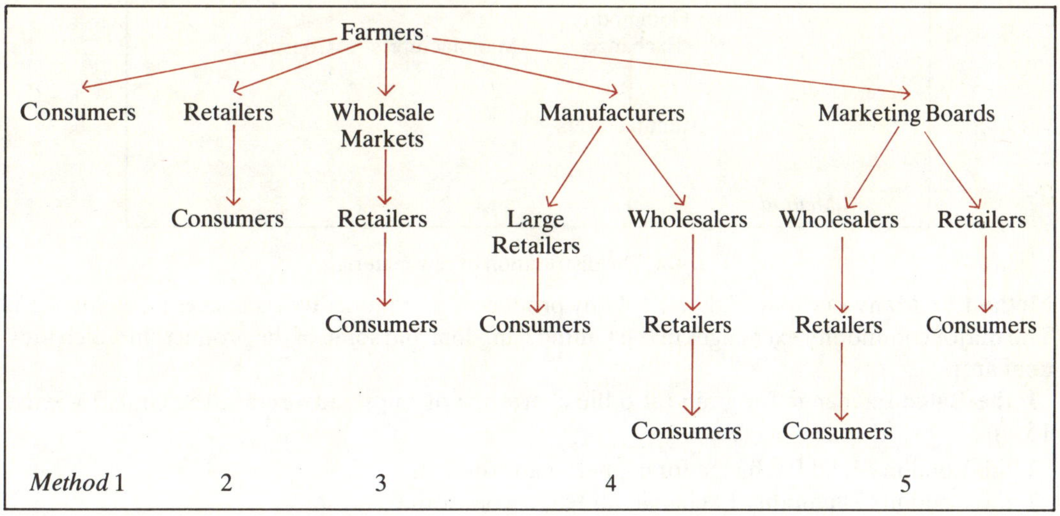

Fig. 4.1 Channels of distribution for foodstuffs

Method 1 Farmers can sell directly to consumers using, for example, farm shops.

Method 2 This is where a producer sells his produce directly to retailers. For example, a greengrocery chain might agree to buy all the potatoes produced by a farmer.

Method 3 Some producers may sell to wholesalers or retailers via a **wholesale (produce) market.** The wholesale markets may be local, serving a particular city, or national, serving the whole country. Examples of national markets include Smithfield (meat), Billingsgate (fish) and New Covent Garden (fruit and vegetables). Other foodstuffs might be sold via commodity exchanges (see Unit 4.5).

Method 4 A manufacturer could agree, in advance, to buy the whole output of a producer of foodstuffs. An example of this would be a vegetable canning firm which signs an agreement with a farmer producing peas. The tinned peas are then distributed directly to large retailers or via wholesalers to smaller retailers.

Method 5 This is where farmers sell to marketing boards (e.g. the **Milk Marketing Board**) which, in turn, sell to wholesalers and retailers.

4.3 Marketing Boards

Marketing boards are set up by Acts of Parliament and usually deal in **agricultural output.** Their functions are to regulate the supply and sale of specified foodstuffs and they can compel producers to sell their output to them. Marketing boards are particularly important in developing countries where agricultural output is an important source of foreign currency.

Benefits to farmers of marketing boards

Marketing boards operate in different ways but they can:

1 guarantee prices for farmers.
2 advertise to stimulate demand.
3 supply, for example, seed and equipment.
4 give advice.
5 provide loans at favourable rates of interest.
6 collect output from farms.
7 provide storage facilities, particularly for non-perishable output.
8 give subsidies to farmers.
9 retail output in some cases.

4.4 The Distribution of Raw Materials

Many raw materials, which include mining and some agricultural output, are distributed via the channels shown in Fig. 4.2. These raw materials can be imported or home-produced.

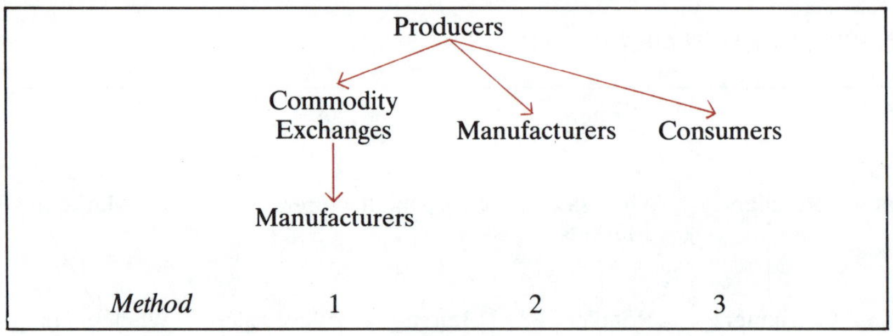

Fig. 4.2 The distribution of raw materials

Method 1 Many raw materials are sold by producers on **commodity exchanges** (see Unit 4.5). The major commodity exchanges in the United Kingdom and some of the products in which they deal are:

1 the Baltic Exchange for grain (also the chartering of ships and aircraft, see Units 15.5 and 15.8)
2 the London Metal Exchange for copper, lead, zinc, tin
3 the London Commodity Exchange for tea, cocoa, coffee, sugar
4 the Liverpool Cotton Exchange for cotton

Method 2 A number of large manufacturers are able to buy in sufficient bulk so they can make contracts directly with producers thus by-passing the commodity exchanges.

Method 3 Some raw materials, e.g. coal, can be sold directly to consumers.

4.5 Commodity Exchanges

A commodity exchange is a market (see Unit 4.6) where primary products can be bought and sold. The methods of selling used on the exchanges are determined by the nature of the commodities involved (Fig. 4.3).

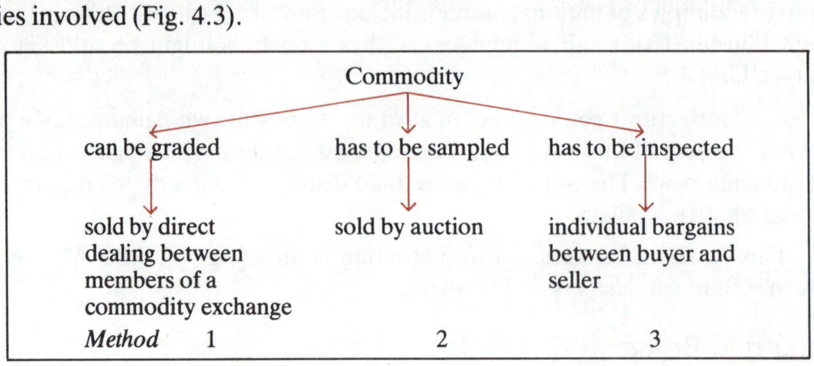

Fig. 4.3 Methods of selling commodities

Method 1 Some commodities can be **accurately graded** and **described** e.g. wheat, cotton, sugar, metals. A manufacturer could, therefore, agree to buy a consignment of US dark northern spring No 1 14% wheat from an importer without first having to see the commodity. The description of the wheat is an accurate guide to its quality.

Method 2 Some commodities, such as tea or wool, **cannot be graded** and have to be sold by **sample.** A buyer will, therefore, inspect a sample taken from a consignment of tea and this sample will be an accurate guide to the quality of the whole consignment. Commodities of this kind are sold by **auction.**

Method 3 Commodities like diamonds cannot be sold by sample because consignments of the commodity vary so much in quality. In this case a **whole consignment** would have to be inspected by potential buyers who would then have to make their own individual agreements with sellers of these commodities.

Spot and futures dealing on commodity exchanges

A **spot** deal is where a contract is signed for the **immediate** delivery of a commodity. The price at which the deal is struck is the 'spot' price and such deals can be arranged in all commodities.

A **futures** deal is an agreement for the delivery of a commodity at a date in the **future** (forward delivery) but at a price agreed on the day the contract is signed. Futures deals are only possible for those commodities which can be **accurately graded.**

Date for delivery	*Price of sugar (£/tonne)*
Spot (10 September)	157
October	168
December	176
March	187

Fig. 4.4 Spot and futures prices of sugar

Fig. 4.4 shows that a buyer of sugar can agree, on 10 September, to pay £187/tonne for a consignment of sugar to be delivered the following March.

Futures dealings are used by:

1 manufacturers who want to be sure of taking delivery of raw materials at a **fixed date** and at a **fixed price** in the future. Uncertainty is reduced for the manufacturers who can more easily plan ahead.

2 speculators whose aim is to make a **profit.** For example, a speculator agrees to buy 500 tonnes of sugar at £176/tonne to be delivered in December (Fig. 4.4). By December, however, the 'spot' price of sugar has risen to £200/tonne. The speculator sells 500 tonnes of sugar at this price and has therefore made a profit of 500 × £24 = £12 000 less dealing expenses.

Speculators:

(a) can contract **to buy and/or to sell** commodities on a futures basis.
(b) can make a **loss** if prices move against them.
(c) never take delivery of a commodity.

3 buyers and sellers of commodities as a **hedge** against future price movements.

For example a manufacturer of flour buys grain, for **immediate delivery,** at the current spot price (*Contract 1*). This grain is to be manufactured into flour which will be on sale in, say, three month's time. If the price of grain falls during those three months the manufacturer will have to accept a lower price for his flour. To cover this possible loss the manufacturer signs another contract to **sell a futures** in grain. (*Contract 2*— the **hedging** contract.)

The price of grain now falls

The manufacturer makes a **loss** on *Contract 1* because the price obtained for flour is less than expected. He has, however, made a **profit** on *Contract 2* because he can buy spot grain at a price lower than that which he receives on his forward sale. In practice, the manufacturer would not have to buy spot grain to fulfil the futures contract but would simply receive from the dealer the **difference** between the spot price and the futures price. The profit on *Contract 2,* therefore, offsets the loss made on the sale of flour.

The price of grain, instead, rises

The manufacturer makes a **profit** on *Contract 1* because the price obtained for flour is higher than expected. A **loss** is made on *Contract 2* because the spot price of grain is now greater than the futures selling price.

Whether there is a price rise or price fall the manufacturer has covered himself and the only 'loss' as a result of the two contracts are the dealing expenses involved. Manufacturers feel that it is worth paying such expenses as a form of 'insurance' against much greater losses which could result from large changes in commodity prices.

4.6 Markets

Commodity exchanges are examples of **markets** because, at these exchanges, **buyers and sellers** are able to **contact one another.** Deals can then be arranged and prices established. Some markets are **carefully regulated** and only elected members are able to buy and sell, as on commodity exchanges and the London Stock Exchange.

A market may be at a **specific location** e.g. the London Metal Exchange. In this market the prices of metals are established using **ring trading.** Ring brokers gather round in a circle and shout out the price at which they are prepared to buy or sell a particular metal. Each metal is traded for a short period of time and a market price for a metal is eventually agreed which satisfies both buyers and sellers.

A market, however, need **not** be in a specific place. Manufacturers wishing to buy large quantities of a metal may prefer to bypass the London Metal Exchange and deal directly with mining firms abroad. Such dealing can be carried out using letter, telephone or telex and the development of quicker systems of communications has helped such markets to develop (as with the foreign exchange market). Once buyers and sellers have made contact, by whatever means, a market has been established.

5 The middlemen of trade

5.1 Introduction

The **middlemen of trade** are involved in the distribution of raw materials, foodstuffs and manufactured goods at home and abroad. Because they operate at stages between industry and the final consumer they are sometimes referred to as **intermediaries** who act as links in the chain of distribution. There are those who buy and sell on their **own** account when they act as **principals** and hope to make a **profit.** They can also act as **agents** for **others** and receive **commission** or **fees.**

5.2 Types of Middlemen

1 Wholesalers

The wholesaler acts as a **link** between the manufacturer and the retailer (see Unit 3).

2 Retailers

The retailer acts as a link between the manufacturer and/or wholesaler and the consumer (see Unit 2).

3 Brokers

A broker is an **agent** who arranges **deals** for buyers and sellers. Thus an importer might employ a broker to sell a consignment of copper for him on the London Metal Exchange. Alternatively a manufacturer could employ a broker to buy a similar consignment. A broker does **not possess** and is **not responsible** for the delivery of the goods in which he deals. He **cannot arrange contracts** in his own name and **must** give the name of his principal. The broker's reward is **commission.**

4 Factors

A factor is an agent responsible for **selling** but not buying goods for his principal. Unlike a broker he **possesses the goods** in which he deals and can **make contracts in his own name.** A factor's reward is **commission.** This type of factor should not be confused with a financial factor (see Unit 11.4).

5 Del credere agents

A del credere agent is one who takes on the additional rôle of **guaranteeing** that a customer is **solvent** and that he **will pay for goods bought.** If the customer does not pay then the del credere agent is **liable** for the debt. Such an agent is paid an additional commission as a reward for the extra risk which he takes.

6 Merchants

In home trade the wholesaler is an example of a merchant and is sometimes described as a **wholesale** merchant. In foreign trade there are **export** merchants and **import** merchants who trade in goods just like a wholesaler. A merchant operates **on his own account** and his reward is **profit.**

7 Export houses

Where a manufacturer does not have the expertise to sell goods abroad he might use an export house to carry out such work for him. An export house can act as a **principal** by buying the goods from the manufacturer or as an **agent** by arranging selling contracts.

8 Forwarding, packing and shipping agents

Their functions are to pack goods safely, usually for export, and then to arrange all the formalities of **transport,** e.g. booking space on a ship. These types of agent earn **fees.**

6 Foreign trade

6.1 International Specialization

International specialization occurs when countries concentrate on the production of particular goods and services e.g.

Saudi Arabia	oil
Brazil	coffee
Switzerland	banking
The United Kingdom	insurance

As a result of specialization a country is able to produce a **surplus,** that is, an output which is greater than that which is required for its own consumption. International or foreign trade, which is the buying and selling of goods and services between countries, is then needed to

exchange the unwanted surplus for the surpluses of other countries. A simplified two-country model of exchange is shown in Fig. 6.1.

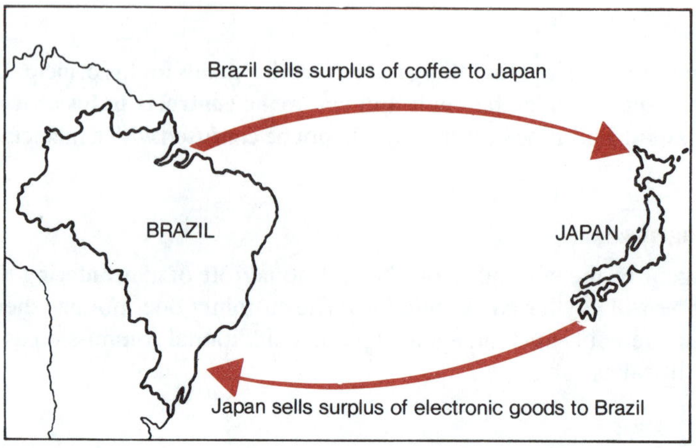

Fig. 6.1 Exchange of surpluses

6.2 Reasons for Specialization

The United Kingdom **cannot produce certain goods** because:

1 some raw materials do not occur naturally in the United Kingdom. Thus, the United Kingdom could not extract large quantities of gold.

2 the United Kingdom does not have the right climate to grow certain products.

3 some goods would be too expensive to produce. Although it might be possible to create, at high cost, the right conditions in which to grow coffee, this coffee would be far too expensive to be able to compete with Brazilian coffee in world markets.

It is therefore, more sensible for the United Kingdom to specialize or concentrate on producing those goods and services at which it is most efficient, that is, at which it has a **comparative advantage.** Thus, the United Kingdom specializes in making aircraft engines and providing insurance services, and the foreign currency earned can be used to buy goods such as coffee. As a result of international specialization and trade all countries can benefit from increased world output.

6.3 The Importance of Foreign Trade to the United Kingdom

Foreign trade is important to the United Kingdom because:

1 some raw materials such as the ores of many metals, do not occur naturally in the United Kingdom and have to be imported so that goods can be manufactured.

2 it is cheaper for other countries to produce certain goods, e.g. Japanese motorcycles.

3 selling goods and services abroad provides the United Kingdom with foreign currency with which to buy imports.

4 the United Kingdom provides many financial services, on an international level, which are dependent on a high level of foreign trade e.g. the insurance of ships and their cargoes by Lloyd's of London.

5 by selling abroad, the United Kingdom gains the benefits of wider markets. Mass production can then occur which brings the benefits of economies of scale (see Unit 1.5).

6 it creates employment in the United Kingdom.

7 consumers in the United Kingdom have a wider variety of goods from all over the world.

8 it increases United Kingdom income which results in a higher standard of living.

6.4 The Balance of Payments

The balance of payments for a country is a record of the foreign currency paid to and received from other countries in a given period of time. Fig. 6.2 gives an imaginary example of the balance of payments figures for the United Kingdom.

The balance of payments records inflows and outflows of foreign currency. **Inflows** of foreign currency arising e.g. from the sale of exports, represent gains in foreign currency and are shown by plus signs. **Outflows** or losses in foreign currency resulting, e.g. from the purchase of imports, are shown by minus signs.

	£m		
Visible exports	+200	a balance of trade (or visible balance) of £−150m	1
Visible imports	−350		
Invisible exports	+500	an invisible balance of £+100m	2
Invisible imports	−400		
Current account balance	−50		3
Investment and other capital flows	−40		4
Total currency flow	−90		5
Official financing			6
Borrowing from the IMF	+40		
Borrowing from foreign central banks	+30		
Fall in reserves	+20		
	+90		

Fig. 6.2 An imaginary example of the UK balance of payments

1 Visible trade is the trade in **goods** between countries. Visible **exports** are the goods which the United Kingdom sells to other countries, aircraft engines to France for example. Visible **imports** are the goods which the United Kingdom buys from other countries. An example of this could be French or German wine.
The **balance of trade** or **visible balance** = **visible exports** − **visible imports.**
In Fig. 6.2 the balance of trade = £200m − £350m = −£150m. This is a **deficit** because there is an overall **loss** in foreign currency as a result of the trade in goods.

2 Invisible trade is the trade in **services** between countries. Invisible **exports** are the services which the United Kingdom sells to other countries, e.g. a foreign ship being insured at Lloyd's of London. Invisible **imports** are the services which the United Kingdom buys from other countries, e.g. UK citizens holidaying in Spain.
The **invisible balance** = **invisible exports** − **invisible imports.**
In Fig. 6.2, the invisible balance = £500m − £400m = +£100m. This is a **surplus** because there is an overall **gain** in foreign currency as a result of the trade in services.

3 The **balance of payments on current account** includes both the trade in goods and services, i.e. visibles and invisibles, and is given by either:
(a) (visible exports + invisible exports) − (visible imports + invisible imports)
In Fig. 6.2, the balance on current account (current balance) = £(200 + 500)m − £(350 + 400)m = £700m − £750m = −£50m; *or*
(b) the **visible balance** + the **invisible balance**
In Fig. 6.2, the balance on current account (current balance) = −£150m + £100m = −£50m.
As a result of the trade in goods and services, therefore, the United Kingdom has a deficit on current account of £50m which represents a loss in foreign currency.

4 Investment and **capital flows** are not directly concerned with the trade in goods and services, which are recorded in the current account, but include items such as
(a) a foreign company spending money to build a factory in the UK which would result in an inflow of foreign currency, *or*
(b) a company moving deposits from a UK bank to a bank in the USA to take advantage of higher American interest rates. This represents an outflow of foreign currency.

In Fig. 6.2 the figure of −£40m for investment and other capital flows represents a net loss of foreign currency.

5 The **total currency flow** shows how much foreign currency has been paid out or received as a result of:
(a) the trade in goods and services, *and*
(b) investment and capital flows.

It thus shows the overall position for the balance of payments of a country. In Fig. 6.2, therefore, the total currency flow of −£90m represents an **overall balance of payments deficit.**

6 Official financing shows the way in which a balance of payments deficit is financed or the purposes to which a balance of payments surplus is put. In Fig. 6.2, the deficit of £90m is financed by:

(a) borrowing from the International Monetary Fund (IMF). The IMF is an international organization with funds available to help countries with balance of payments deficits.

(b) borrowing from the central banks of other countries.

(c) drawing on UK reserves of foreign currency.

Since the balance of payments must always balance, the total for official financing must exactly match the total currency flow. Thus, for Fig. 6.2, the total currency flow of −£90m is exactly matched by official financing of +£90m. A balance of payment **surplus,** in contrast, could be used

(i) for repaying the International Monetary Fund
(ii) for repaying the central banks of other countries
(iii) by the Bank of England to lend to other countries in balance of payments difficulties
(iv) for adding to the United Kingdom's reserves of foreign currency.

6.5 The United Kingdom Balance of Payments on Current Account

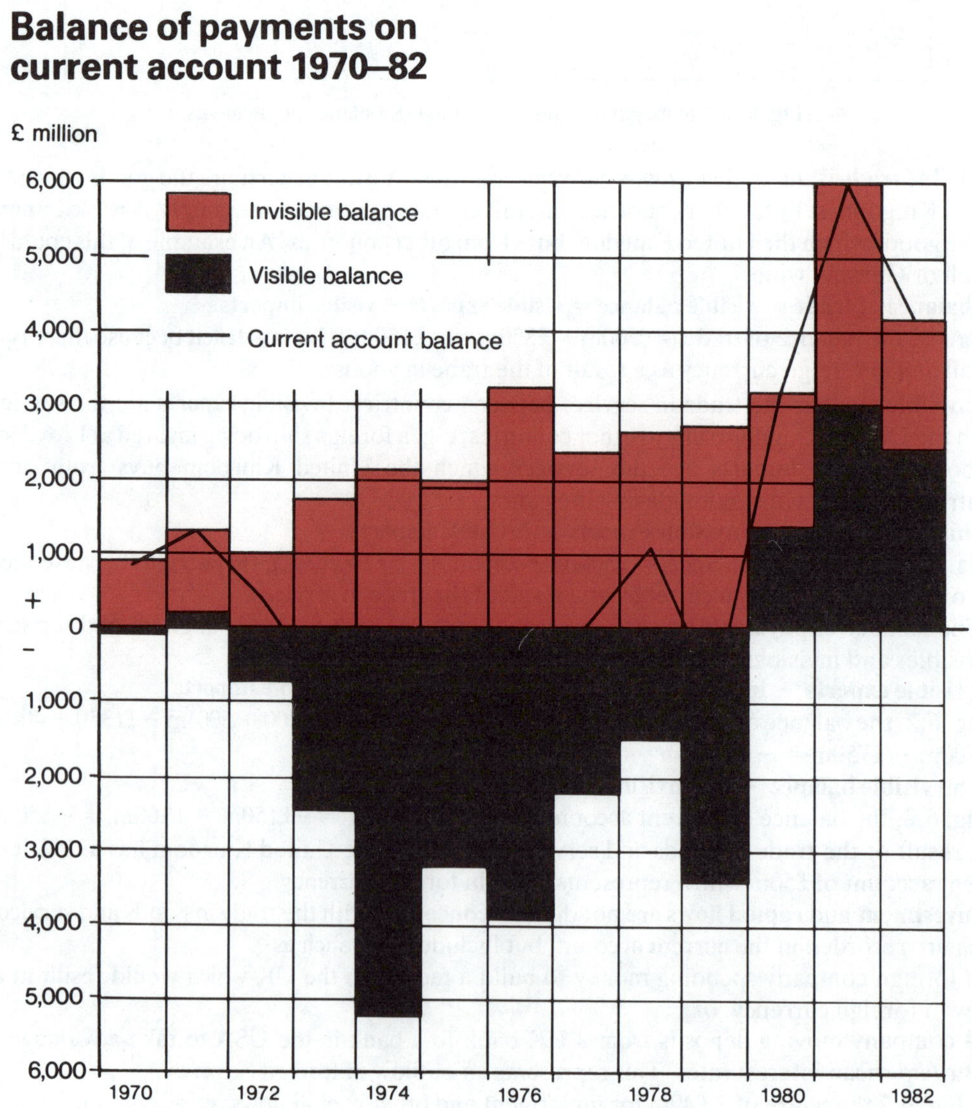

Source: Economic Progress Report May 1983

Fig. 6.3 The UK balance of payments on current account 1970-82

Fig. 6.3 shows the United Kingdom's visible and invisible trade between 1970 and 1982. For many years, the UK has usually had a deficit on visible trade, that is, a greater value of goods has been imported than exported. It can be seen from the graph, however, that this pattern changed in 1980 when the visible balance moved into surplus. The main reason for this was the increasing contribution of North Sea oil to the visible balance.

The invisible balance, on the other hand, has always been in surplus, that is, services exported have been greater in value than services imported. The major contributors to this invisible surplus include:

1 **interest, profits** and **dividends,** e.g. United Kingdom residents receiving dividends on shares in foreign companies.

2 financial services such as **banking** and **insurance,** e.g. an American firm paying bank charges to a UK bank.

3 **tourism,** e.g. an American citizen on holiday in the United Kingdom.

The contribution of services to the United Kingdom balance of payments has always been very important because, until 1980, the invisible surplus each year had gone some way towards meeting the deficit on visible trade. It can be seen, from Fig. 6.3, that in 1978 the invisible surplus was large enough to outweigh the visible deficit to give a current account surplus. From 1980 onwards the invisible balance became less important as the visible balance moved into surplus.

6.6 The Visible Trade of the United Kingdom

	Exports %	*Imports* %
Finished goods	42	41
Semi-finished goods	25	25
Fuels	20	13
Food, beverages and tobacco	7	13
Raw materials	6	8
	100	100

Fig. 6.4 Analysis of UK visible trade 1982 by commodity (to nearest %)

The types of goods in which the United Kingdom trades are shown in Fig. 6.4. **Finished goods,** the most important category for both exports and imports, include items such as cars and machinery which can be immediately used. In contrast, **semi-finished goods** require further processing to change them into finished goods. Examples of semi-finished goods are steel and chemicals. Examples of goods included in the remaining three categories are oil and coal (**fuel**), apples and coffee (**food, beverages and tobacco**) and raw cotton and iron ore (**raw materials**).

	Exports %	*Imports* %
European Economic Community	42	44
Other Western European countries	12	15
North America	15	14
Rest of world	31	27
	100	100

Fig. 6.5 Analysis of UK visible trade 1982 by area (to nearest %)

Fig. 6.5 shows that countries within the **European Economic Community** (see Unit 6.14) are the major trading partners of the United Kingdom. This has not always been the case. The United Kingdom once had stronger trading links with Commonwealth countries such as Australia and New Zealand. As a result of the United Kingdom's membership of the EEC, however, the pattern of trade has moved away from the Commonwealth and towards the EEC.

6.7 Difficulties Faced by Exporters

When a United Kingdom firm exports goods it can encounter difficulties which are not found, or not found to the same extent, in home trade. Such difficulties include:

1 language Documents, labels and catalogues might have to be translated into foreign languages.

2 currency When foreign customers make payments these may be made using German marks, French francs, Japanese yen and so on. Such foreign currency would then have to be converted into sterling which creates extra work for the exporter. An additional difficulty then arises because the prices of currencies, i.e. exchange rates, can change (see Unit 6.10).

3 credit risks In both home and foreign trade there is always the possibility that customers buying on credit will not pay what they owe. It is more difficult, however, for an exporter to establish the credit risk of a firm based in, say, SE Asia than one based in the United Kingdom. It is also more difficult to recover debts from foreign customers.

4 delivery Longer distances are likely to be involved in foreign trade and it is likely to be more difficult for an exporter to be able to state an exact time of delivery.

5 transit risks When the goods are being transported over longer distances there is the increased possibility of theft or damage to goods.

6 standards of products Different countries often set different standards for goods entering a country. Cars exported from the United Kingdom must often be left-hand drive.

7 import restrictions All countries impose some restrictions on imports. Examples are custom duties, quotas and embargoes (see Unit 6.13).

8 obtaining information Since longer distances and different languages may be involved it is particularly difficult for an exporter to obtain information about the types of goods required in other countries.

The difficulties listed above tend to increase costs and may explain why some firms prefer not to take part in foreign trade.

6.8 Government Help for Exporters

1 The **Export Credits Guarantee Department** (ECGD) is part of the Department of Trade and Industry and it helps exporters in two main ways.
(a) It acts like an insurance company by offering **credit insurance.** By paying a premium an exporter can be paid compensation if a customer fails to pay what is owed. The ECGD covers credit risks of:
(i) up to 95% of the loss if it is due to risks such as exchange difficulties, withdrawal of licences and war.
(ii) up to 90% of loss resulting from bankruptcy or other causes of default by the buyer.
(b) It **guarantees export finance.** If an exporter has to borrow from a bank to provide credit to a foreign buyer the ECGD can act as a guarantor and will repay the bank if the exporter fails to do so. The exporter is therefore able to obtain finance more easily because of the security provided by an organization backed by the Government.
2 The **British Overseas Trade Board** (BOTB) is part of the Department of Trade and Industry and helps exporters by providing:
(a) an export intelligence service which gives information about trading opportunities in other countries. Much of such information is obtained from United Kingdom embassies and consulates abroad.
(b) grants to enable exporters to carry out market research in foreign countries.
(c) help for UK exporters to display their goods at trade fairs and exhibitions in other countries.
3 **British embassies** in foreign countries employ trade officials who can directly help United Kingdom firms wishing to sell in those countries.

6.9 Other Help for Exporters

Firms who export on a large scale may be large enough to justify a separate export department which is sufficiently specialized to be able to overcome the difficulties that arise from exporting. Smaller firms, however, often need special help. Some of this can come from the ECGD and BOTB and some from **non-government** sources such as:

1 chambers of commerce. Chambers of commerce are local associations with membership drawn from firms involved in the production of quite different goods and services e.g. the London Chamber of Commerce and Industry. The larger chambers of commerce have specialist committees which are able to give advice on exporting to particular countries. Chambers of commerce also provide translation services and can sign certificates of origin (see Unit 8.2.8).

2 trade associations. Trade associations such as the Society of Motor Manufacturers and Traders are national organizations of firms involved in the provision of similar goods and services. They provide similar services to those of the chambers of commerce.

3 the British Exports Houses Association which publishes a directory listing the activities of export houses (see Unit 5.2) and the products in which they deal.

4 the British Standards Institution (see Unit 13.7) which provides information about technical standards in foreign countries.

5 the clearing banks. Clearing banks provide information about foreign markets, help with the exchange of foreign currency and with the use of documentary credits for payment (see Unit 8.3).

6.10 Exchange Rates

When firms export goods **gains** and **losses** can occur because of **changes** in the **exchange rate of a currency.** For example, on 1 September a UK exporter sells a machine to West Germany for £950. On that day the rate of exchange is £1=4 marks so the exporter fixes the contract price at 3800 marks. Now assume that payment of 3800 marks is made to the exporter on 1 November and that between 1 September and 1 November the pound could either have increased in value (**appreciated**), or decreased in value (**depreciated**).

	Exchange rate of £1	*Contract price*	*Sterling equivalent*	*Sterling gain/loss*
1	£1 = 5 marks	3800 marks	£760	*loss* of 950 − 760 = £190
2	£1 = 3.8 marks	3800 marks	£1000	*gain* of 1000 − 950 = £50

Fig. 6.6 Losses/gains resulting from changing exchange rates

Fig. 6.6 shows that an exporter can lose, in sterling terms, if the pound appreciates. To **prevent** such a loss the exporter could:

1 fix the contract price in terms of sterling so that payment of £950 would be received whatever the exchange rate on 1 November.

2 sell marks forward. By using a forward selling contract the exporter could agree, on 1 September, to sell 3800 marks on 1 November at an exchange rate agreed on the September date. The exporter will then know precisely the amount of sterling which he will receive on 1 November even if the pound changes value in the meantime. The cost of arranging the forward contract can be considered to be a form of insurance premium. Forward dealing on foreign exchange markets, as described above, is very similar to forward dealing on commodity exchanges described earlier (see Unit 4.5).

6.11 Bonded Warehouses

Bonded warehouses are important in foreign trade although they are also used in home trade. Goods on which customs and excise duties have to be paid can be stored in a bonded warehouse. While in 'bond' the goods can be bottled, blended, packaged and graded, but can only be released from 'bond' once duty on the goods has been paid. A bonded warehouse may be owned by a manufacturer, importer, port authority etc but is under the control of the **Customs and Excise.** The owner of the bonded warehouse must give a written undertaking (the bond) to the Customs and Excise that the 'rules' of the bonded warehouse will be kept, e.g. goods will only be released once duty has been paid. If the 'rules' are broken then the owner of the warehouse has to pay a large fine to the Customs and Excise. The amount of the fine will be stated in the original bond signed by the owner.

Advantages of the bonded warehouse to firms

1 Payment of duty is postponed. Goods can be stored and payment of duty made only when the goods are actually needed or sold. Firms, therefore, save on circulating capital which could be expensive to borrow.

2 Goods can be sold while in bond. Payment of the duty will then have to be made by the new owner.

3 Goods for re-export can be stored, and, if necessary, processed in the bonded warehouse. Payment of duty is then eliminated altogether because the goods are for re-export only. (If payment of duty has been made on goods which are re-exported a refund of duty, called **Customs drawback,** can be obtained from the Customs and Excise.)

The principle of non-payment of duty for goods which are re-exported is employed in the system of **freeports.** A freeport is a clearly defined geographical area inside a particular country. Within that area the production of goods, including manufacturing, can be conducted without any taxes on goods having to be paid. When goods leave the freeport for other areas in the country duty becomes payable. For goods being exported, however, no duty is payable. The system of freeports is particularly suitable for entrepôt trade — the system of importing goods which are later re-exported to other countries. For example, a United Kingdom wine merchant imports wine in bulk; he then bottles the wine within the freeport area and later exports the bottled wine to other countries. In 1984 the United Kingdom government announced the establishment of six freeports — Belfast, Birmingham, Cardiff, Liverpool, Prestwick and Southampton.

6.12 HM Customs and Excise

The Customs and Excise have three important functions in foreign trade:

1 Inspection and revenue collection

(a) Vessels, vehicles, aircraft and goods are inspected on entering the country in order to prevent smuggling and the entry of prohibited goods e.g. certain animals.

(b) Customs and excise duties (see Unit 22.3) are collected which provide revenue for the government.

2 Collection of statistics

(a) The value, volume and category of exports and imports are recorded, together with

(b) the origin of imports and destination of exports. These statistics allow the balances of trade and payments to be calculated and information such as that found in Figs. 6.2 to 6.5 to be presented.

3 Control of bonded warehouses

See Unit 6.11.

6.13 Free Trade and Protection

Free trade occurs when firms in different countries can trade with each other with no interference from governments. In all countries, however, governments do interfere with free trade by imposing restrictions such as:

1 **import duties** (tariffs) which may be customs or excise duties (see Unit 22.3). Import duties make imports more expensive and consumption may be discouraged.

2 **quotas.** A quota is a maximum set on the quantity or value of certain imports, e.g. 10 000 Japanese cars per year.

3 **embargoes.** An embargo is a complete ban placed on certain imports e.g. during wartime an embargo would be placed on trade with enemy countries.

4 **subsidies to home producers.** If the United Kingdom government gave subsidies (grants) to home producers this would discriminate against imports by making UK goods cheaper, e.g. a subsidy to UK textile firms would make it easier for them to compete against imported textiles from South East Asia.

Restrictions on imports are imposed by governments to enable them to:

1 raise revenue from import duties.

2 help the balance of payments by restricting imports.

3 help employment in their own country.

4 help particular industries e.g. the UK textile industry.

5 protect infant industries. These are 'new' industries which need time to grow until they are in a position to compete more easily with already established foreign competition.

Disadvantages of protection

When one country imposes trade restrictions there is the danger that other countries will **retaliate** by introducing their own trade restrictions. As a result countries will not be able to obtain the full benefits of comparative advantage. For this reason the **General Agreement on Tariffs and Trade** (GATT) was signed in 1947 with the objective of promoting free trade between countries. Representatives from nations now meet regularly to encourage world trade by reducing trade barriers.

6.14 The European Economic Community (EEC)

The EEC or **Common Market** was set up by the Treaty of Rome in 1957. There are, at present, ten countries in the Community: the United Kingdom, France, West Germany, Italy, Luxembourg, Holland, the Republic of Ireland, Denmark, Belgium and Greece. One of the aims of the Common Market is that trade between member countries should be **'free'**, that is there should be no customs duties. If duties are to be levied then all member countries should charge the same duty. Goods entering the Market from countries outside the Community are faced with a **common external tariff.** Revenue from this external tariff goes towards financing the Community budget e.g. giving subsidies to farmers. The aim of a Common Market is to encourage trade between member countries and to discourage trade with non-members.

7 Business documents used in home trade

7.1 Introduction

Business documents are essential because they provide:

1 **written records** of transactions between firms (an order given over the telephone could be misunderstood and a written confirmation of the order is therefore usually sent).

2 the information which allows firms to keep **systems of accounts** e.g. a supplier needs to keep a record of the amounts owing by different customers.

3 the information which allows **taxes to be assessed** (e.g. VAT (see Unit 22.3), income tax, corporation tax (see Unit 22.2)).

4 the basis for the publication of **Government statistics** on a wide range of business activity, e.g. the number of cars sold in the United Kingdom in a given period of time.

7.2 The Letter of Inquiry

Letters of inquiry are sent from potential customers, e.g. retailers, to potential suppliers, e.g. manufacturers and wholesalers asking for details of:

1 whether certain goods are stocked by a supplier

and if so,

2 the prices of such goods including discounts and taxes charged,

3 date for delivery,

4 whether credit is offered, *and*

5 the costs of delivery.

By sending letters of inquiry to a number of suppliers the customer is able to compare the goods and terms offered by each supplier and is then able to choose the best supplier.

7.3 Quotation, Catalogue and Pro-Forma Invoice

1 In reply to a letter of inquiry the supplier may send a **quotation** which gives the customer the information which is required (Fig. 7.1). (The business terms used in Fig. 7.1 are explained in Unit 7.6.)

2 Some firms do not use quotations when replying to letters of inquiry. Instead, catalogues and price lists are sent to customers. A **catalogue gives:**

(a) detailed descriptions of the goods which a firm supplies;

(b) catalogue numbers for each item;

(c) photographs of goods where necessary.

Prices may be quoted in a catalogue but, often, separate price lists are issued. A **price list** gives:

(a) the prices of goods;

(b) other information such as size of trade discount, terms of payment and terms of delivery.

Separate price lists are issued by suppliers because catalogues are expensive to produce. If

A. SUPPLIER
14 West St,
Newtown NW3 8BJ

Tel: Newtown 42436

J. BUYER
26-32 Midland St,
Newtown, NW8 4BG

5.6.1985

Dear Sir,

QUOTATION

Thank you for your letter of inquiry dated 1 June 1985. We are pleased to offer the following quotations for the goods stated in your letter:

20 boxes	Pens	Cat No 428	at	£24.00 per box
400	Rulers	Cat No 123	at	£0.50 each

The above is subject to trade discount of 20%.
Delivery is within 7 days of receipt of order.
Terms of delivery: carriage paid.
Terms of payment: 5% 14 days, 2% 28 days, net 42 days.

Yours faithfully,

A Supplier

Fig. 7.1 A quotation

changes in prices have to be made it is cheaper to reprint a price list than to have to reprint the whole catalogue.

3 A further means of providing the information a customer wants is for the supplier to send a **pro-forma invoice.** A pro-forma invoice is what the actual invoice would look like (see Fig. 7.2) if the customer did decide to order the goods. This type of invoice is also used when a supplier wants payment before despatching the goods i.e. payment in advance and when goods are sent on approval.

7.4 The Order

Once the customer has decided with which supplier to deal he will send a signed and dated **order** to that supplier stating:

1 the goods that are required.
2 the catalogue numbers of such goods.
3 the prices agreed.
4 the place of delivery.
5 the date on which the goods are required.
6 terms of delivery.
7 terms of payment.

When customers place orders by telephone, written confirmation of such orders is often requested by suppliers. Any confirmation of this kind must also be signed and dated.

7.5 The Advice Note, Delivery Note and Consignment Note

1 The **advice note** is sent by the supplier to advise the customer that the goods have been despatched and will soon be delivered. The customer can then arrange to receive such goods and can advise the supplier if they are not delivered.

2 The **delivery note** accompanies the goods and is signed by the customer as proof that the goods have been delivered.

3 The **consignment note** is used when the supplier employs a transport firm (carrier) to deliver the goods. A copy of the consignment note is signed by the carrier to indicate acceptance of the goods. At a later stage the customer signs the consignment note as proof that the goods have been delivered.

The information shown on these three documents usually includes:

(a) name and address of supplier (consigner);
(b) name and address of customer (consignee);

(c) address for delivery; *and*
(d) description and quantity of goods being delivered.
Prices are not normally shown on these documents.

7.6 The Invoice

The **invoice** is one of the most important documents used in business (Fig. 7.2).

(1) VAT Reg No 46731 | **INVOICE** | (2) No 8641

A. SUPPLIER
14 West St,
Newtown NW3 8BJ
Tel: Newtown 42436

J. BUYER
26-32 Midland St,
Newtown NW8 4BG

(3) Order No S732 dated 21.6.1985

Date 14.7.1985

Quantity	Description	(4) Unit Price (RRP)	Cost (£)
	(5)		
20 boxes	Pens (Cat No 428)	£24.00 per box	480.00
400	Rulers (Cat No 123)	£0.50 each	200.00
	(6)		680.00
	less 20% Trade Discount		136.00
	Amount owing (excluding VAT)		544.00

(7) Terms of delivery: carriage paid

(8) Terms of payment: 5% 14 days, 2% 28 days, net 42 days

(9) E and O E

Fig. 7.2 An invoice

The invoice shown in Fig. 7.2 uses the information given in the earlier quotation (Fig. 7.1). The numbered terms on the invoice are frequently found and are now explained.
(1) VAT Reg No stands for Value Added Tax Registration Number. Many firms have to register with HM Customs and Excise so that VAT can be collected (see Unit 22.3).
(2) Invoice No 8641. Each invoice issued will be individually numbered. It is essential that business documents are numbered so that, by filing them according to these numbers, they can easily be referred to at a later date.
(3) Order No S732. This is the number given by the customer to the order sent to the supplier.
(4) The **unit price** or **recommended retail price** (RRP) is the price at which the manufacturer recommends that a product be sold to the public. For the invoice given, therefore, the recommended price at which the ruler should be sold in shops is 50 pence, excluding VAT. RRP is, however, only a recommended price and many firms sell goods at below RRP.
(5) Cat No 428. Each item sold by the supplier is given an individual catalogue number. When ordering goods the customer need only quote these numbers and detailed descriptions of goods are unnecessary.
(6) Trade discount is an automatic deduction given by traders to other traders but not to the public. It is important to traders because it:
(a) allows buyers to make a profit when they re-sell goods e.g.
the RRP of a ruler is 50 pence.
J. Buyer buys the ruler for 50 pence less 20% = 40 pence.
If the ruler is now sold at the RRP the profit made is 50p − 40p = 10p = amount of trade discount.
(The calculation above is, more precisely, a calculation of gross profit and excludes the effect of VAT.)

(b) encourages traders to buy in greater bulk because the trade discount offered may increase as quantity bought increases (Fig 7.3).

quantity ordered	*trade discount*
below 1000 rulers	20%
between 1000 and 5000	22%
over 5000	25%

Fig. 7.3 Quantity discounts

When trade discount is used in this way it is referred to as **quantity discount** because through buying in greater quantities traders obtain cheaper goods. Suppliers are prepared to give large quantity discounts because it is cheaper to deal with very large orders than with a large number of small orders.

(c) can be altered to allow for changes in the prices of goods. If suppliers wish to increase the prices of goods they could reprint catalogues and/or price lists but this would prove expensive. What suppliers could do, instead, would be to **lower** trade discount on existing unit prices which would result in suppliers' prices being increased.

(7) Terms of delivery. In Fig. 7.2 the goods are carriage paid which means that the supplier pays for the costs of delivery to the customer. Other examples of terms of delivery are:

(a) carriage forward—the customer pays for the cost of delivery.

(b) ex-warehouse—the customer pays for all the costs incurred after the goods leave the warehouse.

(c) free on rail and others (see Unit 8.4).

(8) Terms of payment. When goods are sold on credit, suppliers try to encourage customers to **pay promptly** by offering **cash discount.** In Fig. 7.2, therefore, if J. Buyer settles the bill within 14 days he will receive a cash discount of 5%. He will pay £544.00 − 5% of £544.00 = £516.80. If payment is made between 14 days and 28 days from the date of the invoice or statement (see Unit 7.9) a smaller cash discount of 2% will be deducted. Payment is expected, at the latest, within 42 days when no cash discount is allowed (**net terms**).

It is worthwhile for suppliers to offer cash discount because:

(a) bad debts are reduced.

(b) there is less time taken in sending reminders about payment to customers.

(c) less capital is needed to finance the credit offered to customers.

(d) the rate of cash discount given could be less than the rate of interest which the supplier would have to pay on an overdraft.

(9) E and OE stands for **Errors and Omissions Excepted.** If mistakes have been made on the invoice then the statement 'E and OE' allows the supplier to correct such mistakes afterwards.

When a customer occasionally buys goods from a supplier the invoice sent by the supplier is itself a request for payment. However, when a customer has a number of transactions each month with a supplier then the invoice is not a request for payment but simply states the debt arising from one particular transaction. In such cases a statement of account (see Unit 7.9) is used as the request for payment.

7.7 The Credit Note

Credit notes are issued by suppliers to customers to **reduce the amount charged** on invoices. The original invoice must not be altered.

Credit notes are issued when:

1 a mistake has been made by the supplier and the charges shown on the invoice are too high.

2 damaged goods have been returned to the supplier and these goods have not been replaced.

3 incorrect goods have been supplied and have been returned to the supplier.

4 a charge has been made for packing cases and the cases have been returned by the customer.

The effect of a credit note can be shown by assuming that five of the boxes of pens invoiced in Fig. 7.2 were damaged and were returned by the customer. A. Supplier issues the credit note shown in Fig. 7.4.

It should be noted that the percentage trade discount shown on the original invoice must also be applied to any credit note. The effect of the credit note is to **reduce** the amount which J. Buyer owes. Credit notes are, therefore, normally printed in red to distinguish them from other documents, such as the invoice, which show how much customers owe to suppliers.

VAT Reg No 46731	CREDIT NOTE		No 4013
	A. SUPPLIER 14 West St, Newtown NW3 8BJ	Tel: Newtown 42436	
J. BUYER 26-32 Midland St, Newtown NW8 4BG	Invoice No 8641 dated: 14.7.1985	Date 18.7.1985	

			£
5 boxes	Damaged pens returned (Cat No 428) less 20% Trade Discount	£24.00 per box	120.00 24.00
	Amount credited (excl VAT)		96.00

Fig. 7.4 A credit note

7.8 The Debit Note

Debit notes are issued by suppliers to customers to **correct undercharges** on invoices. As with the credit note the original invoice must not be altered.
Debit notes are issued when:

1 too low a price has been entered on the invoice, e.g. a product with a catalogue price of £20 has been invoiced at £18.

2 more goods have been sent than are shown on the invoice. Assume that, for the invoice in Fig. 7.2, 500 rulers were sent in error and the customer has decided to keep the extra 100 rulers. The supplier will then issue the debit note as shown in Fig. 7.5.

VAT Reg No 46731	DEBIT NOTE		No 1827
	A. SUPPLIER 14 West St, Newtown NW3 8BJ	Tel: Newtown 42436	
J. BUYER 26-32 Midland St, Newtown NW8 4BG	Invoice No 8641 dated: 14.7.1985	Date 21.7.1985	

			£
100	Extra rulers sent (Cat No 123) less 20% Trade Discount	£0.50 each	50.00 10.00
	Amount debited (excl VAT)		40.00

Fig. 7.5 A debit note

As with a credit note the percentage trade discount allowed on the original invoice must also be allowed on the debit note.

The effect of this debit note is to **increase** the amount which J. Buyer owes by £40. A supplier is able to correct the original error on the invoice because of the statement 'E and OE' at the bottom of the invoice. Some firms prefer not to issue debit notes. Instead, they would simply issue a new invoice to correct the original undercharge.

7.9 The Statement of Account

When a customer has frequent transactions with a supplier the supplier will issue a **statement of account** which provides a summary of these transactions for a given period of time, usually one month. Fig. 7.6, for example, shows a statement of account issued by A. Supplier covering all the transactions with J. Buyer referred to earlier in this unit.

VAT Reg No 46731	STATEMENT OF ACCOUNT A. SUPPLIER 14 West St, Newtown NW3 8BJ		Tel: Newtown 42436	No 2352
J. BUYER 26-32 Midland St, Newtown NW8 4BG				Date 3.8.1985
Date	*Details*	*Debit*	*Credit*	*Balance*
1 July	Balance owing			400.00
5 July	Cheque		380.00	20.00
5 July	Cash discount		20.00	0.00
14 July	Invoice (8641)	544.00		544.00
18 July	Credit Note (4013)		96.00	448.00
21 July	Debit Note (1827)	40.00		488.00
1 Aug	Balance owing (excl VAT)			488.00
Terms of payment: 5% 14 days, 2% 28 days, net 42 days.				

Fig. 7.6 A statement of account

In Fig. 7.6 the statement shows that J. Buyer owed £400 on 1 July. Payment was then made within 14 days and a cash discount of 5% of £400 was allowed. The transactions described in Figs. 7.2, 7.4 and 7.5 are then entered. Cheques, cash discount and credit notes are entered in the credit column because they all **reduce** what the customer owes. Invoices and debit notes are entered in the debit column because they **increase** what the customer owes.

This statement of account is important to J. Buyer because:

1 it allows him to **check** the accuracy of entries on the statement against his own records.

2 it **states** the amount owing to A. Supplier viz £488 on 1 August.

3 it **shows** the amount of cash discount available if prompt payment is made.

The method of calculating cash discount does vary from firm to firm. Where invoices but not statements are issued the time allowed for payment is based on the date of the invoice. Where statements are issued the time allowed for payment might be based on the date of the statement. The exact terms of payment should be requested in the letter of inquiry so that a supplier will state precise details of cash discount calculations in the quotation.

7.10 The Receipt

Receipts are issued by suppliers as evidence that payment has been made by customers. Receipts are still used when payment is made by cash but they have become less important because:

1 most payments are made by cheque and the cheque itself is proof that payment has been made.

2 when payment is made by credit transfer (see Unit 9.8) the bank at which the transfer is effected will itself issue a receipt.

8 Business documents used in foreign trade

8.1 Introduction

The business documents used in foreign trade are likely to be **more numerous** than those in home trade because:

1 the Customs authorities in different countries require specific documents to be presented when goods are exported and imported. The information contained in these documents is used to:

(a) compile balance of payments statistics
(b) allow the calculation of any duties which might have to be paid
(c) decide whether the imports are subject to any quota or embargo (see Unit 6.13).

2 the risks in foreign trade are greater. More complex insurance documents have to be prepared to cover credit risks (ECGD, see Unit 6.8) or risks during transit (Lloyd's of London, see Unit 14.15).

3 the distances involved are likely to be greater and a number of different forms of transport may be required, each requiring its own documentation.

4 the number of intermediaries involved in foreign trade is likely to be greater and information for each of these intermediaries will require a greater number of documents.

5 of other differences between home and foreign trade (such as differences in currencies and laws, see Unit 6.7).

8.2 Documents used when Sending Goods

8.2.1 The indent

The importer informs the exporter of the goods required by sending an **indent** (or order). The indent will contain details such as:

(a) a description of the goods required
(b) the quantity of such goods
(c) the prices agreed as stated in the quotation
(d) shipping instructions
(e) address for delivery
(f) date for delivery

Instead of dealing directly with an exporter the importer could, instead, use the services of a **buying agent.** The indent would then be sent to the agent who would in turn, contact the exporter. When an agent is given detailed instructions about the goods to buy the indent is a **closed indent.** If, instead, the agent was simply told the general nature of the goods required but it was left to him to choose the specific items and suppliers the indent would be an **open indent.**

8.2.2 Shipping note, dock receipt and mate's receipt

Once an exporter has received an indent arrangements must be made for the goods to be shipped to the importer. The goods for export must now be prepared and space booked on a ship. When these arrangements have been completed the exporter sends:

(a) a **shipping note** with the goods to the dock. This note contains details of the goods, the name of the ship etc and is handed to the port authority which will issue

(b) a **dock receipt** (or **wharfinger's receipt**) as evidence that the goods have been received. If the goods are delivered directly to the ship, then a **mate's receipt** will, instead, be issued.

8.2.3 Freight note

The **freight note** is prepared by the shipping company and sent to the exporter. It contains details of the freight charges, that is, the cost of shipping the goods.

8.2.4 Bill of lading

The **bill of lading** is provided by the shipping company but is completed by the exporter (see Fig. 8.1).

(1) FAR EASTERN SHIPPING plc Dock St, London	**(2)** BILL OF LADING No 8763
(3) Shipper: Exporter, Birmingham Delivered to: Importer, Hong Kong	Port of loading: London **(4)** Port of destination: Hong Kong **(5)** Vessel: Eastern Trader

NO	(6) DESCRIPTION	WEIGHT
1	Machine	2000 kilos
	(7) FREIGHT PAID	

The goods listed above have been received on ship in good condition and will be conveyed to the port shown.

Signed

(8) D. J. Salt Dated 7.2.1985

Fig. 8.1 A bill of lading

Fig. 8.1. gives a simplified bill of lading which contains:

(1) the name of the shipping company
(2) the number of the bill of lading
(3) the names and addresses of the exporter and importer
(4) the ports of loading and destination
(5) the name of the ship
(6) details of the goods
(7) a statement that the freight charges (shipping costs) have been paid
(8) the signature of the master of the ship to signify:
(a) that the goods have been received on board ship
(b) his agreement to carry the goods to the port of destination stated

The bill of lading is prepared in, at least, **triplicate:**

1 one copy is kept by the exporter
2 one copy is kept by the master of the ship
3 one copy is sent to the importer by **airmail.** (It is, however, more usual for a number of copies of the bill of lading to be sent to the importer by different airmails in case some go astray.)

The bill of lading is a very important document in foreign trade because it fulfils three main functions.

1 It is a **receipt** to show that the goods have been received on board ship ((**8**) in Fig. 8.1). If the goods are damaged when they are accepted by the master of the ship the extent of the damage would be indicated on the bill which would become a **dirty bill of lading.** If the goods are in good condition the bill of lading would not be altered and it would remain a **clean bill of lading.**

2 It is **evidence of the terms of the shipping contract** between the shipping company and the exporter ((**8**) in Fig. 8.1) and it can also indicate that the **freight charge** has been paid ((**7**) in Fig. 8.1).

3 It is a **quasi-negotiable document of title** to the goods. The importer **must** receive the bill of lading because it **allows him to claim ownership** of the goods stated on the bill, i.e. it is a document of title. The bill of lading can be **transferred** to another person or firm and ownership of the goods would then be transferred as well. In any transfer, however, the bill remains a 'not negotiable' instrument (see Fig. 9.5) i.e. it is quasi-negotiable.

8.2.5 Export invoice

The export invoice gives details of the transaction between the exporter and importer and it therefore fulfils the same functions as the invoice used in home trade (see Unit 7.6). The export invoice contains:

(a) the names and addresses of exporter and importer
(b) the place and date of issue of the invoice
(c) the order number
(d) a description of the goods
(e) the quantity of such goods
(f) the amount of freight and dock charges
(g) the amount of insurance premiums
(h) the total amount payable
(i) the terms on which the goods have been sold e.g. cif, fob (see Unit 8.4).
(j) the signature of the exporter

A copy of the export invoice is usually attached to each bill of lading and additional copies are needed for customs authorities for entry and specification purposes (see Unit 8.2.10).

8.2.6 Certificate of insurance

The **certificate of insurance** or **insurance policy** gives details of the insurance cover provided for goods that are being exported and imported. Regular exporters normally arrange an open insurance contract to cover all exports during a specific period. This avoids having to obtain separate cover for each shipment.

8.2.7 Consular invoice

When goods enter a country ad valorem customs duties (see Unit 22.3) may have to be paid on these imports. The amount of duty paid will be based on the prices shown in the export invoice. If the prices are deliberately set low then some evasion of duty will occur. A **consular invoice** overcomes this because the consul (or agent) of the importing country, who is resident in the exporting country, will certify on a consular invoice that the prices shown are correct. Copies of the consular invoice will then be given to the exporter who can attach them to the other documents sent to the importer. Other copies will be directly sent to the Customs authorities in the importing country.

8.2.8 Certificate of origin

A certificate of origin states the country of extraction or manufacture of the goods being exported, and is signed by the exporter or the chamber of commerce in the exporting country or the consul of the importing country resident in the exporting country. The certificate of origin is needed because:

(a) the rate of duty levied by countries on imports often varies with the country of origin of such imports, e.g. duty is charged on imports entering EEC countries from countries outside the EEC while trade between EEC countries is duty-free (see Unit 22.3).

(b) an embargo might have been placed by one country on trade with another country and the certificate of origin certifies that any imports are not from that other country.

8.2.9 Import licence

Before goods are allowed into many countries an **import licence** must be obtained. This licence shows that the government of the importing country is prepared to allow those goods into the country (e.g. the goods may be explosives) and that foreign currency will be available to pay for the imports.

8.2.10 Custom's entry and specification

Customs authorities in the **importing** country require a customs **entry** to be completed while the Customs in the **exporting** country require a Customs **specification.** Both these documents list the goods being traded so that the Customs can assess duties payable and obtain information for balance of payments statistics.

8.2.11 Ship's manifest and report

Full details of cargo carried and dutiable articles contained on board ship are included in the **ship's manifest** which must be presented to port and customs authorities for ships **leaving** the country. The equivalent document for ships **entering** the country is the **ship's report.**

8.2.12 Air waybill

An **air waybill** (or **air consignment note**) is used instead of a bill of lading when goods are sent by air. Like the bill of lading it is prepared in a set of at least three; one copy is kept by the exporter, one by the airline and one is carried with the goods to the importer. Unlike the bill of lading the air waybill is not a document of title but it is **evidence of a contract of carriage.**

8.3 Documents used for Payments in Foreign Trade

Within the United Kingdom, sellers of goods face relatively little difficulty in receiving payments because:

1 the creditworthiness of a customer can be more easily established;
2 the UK banking system, with its many banks and branches, allows payments to be easily made; *and*
3 a single currency is used within the country.

Receiving payments from customers who live abroad is likely to be more difficult because:

1 the creditworthiness of a customer is more difficult to establish because of the distances which separate supplier and customer;
2 in some countries a less sophisticated banking system makes it more difficult to collect payments; *and*
3 problems arise because of different currencies.

Special methods of payment are, therefore, needed in foreign trade and these include:

8.3.1 Bill of exchange

A simplified **bill of exchange** is shown in Fig. 8.2 and it relates to the transaction described earlier in the bill of lading shown in Fig. 8.1.

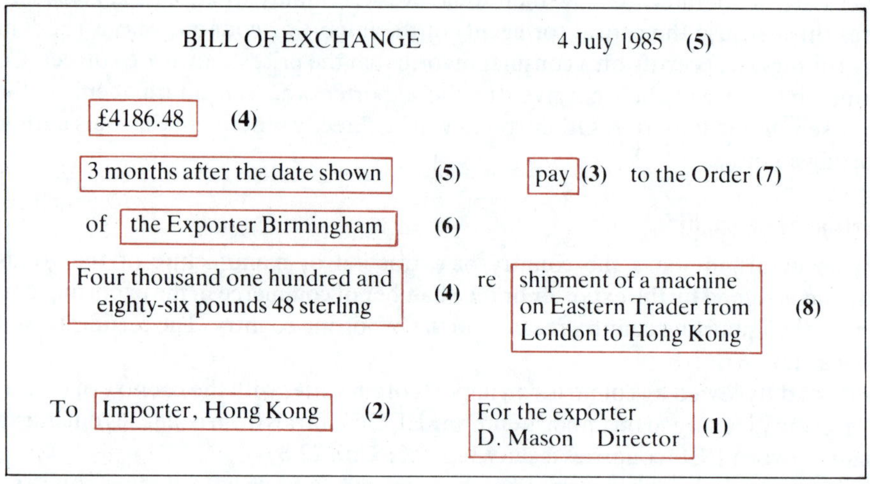

Fig. 8.2 A bill of exchange

(1) The bill of exchange is drawn up by the exporter and
(2) sent to the importer who signs and writes 'accepted' to signify
(3) that he will make payment of
(4) £4186.48 in sterling on
(5) 4 October 1985, i.e. 3 months after 4 July 1985,
(6) to the Exporter, Birmingham
(7) or Order, i.e. the exporter can order the importer to pay someone else,
(8) the bill of exchange being payment for a machine.

Once the bill has been 'accepted' by the importer it will be returned to the exporter who will then have to wait until October 1985 for payment. The exporter may, however, need cash immediately to pay wages or to buy more raw materials. He can, therefore, sell the bill of exchange to a clearing bank, merchant bank or discount house or can transfer the bill to a third party in payment for goods and/or services. The money received for the bill of exchange will be **less than its face value** and, for this reason, the process of selling a bill of exchange is known as **discounting** the bill of exchange.

The difference between the price paid by the bank for the bill and the bill's face value represents the bank's reward for, in effect, lending to the exporter for a number of months and for taking the risk that the importer will not honour the bill of exchange when it falls due.

In practice, banks will minimize the risk of non-payment by buying only those bills of exchange which have been drawn on importers of sound reputation and, where the name of the trader owing the money is not well-known, insisting that the bill is first 'accepted' by an **accepting house.** In return for a fee the accepting house will **guarantee to meet the debt** if the importer fails to pay.

8.3.2 Documentary bills of exchange

When bills of exchange are used in foreign trade it is more usual for them to be supported by the documents which relate to the transaction for which payment is to be made. The major supporting document is the bill of lading together with other documents such as the export invoice and insurance policy. A **documentary bill of exchange,** as the bill of exchange is now called, is designed to cope with two specific problems:

1 The exporter will not allow the bill of lading to be transferred to the importer until the importer has accepted the bill of exchange.

2 At the same time the importer will not accept the bill of exchange until ownership of the goods has been passed to him through the transfer of the bill of lading.

To satisfy both exporter and importer the following procedure is adopted:

1 The exporter sends the bill of exchange with the supporting documents to his bank which
2 transfers them to a bank in the importer's country which
3 then informs the importer that the documents are ready for collection once the bill of exchange has been accepted.
4 The importer then signs the bill of exchange and receives the bill of lading and other documents, and
5 the accepted bill of exchange is sent to the exporter who will have to wait for payment unless he discounts or transfers the bill.

If the exporter does not wish to extend credit to his customer he could, instead, issue a 'sight' bill of exchange which would mean that payment would have to be made by the importer whenever the bill was presented i.e. it could be presented immediately.

8.3.3 Documentary letters of credit

The problem with documentary bills of exchange, which allow a period of credit, is that the importer may eventually fail to pay. For this reason **documentary letters of credit** (or **documentary credits**) have been developed. For the exporter the documentary credit is a **safer** method of credit because a bank guarantees payment for the goods exported.

The procedures involved in paying by documentary credit are:

1 The importer arranges for a bank in his own country (the issuing bank) to open a documentary letter of credit by
2 delivering the letter to a bank in the exporter's own country (the advising bank).
3 The letter states the terms under which payment will be made and the advising bank informs the exporter of these terms e.g. payment will be made if a correctly drawn up bill of lading is deposited by the exporter at the advising bank.
4 The goods are now despatched to the importer.
5 The exporter presents the necessary shipping documents to the advising bank.
6 The advising bank pays the exporter and then
7 forwards the shipping documents to the issuing bank which
8 pays the advising bank and
9 after receiving payment from the importer
10 releases the documents so that the importer can claim the goods.

The importance of the documentary letter of credit is that the issuing bank guarantees payment and the exporter need not worry about the creditworthiness of the importer. The issuing bank bears the risk that the importer will not pay but safeguards itself by not releasing the bill of lading until payment has been made. The issuing bank could also ask the importer to sign a **letter of hypothecation** which would allow the bank to sell the goods named on the bill of lading if the importer did not pay the bank.

Documentary letters of credit can be

1 **revocable:** the credit can be cancelled by the importer at any time;
2 **irrevocable:** the credit cannot be cancelled without the agreement of the exporter; *or*
3 **confirmed:** the advising bank will agree to pay the exporter if there is any default by the importer or the issuing bank.

For the exporter, therefore, a confirmed credit is the safest form of documentary credit.

8.3.4 Direct transfer of funds

One further method of payment is for the importer to deposit funds into his own bank account or into a branch of the exporter's bank located in the importer's country. The funds would then be **transferred by cable** to the exporter's own bank branch. This method of payment is only used for customers that the exporter can trust although, for credit transactions, the exporter would probably still arrange credit insurance with the ECGD (see Unit 6.8) to cover the transaction.

8.4 Price Quotations used in Foreign Trade

It is important for traders to know precisely what charges are included in the quoted prices of goods. For example, does the price of a product include the cost of shipping? For this reason the following terms are used when prices are quoted in foreign trade.

1 **ex-works (ex-factory):** if the price of a machine is quoted as £10 000 ex-works this price only covers the cost of the machine. The buyer must pay for all the charges after the machine leaves the factory.

2 **for** (free on rail): the price includes delivery to the railway terminal nearest the seller.

3 **fas** (free alongside ship): the price only includes delivery to the dockside. Loading, freight and insurance charges, for example, would have to be met by the buyer.

4 **fob** (free on board): the price is as for fas but also includes loading charges.

5 **c and f** (cost and freight): as for fob plus freight charges.

6 **cif** (cost, insurance and freight): as for c and f plus insurance premiums to the port of destination.

7 **landed:** as for cif plus unloading charges at the port of destination.

8 **franco:** all charges are paid by the seller up to the delivery of the product to the buyer's premises.

9 Banking: the commercial banks

9.1 Introduction

The major **commercial** or **clearing** banks are:

1 Lloyds
2 National Westminster
3 Barclays
4 Midland

They are called clearing banks because they are members of the **Bankers' Clearing House** (see Unit 9.12). These banks, which are also referred to as joint-stock banks, have three main functions:

1 To **make and receive payments** on behalf of customers
2 To **keep money safely** for customers
3 To **lend** to customers

These functions are carried out through holding accounts for customers.

9.2 Types of Account

The clearing banks offer different types of accounts because the needs of customers vary.

9.2.1 Current account

In a current account money is being constantly **paid in** and **withdrawn** and the **balance** of money in the account, therefore, **frequently changes.**

Advantages to the customer of a current account

1 Cheques can be used for payment (see Units 9.3 to 9.7).
2 Money can be withdrawn on demand.

3 Overdrafts are possible (see Unit 9.10.2).

4 The bank sends regular statements of account showing the balance in the account (see Unit 9.9).

5 Payments can be made by, for example, standing order and direct debit (see Unit 9.7).

6 The customer can arrange for his employer to pay his wages directly into the current account by means of a credit transfer (see Unit 9.8).

Disadvantages to the customer of a current account

1 Generally, no interest is earned although some commercial banks now allow interest on current accounts with high minimum balances.

2 There may be bank charges e.g. if the current account is frequently used yet the average balance in the account is small then bank charges will be payable.

Before a clearing bank allows a customer to open a current account it will first ask for an **application form** to be completed. This form will ask for:

1 the name and address of the applicant

2 the name and address of the applicant's employer

3 the name of a referee to vouch for the applicant's honesty

4 a specimen signature which can be checked against the signature used on cheques which are issued

9.2.2 Deposit account

This account is used for **savings** e.g. for the savings of the public or for the spare cash of firms.

Advantages to the customer of a deposit account

1 There are no bank charges.

2 Interest is earned.

Disadvantages to the customer of a deposit account

1 Cheques cannot be used for payments.

2 Other money transfer services cannot be used e.g. standing orders.

3 Overdrafts are not possible.

4 Seven days notice of withdrawal is required. In practice banks normally do allow immediate withdrawal, except for very large sums, but seven days' interest is then lost.

9.2.3 Budget account

A customer holding a current account can also open a budget account for which a **special cheque book** is issued in addition to the current account cheque book. Before using a budget account the bank will ask the customer to complete a budget account schedule which lists the payments which the customer expects to make from the budget account (Fig. 9.1).

Nature of payment	*Estimated maximum annual expenditure* £	*Payment due on*
Rates	600	1 April, 1 October
Electricity	400	1 April, 1 July, 1 October, 1 January
Gas	400	1 April, 1 July, 1 October, 1 January
Telephone	200	1 April, 1 July, 1 October, 1 January
Total	1600	
Service charge	80	
	1680	

Monthly transfer from current account = £1680 ÷ 12 = £140

Fig. 9.1 A budget account schedule

The budget account holder agrees to transfer a fixed amount, (in Fig. 9.1 £140), every month from the current account to the budget account, and to use only the budget account cheque book to pay those bills agreed with the bank **in advance** e.g. rates and electricity.

The budget account has been designed to overcome the problem of expenditure being unevenly spread throughout the year. In Fig. 9.1, for example, on 1 April the customer expects to be faced with bills of £550 (rates £300, electricity £100, gas £100 and telephone £50). The budget account holder would find it difficult to pay these bills so the bank allows him to overdraw by £410; (£550 less the monthly transfer of £140). The bank is prepared to do this because over the full year the customer will transfer sufficient funds to meet all the specified payments, and the bank earns £80 by providing this service.

9.2.4 Savings account

Clearing banks often provide savings accounts for small sums of money, e.g. the savings of children. A lower rate of interest is paid but the savings can be withdrawn on demand.

9.3 Cheques

Payments from a current account (or budget account) can be made using cheques.

A cheque is an order:

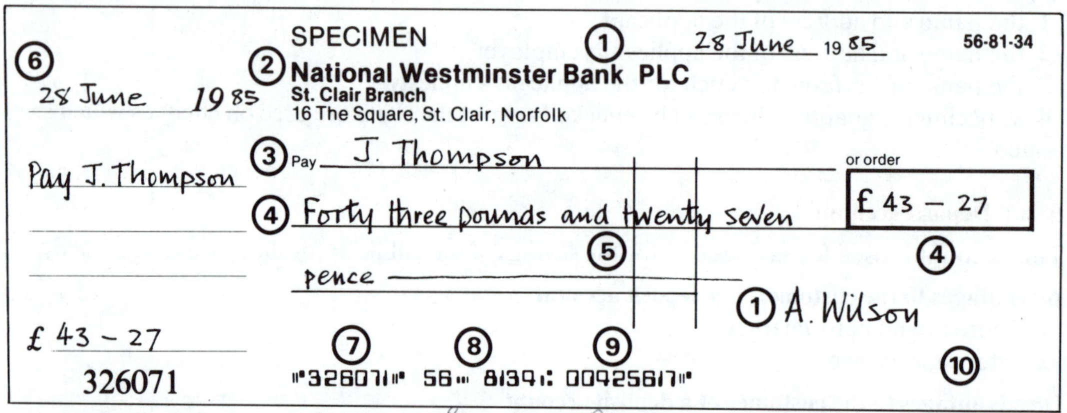

Fig. 9.2 A cheque

(1) **signed and dated** by the **drawer** of the cheque—A. Wilson
(2) to the **drawee**—National Westminster Bank, St Clair branch which is the drawer's bank
(3) to pay the **payee**—J. Thompson. ((1), (2) and (3) are the **parties** to a cheque).
(4) The amount to be paid is written in **words and figures.**
(5) This cheque is **crossed** (see Unit 9.4) and
(6) a **counterfoil** is kept by the drawer as a record of the payment.

At the bottom of the cheque are identifying numbers printed in magnetic ink which are used to facilitate clearing (see Unit 9.12).

(7) is the number of the cheque (326071).
(8) is the bank and branch number (56-81-34).
(9) is the drawer's account number (00925617).
(10) Where the figure (10) appears on the cheque, the bank adds, at a later stage, a magnetic encoding for the amount being paid (in this case £43.27). This enables a computer to debit the account automatically.

9.4 Open and Crossed Cheques

An **open** cheque has **no crossing** on its face. The payee named on an open cheque can obtain cash for it at the **bank** and **branch named on the cheque** i.e. from the drawee. Open cheques are unsafe because any person finding an open cheque might be able to obtain cash for it over the counter.

For this reason most cheques are now **crossed** and are **preprinted** with the crossing before a customer is given a cheque book. The effect of crossing a cheque is that the cheque **must** be paid into a bank account and cash **cannot** be obtained for it over the counter. There are two types of crossing.

9.4.1 Special crossings

A cheque which has been specially crossed must have the name of a bank and branch, written by the drawer, between the crossings. (Fig. 9.3).

The special crossing means that the cheque must be paid into an account at the bank named within the crossings. In most cases, however, the drawer would not know the name of the bank and branch of the payee and, instead, a general crossing would be used.

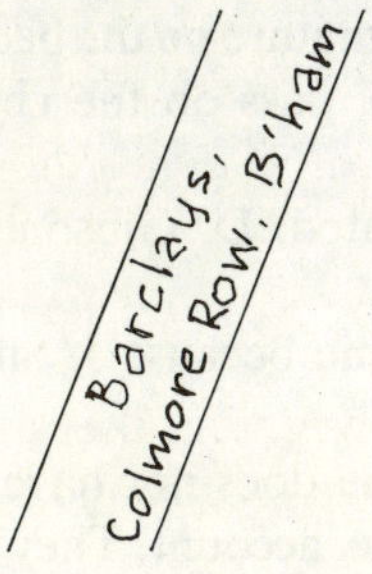

Fig. 9.3 A special crossing

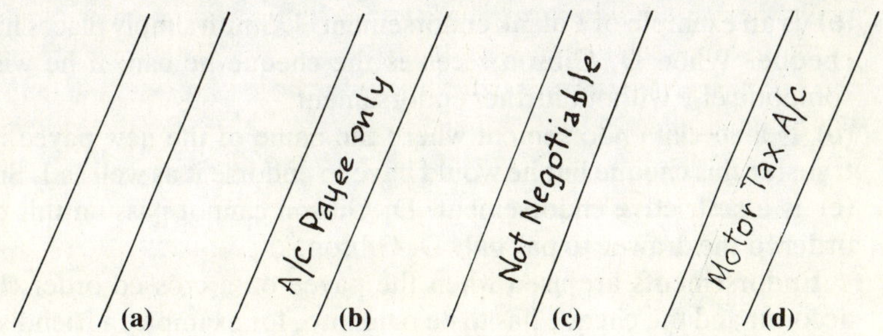

Fig. 9.4 General crossings

9.4.2 General crossings

A cheque which has a general crossing must be paid into a bank account but the name of the bank and branch into which the cheque must be paid is not named. Examples of general crossings are shown in Fig. 9.4.

(a) gives the preprinted crossing on a cheque when it is received by the current account holder. The drawer can leave the crossing as shown in **(a)** or he could add
(b) account payee only—this cheque must now be paid into the payee's bank account and it cannot normally be transferred to anyone else (see Unit 9.5).
(c) is **not negotiable**—this cheque can be transferred (see Unit 9.5) but the new owner of the cheque has no better title (claim to ownership) to it than the person from whom he received it. Thus an honest person who accepts a stolen cheque with a 'not negotiable' crossing has no legal right to the cheque and the cheque can be taken from him (Fig. 9.5).

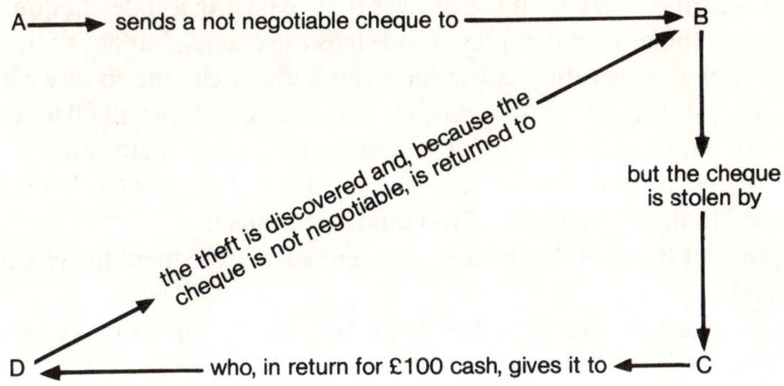

Fig. 9.5 A not negotiable cheque

(d) shows a motor tax account—a payee can often request the drawer of a cheque to use a particular crossing. In this case a person taxing his car is asked to write 'motor tax a/c' within the crossing which means the cheque must be paid into that account.

Although crossings **(b)** to **(d)** contain instructions they remain general crossings because the **name of a bank has not been specified** within the crossing.

9.5 Order and Bearer Cheques

1 Most cheques are **order** cheques because they contain the instruction 'Pay ..... OR ORDER'. The drawee (bank) is, therefore, instructed to pay the payee or the payee can order the bank to pay to a third party. For example, J. Smith is named as the payee on a cheque. He can order the drawee to pay someone else by **endorsing** the cheque, that is, by signing his own name on the back of the cheque. The endorsed cheque can then be handed over to the new payee. Fig. 9.6 gives examples of possible endorsements which can be used when J. Smith transfers a cheque to D. Gibson.

(a)	(b)	(c)
J. Smith	Pay D. Gibson J. Smith	Pay D. Gibson only J. Smith

Fig. 9.6 Endorsing a cheque

(a) is an example of a **blank** endorsement. J. Smith simply places his signature on the back of the cheque. When D. Gibson receives the cheque he can, if he wishes, pass on the cheque to someone else without further endorsement.
(b) is a **special** endorsement where the name of the new payee is stated. D. Gibson can still transfer this cheque but he would have to endorse it as well as J. Smith.
(c) is a **restrictive** endorsement. D. Gibson cannot pass on this cheque because J. Smith has ordered the drawee to pay **only** D. Gibson.

Endorsements are used when the payee on a crossed order cheque does not have a bank account and the cheque has to be paid into, for example, a friend's bank account. They are also used when the payee wishes to place the cheque into a building society account instead of his own current account.

2 Bearer cheques, which may be open or crossed, carry the instruction 'Pay ..... OR BEARER'. The bank must pay the payee or the bearer, i.e. the person holding the cheque. This is clearly unsafe because any person possessing an open bearer cheque can obtain cash for it over the counter. It is for this reason that bearer cheques are used infrequently.

9.6 Other Features of Cheques

1 A customer can withdraw cash from his current account by writing **'cash'** or **'self'** after the word 'Pay' on the cheque. The cheque can then be presented at his **own branch of the bank.** If the cheque is presented at any **other** branch then a maximum of £50 can be withdrawn in cash on presentation of a **cheque guarantee card** (see Unit 9.7).

2 Alterations to a cheque must be accompanied by the initials of the drawer.

3 A **post-dated** cheque bears a date later than that on which it was written and will not be paid by the drawee until that date.

4 A **stale** cheque is one presented for payment more than six months after the date on the cheque. The bank will first check with the drawer before paying a stale cheque.

5 On a **blank** cheque the drawer completes and signs the cheque but does not fill in the amount to be paid. For example, a secretary could be given a blank cheque to buy office supplies at a local shop. When the total cost of these items is known the secretary will fill in this amount on the cheque. Blank cheques are used infrequently because they could be unsafe.

6 If the drawee writes **'refer to drawer'** across a cheque the cheque has been **dishonoured** and the bank has refused to make payment. This could be because:
(a) there are **insufficient funds** in the drawer's current account to meet the cheque; in effect, the cheque has bounced,
(b) the drawer has asked the bank to **stop** payment, i.e. refuse to make payment when the cheque is presented,
(c) there is a **mistake or omission** on the cheque. It could be that the amount given in words does not correspond with the amount shown in figures or it has not been signed.

Advantages of paying by cheque

1 Paying by cheque is safer and more convenient than having to carry large sums of cash.
2 The payment of a cheque through a bank is legal evidence that payment has been made.
3 Payment can be stopped by the drawer if necessary.
4 The bank keeps a record of cheque payments which is regularly sent to the customer in the form of a bank statement of account (see Unit 9.9).

9.7 Withdrawals from a Current Account

9.7.1 Cheque guarantee card

The main form of **withdrawal** or **payment** from a current account is by means of **cheques** which have been described in detail in Units 9.3 to 9.6. Such payments are often **supported by cheque guarantee cards** which are issued to some holders of bank current accounts.

Shops are reluctant to accept payment by cheque because there is always the danger that the cheque may bounce. For this reason cheque guarantee cards are used. When payment is made by cheque the drawer's cheque guarantee card (Fig. 9.7) is presented to the payee who will write the number of the card on the back of the cheque. If the cheque is then dishonoured the bank will normally guarantee to pay the payee. This guarantee only applies to cheques of amounts up to £50. Cheque guarantee cards must also be used when a current account holder wishes to withdraw cash (£50 maximum) at a bank branch other than his own.

Fig. 9.7 Cheque guarantee card

Other methods of withdrawal from a current account include standing orders, direct debits and cash dispensing machines.

9.7.2 Standing orders

A **standing order** is used when a **current account holder** authorizes the bank to make **regular** payments of a **fixed** amount from the current account e.g. monthly mortgage repayments to building societies. When the amount has to be altered the current account holder will have to inform the bank of the new amount.

9.7.3 Direct debits

A **direct debit** is used when payments are either **irregular** and/or of **varying** amounts e.g. a subscription to a club which is increased each year. With a direct debit the current account holder authorizes the bank to make any payment requested by a payee. It is, therefore, the responsibility of the payee to tell the bank of any changes in the amount to be paid and a new direct debit authorization does not have to be signed by the current account holder.

The advantages to a current account holder of paying by standing order or direct debit are that individual cheques do not have to be written and the account holder does not have to remember to make the payments.

9.7.4 Cash dispensing machines (cash dispensers)

Cash dispensing machines are placed inside or outside banks and allow current account holders to withdraw cash without presenting a cheque. The holder is issued with a cash card which is inserted into the dispensing machine (Fig. 9.8). The holder then types in his own personal identification number (PIN) and the amount needed in cash. Some cash dispensers have additional keys which allow a current account holder to:

(a) receive details of the present balance in the current account,
(b) order a new cheque book, *and*
(c) order a bank statement.

Fig. 9.8 A cash dispensing machine

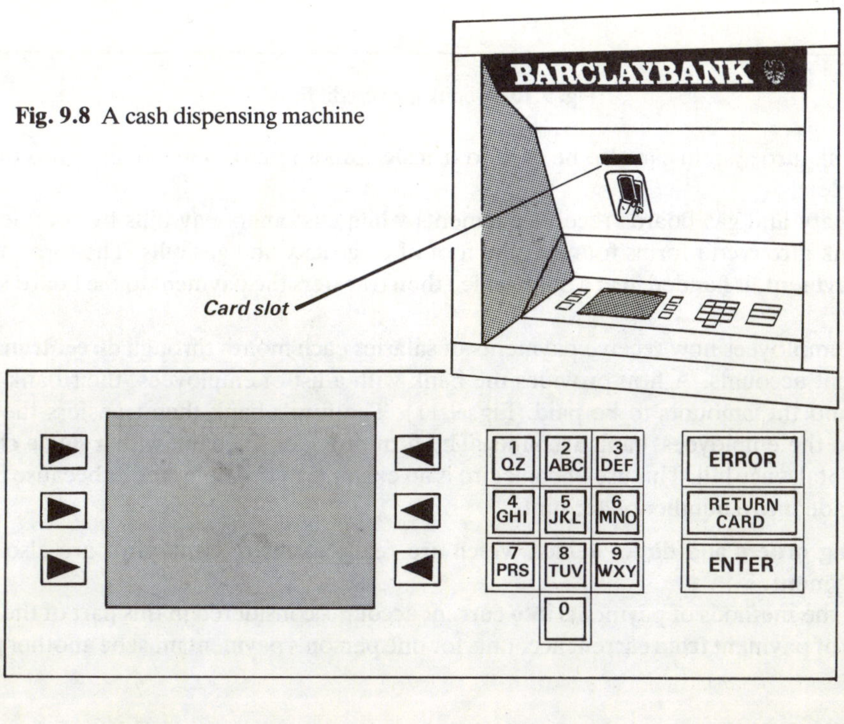

9.8 Payments into a Current Account

1 A current account holder can deposit cash and cheques directly **with his own bank branch** by completing a **paying-in slip** (Fig. 9.9). A receipted counterfoil is retained by the customer as evidence of in-payment or deposit.

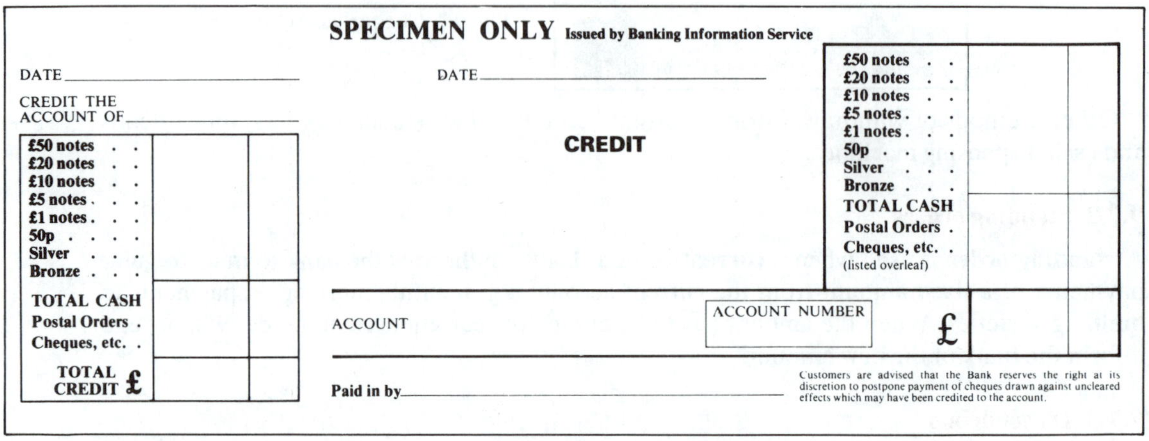
SPECIMEN ONLY Issued by Banking Information Service

DATE
CREDIT THE ACCOUNT OF
£50 notes
£20 notes
£10 notes
£5 notes
£1 notes
50p
Silver
Bronze
TOTAL CASH
Postal Orders
Cheques, etc.
TOTAL CREDIT £

DATE
CREDIT
ACCOUNT
ACCOUNT NUMBER
Paid in by

£50 notes
£20 notes
£10 notes
£5 notes
£1 notes
50p
Silver
Bronze
TOTAL CASH
Postal Orders
Cheques, etc. (listed overleaf)
£

Customers are advised that the Bank reserves the right at its discretion to postpone payment of cheques drawn against uncleared effects which may have been credited to the account.

Fig. 9.9 A paying-in slip

2 If a current account holder wishes to pay money into his own bank account but **at another bank or branch** then a **bank giro credit form** is used (Fig. 9.10).

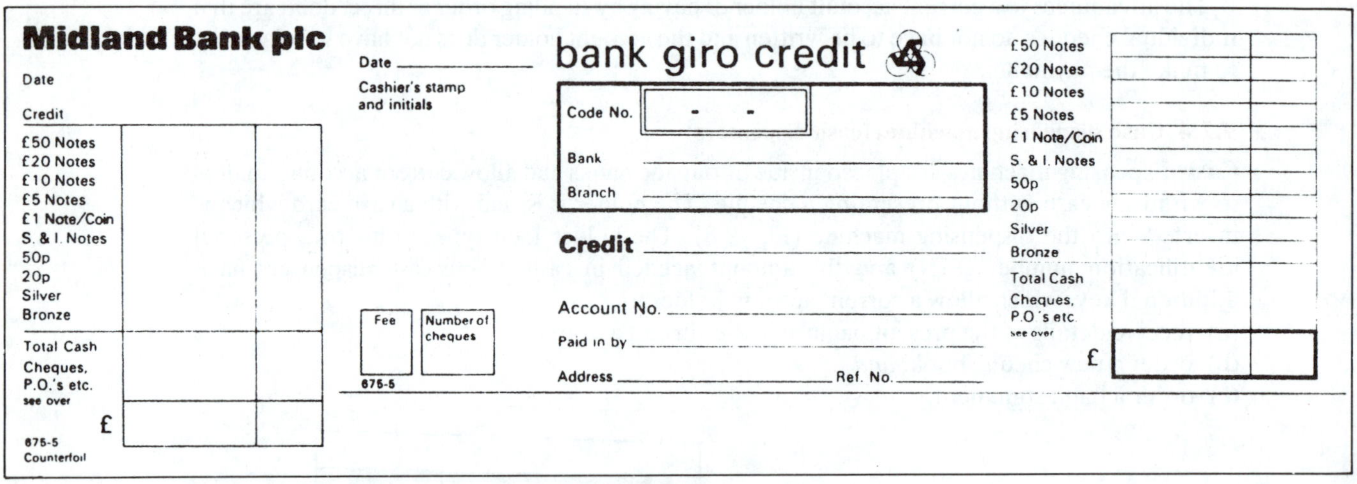
Midland Bank plc
Date
Credit
£50 Notes
£20 Notes
£10 Notes
£5 Notes
£1 Note/Coin
S. & I. Notes
50p
20p
Silver
Bronze
Total Cash
Cheques, P.O.'s etc. see over
£
675-5 Counterfoil

Date
Cashier's stamp and initials
Fee
Number of cheques
675-5

bank giro credit
Code No.
Bank
Branch
Credit
Account No.
Paid in by
Address
Ref. No.

£50 Notes
£20 Notes
£10 Notes
£5 Notes
£1 Note/Coin
S. & I. Notes
50p
20p
Silver
Bronze
Total Cash
Cheques, P.O.'s etc. see over
£

Fig. 9.10 A bank giro credit form

3 The bank giro system can also be used to **transfer funds** into the current accounts of others. For example:

(a) Electricity and gas boards receive payments when customers pay bills by completing the special bank giro credit forms found at the foot of electricity and gas bills. The form, together with the payment, is handed in at a bank which then transfers the payment to the board's current account.

(b) Many employees now receive payments of salaries each month through **direct transfer** into their current accounts. A firm provides the bank with a list of employees, their bank account numbers and the amounts to be paid (Fig. 9.11). The firm's bank then transfers the various amounts to the employees' bank accounts. The firm provides the bank with a **single cheque** to cover the total wage bill. This use of bank giro is an example of multiple credits because payment is being made into a number of accounts.

4 **Standing orders** and **direct debits,** which are really forms of bank giro, are also used to receive payment.

Most of the methods of payments **into** current accounts considered in this part of the unit are also forms of payment **from** current accounts for one person's payment must be another person's receipt!

BANK GIRO CREDIT TRANSFER SCHEDULE

To The ....

Branch at ....

List No. .... Date ....

Kindly distribute the attached credit slips, as arranged with the recipients, and debit our Account No. .... with the amount of £.............. for which our cheque is enclosed.

Signature..............................

Bank Code	*Bank and Branch*	*Payee's Name*	*Net Amount*
		TOTAL	

Fig. 9.11 A bank giro credit schedule

9.9 Bank Statement of Account

A bank statement of account is a **record of payments into** and **from** a **current account** for a given period of time and is usually sent regularly to the current account holder.

Fig. 9.12 gives a simplified bank statement where payments **into** the account are shown in the **receipts** or **credit** column and payments **from** the account are in the **payments** or **debit** column. The abbreviations used are defined at the foot of the statement except for:

(1) 382 and 383 which are the last three digits of each of the cheques debited on 14 and 16 May.

(2) the sundry credit on 10 June which could have been a deposit of cash and/or cheques using a paying-in slip.

BARCLAYS BANK
LIVERPOOL

Title of Account: B. Edwards — Account No 983467

Date	*Details*		*Payments*	*Receipts*	*Balance*
1985	Balance forward				150.00
14 May		382	90.00		60.00
16 May		383	180.00		120.00 DR
28 May	Salary	BGC		400.00	280.00
1 June		SO	20.00		260.00
4 June		DD	40.00		220.00
5 June		CD	10.00		210.00
8 June		CHS	2.00		208.00
10 June	Sundry credit			54.00	262.00

Abbreviations

BGC	Bank Giro Credit	CD	Cash Dispenser
DD	Direct Debit	CHS	Bank charges
SO	Standing Order	DR or OD	Overdrawn balance

Fig. 9.12 A bank statement of account

9.10 Bank Lending

When a customer wishes to borrow from a bank his branch manager will have to consider the following points before deciding whether to lend.

1 The **character of the customer.** Is the customer honest and has his banking record been sound?

2 The **amount** needed. Has the customer asked to borrow enough money and does he have any savings which can be used alongside the loan?

3 The **period of repayment.** For how long does the customer need the money?

4 The **purpose** of the loan. For what is the money to be used?

5 The **capability of the customer to repay the loan.** Will the loan be used to give sufficient profit to repay the loan or does the customer have sufficient income from other sources?

6 The **collateral security** available. Does the customer have any assets, e.g. a house or share certificates, which can be used as security for the loan? If the customer is unable to repay then the security can be sold in order that the bank may obtain its money.

7 **Government guidelines** with respect to bank lending. As part of its general economic policy the government might instruct banks to give preference to certain types of borrowers, e.g. exporters.

9.10.1 Loans

1 A **loan** is for a **stated sum of money,** e.g. £200,
2 for a **stated** period of time, e.g. for two years.
3 The rate of interest is **fixed for the length of the loan**
4 and is **based on the principal** (the full amount borrowed)
5 **whether or not** it has been used.

When a loan is agreed, a **separate loan account** is created for the customer. This loan account is **debited** with the amount borrowed, while at the same time the customer's current account is **credited** with that amount. The customer can then spend this sum immediately from his current account and repayments will be made every month to the loan account, usually by standing order, until the loan **plus interest** is repaid. Before granting a loan the bank manager will ask the customer to complete a loan application form so that the manager can assess the ability of the customer to repay.

9.10.2 Overdrafts

An **overdraft** occurs when the holder of a current account

1 is allowed to issue cheques for **more** than the holder has in his account **up to an agreed maximum.**
2 The rate of interest can **vary** during the period of the overdraft
3 and is charged **only on the amount overdrawn** on a **day-to-day basis.**
4 Overdrafts can be **repayable on demand** although in practice, banks rarely insist on this.

Before granting an overdraft the bank manager will probably not ask for an application form to be completed but will simply talk to the applicant. An overdraft is, therefore, a **less formal method** of lending, although the manager must still ensure that the overdraft will be repaid.

A firm will use a loan when buying fixed assets (see Unit 17.2) e.g. machinery or vehicles, where the **precise** amount to be spent and the **time when required** are known. A **personal loan** can be taken out by an individual to buy, say, a car.

A firm will use an overdraft as **working capital** (see Unit 17.2) to buy stock, pay wages etc where the amount needed is not known exactly and may vary from day to day. An individual can take out an overdraft to cover the period, for example, when he suffers a temporary loss of income, or when he has to meet unexpected expenses.

9.11 Other Services Provided by Banks

Credit cards. These are not issued by the banks themselves but by separate **credit card companies** which are, however, owned by the banks, e.g. **Barclaycard** (Barclays) and **Access** (Lloyds, National Westminster, Midland and Williams and Glyn's). The holder of a credit card (Fig. 9.13) is allowed to buy goods and services on credit, **up to an agreed maximum,** at those firms which accept that particular credit card. The sequence of events in a credit card transaction is:

1 The card holder buys goods from a shop and signs a special voucher.

2 The voucher is sent to the credit card company which
3 pays the shop for the goods less a commission for the credit card company.
4 The credit card holder then sends a monthly statement to the cardholder (Fig. 9.13) who can
5 pay **all** that is owed when **no interest** may be charged or
6 in the case of some cards, pay **some** of what is owed and **interest will be charged on the remainder.**

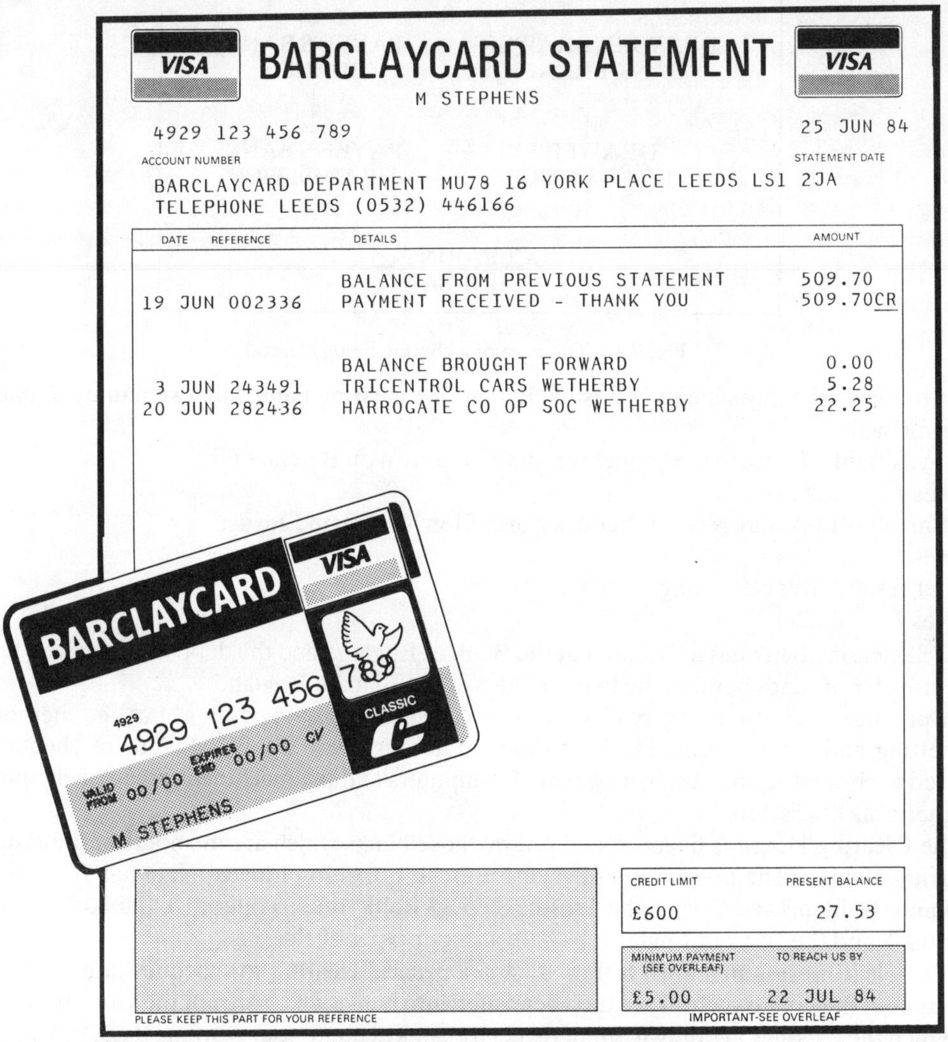

BARCLAYCARD STATEMENT

M STEPHENS

4929 123 456 789 — ACCOUNT NUMBER

25 JUN 84 — STATEMENT DATE

BARCLAYCARD DEPARTMENT MU78 16 YORK PLACE LEEDS LS1 2JA
TELEPHONE LEEDS (0532) 446166

DATE	REFERENCE	DETAILS	AMOUNT
		BALANCE FROM PREVIOUS STATEMENT	509.70
19 JUN	002336	PAYMENT RECEIVED - THANK YOU	509.70CR
		BALANCE BROUGHT FORWARD	0.00
3 JUN	243491	TRICENTROL CARS WETHERBY	5.28
20 JUN	282436	HARROGATE CO OP SOC WETHERBY	22.25

CREDIT LIMIT	PRESENT BALANCE
£600	27.53

MINIMUM PAYMENT (SEE OVERLEAF)	TO REACH US BY
£5.00	22 JUL 84

PLEASE KEEP THIS PART FOR YOUR REFERENCE

IMPORTANT-SEE OVERLEAF

Fig. 9.13 A credit card and credit card statement

Some credit cards, such as Barclaycard, can also be used
(a) to **withdraw cash** from any branch of Barclays bank when, in effect, the credit card company is lending cash to the cardholder. In this case interest is immediately charged on the amount withdrawn
(b) as a **cheque guarantee card** (see Unit 9.7.1)
(c) as a **cash card** (see Unit 9.7.4)

Cards such as American Express and Diners' Club are not like Barclaycard or Access because the full amount owing has to be repaid each month. Credit is, therefore, only allowed for at most one month.

Night safes A night safe allows firms to deposit money when the bank is closed.

Miscellaneous services provided by a bank include:
1 the safe custody of valuables.
2 the issue of travellers' cheques which can be used by, for example, holidaymakers when abroad.
3 the sale and purchase of securities for customers.
4 executor departments which deal with wills.

9.12 The Clearing of Cheques

The use of cheques for payments often results in a **transfer of funds** between branches of different banks. The purpose of the clearing system is to **effect** this transfer. Fig. 9.14 shows the path of a cheque which has to undergo clearing.

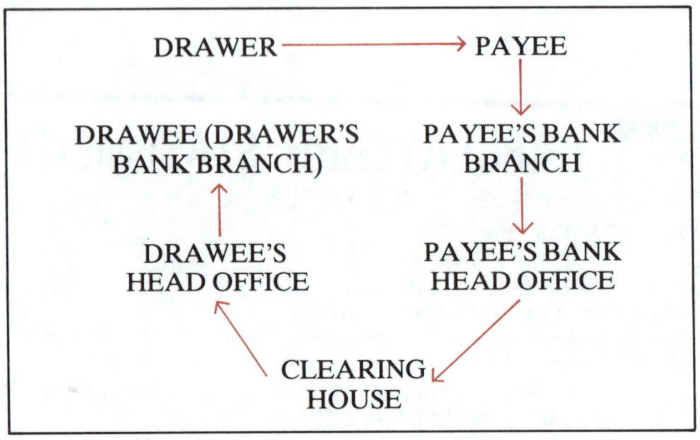

Fig. 9.14 The path of a cheque being cleared

At the end of a day's clearing it is likely that one clearing bank will owe money to another clearing bank.
If Lloyds Bank (*L*) receives cheques worth £20m drawn on Barclays (*B*);
B owes *L* £20m
but Barclays Bank may receive cheques worth £18m drawn on Lloyds:
L owes *B* £18m
the net result, after off-setting, is that
B owes *L* £2m

Each clearing bank has an account at the Bank of England and the debt of £2m will be settled by a transfer of funds beween the two accounts at the Bank of England.

In practice more than two banks are involved in the clearing system but the methods of off-setting and settling using Bank of England accounts still apply. Millions of cheques are cleared each working day using a system of computers and the machine-reading of cheques via magnetic ink characters.

The Clearing House is financed and run by those banks which are members of the **Bankers' Clearing House.** (The present members are Barclays, Coutts, Lloyds, National Westminster, Midland, Williams and Glyn's, the Trustee Savings Bank, the Co-operative Bank, the National Girobank and the Bank of England.) There are four types of clearing:

1 The clearing system shown in Fig. 9.14 is a **general** clearing for cheques drawn on banks throughout the country which are then deposited into banks which are **not** the same as the banks on which the cheques are drawn. General clearing takes about four working days.

2 **Town** clearing is for cheques drawn on banks within the City of London only.

3 **Internal** clearing is for cheques drawn on **one branch** and paid into **another branch** of the **same** bank. Another form of internal clearing is **branch** clearing which is for cheques drawn on and paid into accounts at the **same** branch. There is no need for 'internal' cheques to enter general clearing and for the Clearing House to be involved.

4 **Credit** clearing is used for transfers resulting from, for example, bank giro credits and standing orders.

10 Other kinds of bank and methods of payment

10.1 The Bank of England

The Bank of England is the central bank of the United Kingdom. It is owned by the **Government** and:

1 controls the **issue of notes and coins** in England and Wales (the **Royal Mint** is responsible for the **manufacture** of coins).

2 holds the United Kingdom's **gold and foreign currency reserves.**

3 is the **Government's bank.** The Government has an account at the Bank of England in the same way as individuals have current accounts at clearing banks.

4 is the **bankers' bank.** The clearing banks have accounts at the Bank of England which are used for the settlement of inter-bank debts which result from cheque clearing (see Unit 9.12).

5 enforces part of government **economic policy** in accordance with the wishes of the Government, e.g. by influencing interest rates.

6 manages the Government's debt. The Bank of England is responsible for borrowing on behalf of the Government by issuing Government stock and for making interest payments and capital repayments to those who hold Government stock.

10.2 Merchant Banks

Merchant banks, such as Hambros and Rothschild, provide services to **firms** rather than to individuals. Their services include:

1 advice. Many companies employ merchant banks to give advice about the running of a company particularly with regard to share issues, take-overs and mergers.

2 finance. Merchant banks lend to firms and can also provide factoring (see Unit 11.4.3), hire purchase finance (see Unit 11.2), leasing (see Unit 11.4.2) and the acceptance of bills of exchange (see Unit 8.3).

3 dealing in foreign exchange. When a United Kingdom firm wants to borrow from an organization in a foreign country the merchant bank can arrange the loan for the firm and then convert the foreign currency into sterling.

10.3 National Girobank

The National Girobank operates through the **national network of post offices.** Both individuals and firms can open Girobank accounts which are **all** held centrally at a single **computer** centre. Paragraphs 10.3.1 and 10.3.2 deal with services provided by the National Girobank.

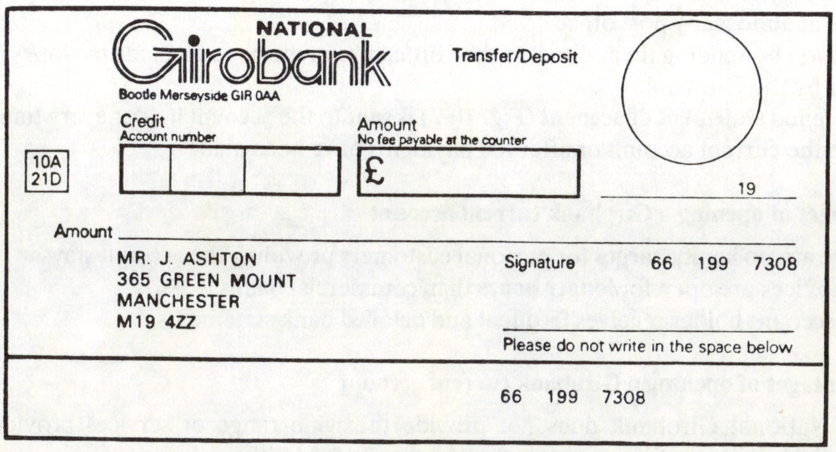

NATIONAL Girobank

Bootle Merseyside GIR 0AA

Transfer/Deposit

Credit
Account number

Amount
No fee payable at the counter

10A
21D

£

19

Amount

MR. J. ASHTON
365 GREEN MOUNT
MANCHESTER
M19 4ZZ

Signature 66 199 7308

Please do not write in the space below

66 199 7308

Fig. 10.1 A Girobank in-payment form

10.3.1 Current accounts

1 A current account holder can make payment to others by:

(a) completing an **in-payment form** (Fig. 10.1) to pay those who **possess Girobank accounts.** The form can be handed in at a post office or sent by post to the Girocentre. The sum to be paid is then **transferred** between accounts at the computer centre and cheques or cash are **not** used. Many household bills such as gas and electricity have Girobank transfer slips already attached so that payment can be made in a similar way.

(b) using a **Girocheque** (Fig. 10.2) to pay those who do **not** possess Girobank accounts. Girobank current account holders are issued with cheque books and many also possess Girobank **cheque guarantee cards** (see Unit 9.7).

Fig. 10.2 A Girobank advertisement showing a cheque-book, cheque card, statement and pre-paid envelope

(c) **standing order** (See Unit 9.7)

(d) **automatic debit transfer** which is similar to direct debit (see Unit 9.7)

2 **Withdrawals** can be made by **cashing a Girocheque.**

(a) The current account holder is allowed to withdraw on demand up to £50 in cash, every other working day, at either of **two named** post offices. For larger sums a few day's notice of withdrawal is required.

(b) If the account holder has a cheque guarantee card then Girocheques can be cashed on demand every other working day. Up to £50 can be withdrawn at **any** post office or up to £100 at a **named** post office.

3 **Payments into** a current account can be made by depositing:

(a) **cash,** at almost any post office

(b) **cheques,** by sending them direct to the Girocentre in the postage-paid envelopes (Fig. 10.2) provided by the Girobank

4 A detailed **statement of account** (Fig. 10.2) is sent to the account holder every time money is paid into the current account or after ten payments have been made.

Advantages of opening a Girobank current account

1 There are **no bank charges** for personal customers providing the account stays in credit.

2 Post offices are open for **longer hours** than commercial banks.

3 The account holder receives **frequent** and **detailed** bank statements.

Disadvantages of opening a Girobank current account

1 The National Girobank does not provide the wide range of services provided by the commercial banks e.g. there are only **limited overdraft facilities.**

2 Only **limited** sums of money can be withdrawn **on demand.**

10.3.2 Deposit accounts

Deposit accounts, which carry interest, can be opened by any Girobank current account holder. No notice of withdrawal is required but the method of withdrawal is by **transfer** to the deposit account holder's Girobank current account.

10.3.3 Budget accounts

The budget accounts run by the National Girobank are similar to the budget accounts of the commercial banks (see Unit 9.2).

10.3.4 Personal loans

There are only limited overdraft facilities for current account holders and the only way of borrowing from the National Girobank is by a personal loan which can be for periods of up to three years.

10.3.5 Travellers' cheques

The National Girobank will issue travellers' cheques and **foreign currency.**

10.3.6 Transcash

Transcash allows those who do **not possess** Girobank accounts to send payment to those who **do.** A Transcash form is completed and handed in at a post office which forwards the form and payment to the Girocentre. A small administration fee is charged by the post office for providing this service.

10.4 Trustee Savings Banks

The Trustee Savings Banks (TSB) were originally set up as savings institutions under government control. They still offer **savings** facilities but have gradually introduced similar services to those provided by the clearing banks for **individuals** e.g. current accounts, cheques, cheque guarantee cards, credit cards, personal loans and overdrafts, as well as mortgages.
Unlike the other clearing banks the TSB:

1 are **non-profit making.**

2 provide services mainly for **individuals** and **non-profit making organizations** rather than firms.

3 are **public bodies** under the control of the **Treasury** although there are plans to change them into public limited companies.

10.5 The National Savings Bank

The National Savings Bank (NSB) operates through the network of post offices. Unlike the Trustee Savings Banks which offer a wide range of banking services, the NSB mainly provides facilities for **savings** through its ordinary and investment accounts (see Unit 21.4).

10.6 Other Methods of Payment

The payment facilities described in Units 9, 10.3 and 10.4 are provided by the **banks** and allow payment to be made by cheque, transfer between bank accounts, e.g. by standing order, and credit cards.

Such facilities are needed because payment by **cash** (notes and coins), although suitable for low value purchases, is unsafe for larger amounts. Those who do not possess bank accounts (the **unbanked**) cannot generally use the payment services provided by the banks but can use the methods of payment provided by the **Post Office.** These include:

1 postal orders. Postal orders can be obtained at any post office for varying amounts up to £10. Those buying postal orders have to pay an additional charge called **poundage** which covers the cost of providing the order. A postal order can be **crossed** (see Unit 9.4) which means that the payee has to pay the order into a bank account.

2 inland telegraphic payment orders. Inland orders can be used for sending payments of up to £100 to destinations within the United Kingdom. **International payment orders** are available for sending sums of up to £50 overseas.

3 registered post. Cash and other valuables can be sent by registered post (see Unit 16.2).

4 cash on delivery (COD). A customer must pay the postman **before** mail order goods are handed over.

11 Buying and selling on credit

11.1 Introduction

When people buy goods on credit, **possession** of these goods, but not necessarily their **ownership,** can be immediately obtained. Full payment for the goods is then made at a **later** date or dates. Goods can be bought on credit by members of the public (**consumer** credit) and by firms (**business** credit). One form of business credit is **trade** credit which is given between traders e.g. by a wholesaler to a retailer.
If credit is **not** used then the goods can be obtained by:
1 **paying for them in full:** ownership is immediately acquired
2 **renting, hiring or leasing** (see Unit 11.4): ownership **never** passes to those possessing and using the goods.

11.2 Hire Purchase and Credit Sale

Hire purchase (HP) and credit sale are two important forms of credit used by consumers and firms to purchase goods.

11.2.1 When buying on **hire purchase** a consumer signs an agreement to pay a **deposit** followed by a number of monthly **instalments.** Buying on hire purchase usually costs **more** than the immediate payment (Fig. 11.1).

Cash price	*Deposit*	*Monthly instalments*	*HP price (total)*
£400	20% of £400 = £80	24 at £20 = £480	£560

Fig. 11.1 The cost of buying on hire purchase or credit sales

When buying goods under a hire purchase contract the consumer:
1 **is not the owner** of the goods until the **final** instalment has been paid
2 cannot **sell** the goods until the **end** of the contract
3 must **look after** the goods because he does not own them
4 must **pay the agreed instalments.** If instalments are not paid the seller can **repossess** the goods. If, however, **one third** or more of the total HP price has been paid the seller must first obtain a court order
5 can **withdraw** from the agreement within the first five days and return the goods. This is known as a **cooling-off period** and has been designed to help those consumers who might be pressured by door-to-door salesmen into signing credit agreements. If, however, the HP agreement has been signed on **trade premises,** for example, in a shop, then **no withdrawal** is possible
6 can **cancel** the agreement at any time and return the goods but at least **half** of the total HP price must first be paid

11.2.2 Buying on **credit sale** (**deferred payment**) is similar to buying on hire purchase because the consumer:
1 agrees to pay a **deposit** followed by **instalments** (Fig. 11.1), *and*
2 is given a **cooling-off period** as for hire purchase (see 5 above).
However there are important differences. Under credit sales the consumer:
1 **owns** the goods **immediately the agreement is made.**
2 can **sell** the goods at **any time** but will still have to pay what is owing.
3 can only be **sued** for the **amount owing** if instalments are not paid. The goods **cannot be repossessed by the seller.**

4 cannot **cancel** the agreement and return the goods.

The regulations relating to hire purchase and credit sale described above are contained in the **Consumer Credit Act 1974.** Further details of this important Act are given in Unit 11.6.

Goods sold on hire purchase are those which are more expensive, have a long life and also have a good re-sale value. Examples of such goods are cars, furniture and television sets. It is worthwhile for a supplier to repossess these types of goods in the event of non-payment of instalments.

Goods sold on credit sale are those which are suitable for one person only and which have a poor re-sale value e.g. clothing. Credit sale, and not hire purchase, is also used when repossession could be difficult as in the case of mail order goods e.g. televisions.

11.3 Other Forms of Credit

11.3.1 Monthly (or weekly) accounts

Monthly (or weekly) accounts are operated by, for example, department stores and garages. Customers sign for goods bought during the month (or week) and the amounts owing are expected to be **settled in full** at the end of each month (or week). Retailers sometimes charge customers for providing this service. Trade credit operates in a similar way when a firm settles an account with a supplier often monthly or possibly three-monthly.

11.3.2 Shop budget accounts (or revolving credit)

The shop budget accounts operated by department stores and some chain stores should not be confused with the budget accounts provided by banks (see Unit 9.2.3). With a shop budget account a customer agrees to make **monthly payments** of, say, £10 to a shop. He is then allowed to buy goods to the value of, say, £200 (twenty times the monthly payment). As the customer repays what he owes this allows him to buy more goods providing the credit purchases do not exceed £200 (Fig. 11.2). Retailers normally charge for providing this service.

Month	*Payment*	*Goods bought*	*Amount owing*
January	£10	£200	£190 (200 − 10)
February	£10		£180
March	£10		£170
April	£10	£15	£175 (170 − 10 + 15)

Fig. 11.2 A shop budget account where there is no service charge

11.3.3 Trading checks

Check trading companies employ **agents** to call on customers, say, every week. A customer could buy a £40 trading check (or voucher) which allows him to buy goods up to the value of £40 **at those shops which accept the trading check.** The retailer indicates on the check the value of goods bought so that the maximum of £40 is not exceeded. The customer would pay something like £5 to buy the check followed by twenty weekly payments of £2. The total amount paid is therefore, £45, the extra £5 being the charge made by the check trading company. Although trading checks are convenient for borrowers it is an expensive form of credit. The check trading company pays retailers for the goods bought by customers who have used its trading checks, but charges the retailers a commission for providing the service. Shops are prepared to pay this commission because, by accepting checks, extra business is obtained.

11.3.4 Credit cards

These are issued by banks and credit card companies (see Unit 9.11). Some retailers also issue credit cards for use at their own branches.

11.3.5 Loans and overdrafts

See Units 9.10.1 and 9.10.2

11.4 Finance Houses

Finance houses, or companies, which are often linked with clearing banks, obtain funds by

attracting deposits from the public and businesses, **borrowing** from the clearing banks, and **selling** shares and debentures.

These funds are then used to finance credit transactions, leasing and the factoring of debts.

11.4.1 Financing credit transactions

Goods bought on hire purchase or credit sale are often financed by a finance house. The finance house pays the shop for the value of goods bought and then receives payments from the customer by deposit and instalments (Fig. 11.3).

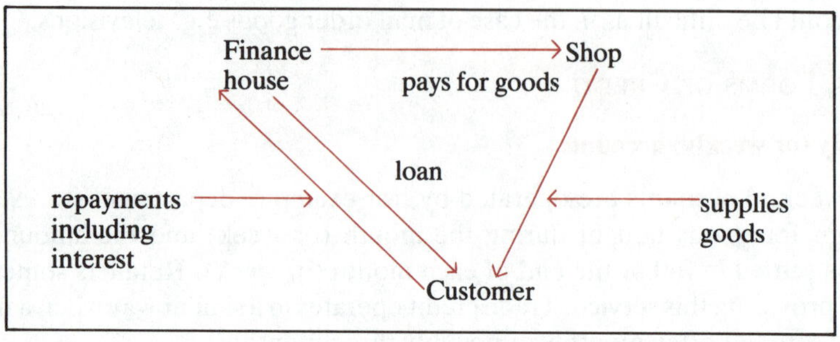

Fig. 11.3 The rôle of the finance house

Although the shop itself arranges the contract by dealing with the paperwork, accepting the deposit and sometimes the monthly instalments, it is acting on behalf of the finance house. Finance houses are important because many smaller retailers do not have sufficient funds to finance credit transactions.

Some consumers may borrow directly from a finance house, for example, to purchase a car or install double-glazing. In this case the retailer is not a party to the credit transaction.

11.4.2 Leasing

Instead of buying assets on credit firms often prefer to lease (or rent) such assets. Assuming that a firm wishes to obtain a new computer and has decided on the make and model required, it could use a finance house or specialist leasing company which would pay the supplier for the equipment and then lease it to the firm. The leasing agreement would involve monthly rental payments to the finance house over an agreed number of years. Under a leasing agreement the firm using the equipment possesses but never owns the equipment. At the end of the leasing period the finance house, which is the owner of the equipment, can re-lease the equipment to the user firm at a favourable rent, lease the equipment to another firm or sell the equipment.

Advantages to a firm of leasing equipment

1 It saves the high lump-sum capital expenditure which would be involved if the equipment was bought outright.

2 In the case of technical goods like computers more advanced equipment is being continually introduced. A series of short-term leases allows a firm continually to update its equipment.

3 By leasing firms may be able to receive tax advantages which could make leasing cheaper than buying outright.

11.4.3 Factoring of debts

The work of a financial factoring business (financial factor) (which should not be confused with the work of the factor engaged in wholesale trade (see Unit 5.2)) is to take over the trade debts of firms. When a firm sells goods on credit to other businesses, at any one time there may be large sums of money owing to the firm. Part of the firm's capital is, therefore, tied up in the form of debtors and the firm may be short of working capital to buy more raw materials or stock. The financial factor helps the firm to convert sums owing into cash in the following way.

The firms send copies of the relevant **invoices** to the factor which will immediately pay a large percentage of their value, less a **service** charge. The balance, less an **interest** charge, will be paid at a later date when the debtors have settled their accounts with the factor and when the factor is able to calculate the interest to be charged. The factor, therefore, takes over the debts of the firm. It can also administer the sales ledger of the firm which will save the firm administrative costs such as computer time, postage and salaries.

An additional benefit to the firm is provided if **non-recourse** factoring is used. If any debtor fails to pay what it owes it is the factor which bears the loss. The factor cannot claim from the client firm the latter of which will benefit from the provision of **100%** bad debt cover.

A financial factor needs large sums of money to carry out the factoring of debts and for this reason is often linked to a finance house or clearing bank.

11.5 Building Societies

Building societies provide loans to individuals who wish to buy or improve property. These loans are financed from the **deposits** which the public place with the societies. Building societies lend by means of a **mortgage** in which the property being bought is given as **security** for the loan. If the borrower fails to repay what is owed the building society can sell the property to recover the debt. Mortgages are usually given as a percentage of the value of a property to be purchased e.g. a 90% mortgage would mean that a borrower would have to find 10% of the value of the property from other sources. Mortgages are good examples of long-term loans which can extend over twenty years or more. **Insurance companies, local authorities** and the **clearing banks** also provide mortage finance.

11.6 The Consumer Credit Act 1974

The Consumer Credit Act 1974 covers most credit transactions and gives consumers a number of basic rights.

1 The right to information. A consumer wishing to buy a product on credit must be given **written details** of:
(a) the product's **cash price;**
(b) the **total cost** if bought on credit;
(c) the **true** rate of interest or **annual percentage rate** (APR) which is usually **greater** than the quoted or nominal rate of interest. If a consumer borrows £1000 over ten months he could agree to pay it back at £100 per month. If the lender charges interest of 2% per month (or 24% per year) **based on the amount originally borrowed,** a monthly interest payment of £20 is obtained. Each month, therefore, the consumer pays £120. For the final month, however, the consumer only owes £100 but still pays interest of £20 which is equivalent to an annual rate of interest of 240%. The quoted rate of interest of 24% per year is therefore much less than the true rate of interest which is being charged;
(d) the goods themselves e.g. a description of them;
(e) his **rights** and obligations under the Consumer Credit Act 1974, e.g. the right, if any, to cancel the agreement.

The Consumer Credit Act 1974 also lays down rules about what credit information must be displayed in **advertisements.**

2 the right to **withdraw** from the agreement (see Unit 11.2);
3 the right to **cancel** the agreement (see Unit 11.2);
4 protection against repossession (see Unit 11.2);
5 the payment of **rebates** to customers who make early settlements of what they owe;
6 if the product bought on credit is **faulty** the buyer can claim against the seller or, if necessary, the provider of credit e.g. the finance company where the loan is tied to some specific item or service.

The Consumer Credit Act 1974 also provides that those dealing in credit must first obtain a **licence** from the **Office of Fair Trading** (see Unit 13.4). A licence lasts for ten years and is renewable but can be withdrawn at any time in the event of the misconduct of the licence holder.

Those who have to register are:
1 the providers of credit e.g. clearing banks, finance houses;
2 those arranging the credit e.g. retailers; *and*
3 those indirectly involved e.g. credit reference agencies.

Credit reference agencies keep lists of consumers showing those who have defaulted on credit agreements and are thus poor credit risks.

Credit transactions **not** covered by the Consumer Credit Act 1974 include:
1 consumer credit transactions below £50 and over £15 000
2 house mortgages
3 credit given to corporate bodies e.g. companies

11.7 Advantages and Disadvantages of Buying on Credit

Advantages

1 Buying on credit allows **immediate use** of goods with the payment being made at later dates. A firm can buy a machine on credit and then use the profits from the output of the machine to repay what has been borrowed.

2 Without credit it would be impossible for most people to be able to afford **expensive** items e.g. a house.

3 Buying on credit allows a consumer to take advantage of **special reductions** in the prices of goods which are likely to be only temporary e.g. during January sales.

4 A consumer can benefit if the rate of inflation on the goods bought is **greater** than the true rate of interest charged in obtaining credit.

5 The availability of credit increases total spending which allows mass production resulting in **cheaper goods** for consumers.

Disadvantages

1 Buying on credit is **more expensive** than paying cash for goods.

2 Credit purchases often require **forms** to be completed and buying can then take longer than when paying by cash.

3 If credit is easily available consumers may be tempted to buy **more** than they can afford.

4 Buyers on credit could suffer from **disreputable traders** although the Consumer Credit Act 1974 attempts to reduce this possibility.

11.8 Advantages and Disadvantages of Selling on Credit

Advantages

1 By granting credit a firm can **increase sales.** This is particularly important for expensive items such as cars.

2 The **profits** derived from extra sales can outweigh the cost of borrowing to finance the credit sales.

3 Selling on credit might encourage **impulse buying** (see Unit 2.4).

4 Selling on credit encourages **customer loyalty.** For example, a person with a budget or monthly account at a shop is more likely to buy goods from that shop.

5 A finance house might pay a shop **commission** for credit transactions arranged on its behalf.

Disadvantages

1 Consumers may **fail** to pay what they owe and bad debts will result.

2 There are **extra administrative costs** when selling on credit e.g. keeping records of what customers owe.

3 There could be **extra costs** in having to **borrow** because more capital is tied up in debts.

4 Payment might have to be made to **other businesses** for providing credit facilities e.g. a retailer paying commission to a credit card company.

5 Those selling on credit have to abide by the **regulations** contained in the Consumer Credit Act 1974.

12 Advertising and marketing

12.1 The Purposes of Advertising

Advertising is used by firms to make other firms and consumers more aware of their products. It is an aid to trade and successful advertising will:

1 increase sales. By selling more a firm increases revenue and might also obtain economies of scale which results in lower average costs of production. The net profit of the firm would then increase if these benefits are greater than the costs of advertising.

2 give information. Through advertising a manufacturer can inform the public of, for example, the names and addresses of retailers stocking its products.

3 promote a brand name. Many products sold in shops are branded, that is, they are given brand names or **trade marks** to distinguish them from similar products. Examples include *Persil* washing powder and *Nescafé* coffee. Brand names are registered so that they cannot be copied by competitors. Some brand names are so well known that advertisements often show only the brand name and the product itself is not mentioned.

4 make consumers aware of new products. When a new product has been developed advertising is essential if consumers are to know of the new product and how, in some cases, it is different from existing products.

Advertising is not only undertaken by firms. The Government uses advertising to give details of, for example, changes in dental charges and National Insurance contributions. The public uses the 'small-ads' columns in newspapers when selling second-hand goods or advertising a service. Fig. 12.1 shows the amounts spent on advertising in the UK in 1982.

	£m	%
Press	1986	63.5
Television	928	29.7
Poster and Transport	124	4.0
Radio	70	2.2
Cinema	18	0.6
	3126	100.00

Source: Advertising Association

Fig. 12.1 Media spending in the United Kingdom in 1982

12.2 Persuasive, Informative and Competitive Advertising

Advertising can be divided into: **1** persuasive advertising, **2** informative advertising, and **3** competitive advertising.

1 Persuasive advertising is aimed mainly at consumers when firms are trying to increase sales. This advertising is helped by the use of brand names (see Unit 12.1).

Sometimes a group of similar firms act together to advertise a common product or service e.g. 'join the tea-set' and 'drink more milk'. This type of persuasive advertising is called **collective** or **generic** advertising.

2 Informative advertising is designed to give information which could be of benefit to firms or the public e.g.

(a) details of a new bus timetable

(b) information about increased postal charges

Informative advertising may, however , contain some elements of persuasion e.g.

(c) the dangers of smoking cigarettes

3 Competitive advertising is used by firms to encourage consumers to buy their products in preference to those of rival firms. Competitive advertising is often persuasive but can be **informative** e.g. discount stores displaying detailed price lists in newspaper advertisements.

12.3 The Media and Devices used in Advertising

The **medium** is concerned with **where** the advertisement is to be placed e.g. in a newspaper or on television. The **device** or **method of appeal** is concerned with **how** the advertisement is to be presented e.g. should a well-known personality be used in the advertisement?

The media available to advertisers include:

1 Commercial television

Advantages of television advertising are that:
(a) the advertisement can be directed at national or regional audiences
(b) the time chosen can suit the audience e.g. toys can be advertised during children's programmes
(c) it can be effective because it combines sound and colour vision as well as movement
Disadvantages of television advertising include:
(a) the expense, especially during peak hours
(b) the unsuitability when detailed information has to be given
(c) the fact that certain products cannot be advertised on television e.g. cigarettes

2 The national press

The **advantages** of using the national press, i.e. **newspapers** and **magazines** which sell throughout the country, for advertising are that:
(a) a national audience is possible.
(b) technical and detailed information can be given.
(c) the advertisement can be cut out and kept by the reader for future reference.
(d) it is less expensive than television.
(e) the particular audience at which the advertisement is directed can be more easily achieved, e.g. a firm selling computer programs could advertise in a computer magazine or a firm selling cash registers could advertise in the **trade journals** read by retailers.
The **disadvantages** of using the national press for advertising are that a newspaper advertisement:
(a) cannot have the same impact as a television advertisement,
(b) may not 'stand out' when placed among many other advertisements.

3 The local press

This includes newspapers and magazines which sell only in a **small geographical area.** The local press has some of the advantages and disadvantages of the national press but its main advantage is that it can be used when the audience must be a **local** one e.g. advertising the opening of a new shop.

4 Posters

These can be found, for example, on large hoardings by the side of roads or in shop windows. The message displayed is **short** so that passers-by can quickly read it. Some posters are left in position for months so the message need not be topical, although some messages are e.g. the times of a football match or a new television programme.

5 Other media

(a) commercial radio
(b) cinemas
(c) placards on buses and taxis
(d) catalogues and leaflets
(e) window displays
(f) illuminated signs

The **devices** used by advertisers include:

1 ambition and success: if the consumer buys a particular brand of clothes he could get a better job.

2 romance: if a woman buys a particular perfume she could become more attractive.

3 social acceptance: a consumer could make more friends if a particular brand of deodorant is used.

4 hero worship: a well-known personality is used to advertise a product. It is hoped that the consumer will buy the product because of the appeal of the personality.

5 the desire for an easy life: buying a new brand of washing machine will give the consumer more leisure.

6 comedy: if an advertisement is amusing the product shown will be remembered by the consumer who might then buy it.

The advertiser will have to consider both the media and the devices available before deciding which particular medium and device to use. In many cases more than one medium and one device will be used in an **advertising campaign.** A successful campaign will have appealed sufficiently to consumers to persuade them to buy the product advertised.

12.4 Advertising Agencies

Firms can arrange their own advertising, but when large sums of money are involved they often employ specialists to handle it for them. These specialists are **advertising agencies** which have five main functions.

1 **Market research** (see Unit 12.8.7).

2 **Creating** the advertisement. The agency will decide on the medium and device to be used and will bear in mind the information obtained from market research. A slogan or the selection of a tune would have to be decided at this stage.

3 **Producing** the advertisement. The advertisement is now drawn, filmed etc.

4 **Booking space** for the advertisement. The agency will book space in newspapers or time on television.

5 **Advice.** The agency will monitor the advertisement to see if it has been successful and will advise the manufacturer on what should be done next.

12.5 Control of Advertising

There is always the danger that advertising can mislead consumers by making untrue statements about products. Consumers are protected in the following ways:

1 The **Advertising Standards Authority** is financed by the advertising industry. Its rôle is to **investigate complaints** about advertisements placed in all media except commercial television and commercial radio. It publishes a **British Code of Advertising Practice** which requires all advertisements to be **'legal, decent, honest and truthful'.** Within the Code there are very strict rules about advertisements directed at children.

2 The **Independent Broadcasting Authority** (IBA) supervises advertisements on commercial television and commercial radio and investigates complaints about advertising appearing in these two media. In addition advertisements for some products, e.g. cigarettes, cannot be shown on television.

3 The **Trade Descriptions Act 1968.** Advertisers must not give incorrect or misleading descriptions of the products which they are advertising (see Unit 13.2.3).

4 The **Consumer Credit Act 1974.** When goods are sold on credit, the cash price, the price if bought on credit and the true rate of interest charged must be shown in advertisements for the goods (see Unit 11.6).

12.6 Benefits of Advertising

1 Advertising **informs** consumers of goods available and this allows them to make a more sensible choice when buying goods.

2 The existence of advertising **encourages competition** between firms which results in lower prices and better quality products.

3 Because of advertising firms are able to sell more. Mass production can then take place which **lowers prices.**

4 It keeps the **prices of newspapers low** and provides the **finance for commercial radio and television.**

12.7 Criticisms of Advertising

1 Advertising is expensive and, if it is unsuccessful, can result in **higher prices.**

2 It persuades consumers to buy goods they really **do not want.**

3 Consumers may also be persuaded to buy goods they cannot **afford.**

4 Advertising can be **misleading** and consumers could be disappointed with the advertised goods they have bought.

5 It **exploits** consumers by appealing to their emotions and places undue emphasis on material possessions.

12.8 Marketing

Advertising is often necessary if goods are to be sold to consumers. Without informative advertising, for example, consumers might be unaware of where to buy a particular product which would then remain unsold. Advertising is, however, just one of the many marketing activities needed in order that goods and services will eventually be bought by consumers. The activities which make up **marketing** include:

12.8.1 Product development

A manufacturer must continually develop new products to meet the **changing needs** of consumers and to meet **competition** from rival firms.

12.8.2 Packaging

A product must be **packaged** and **labelled** so that it **attracts** consumers. For example a bottle of shampoo should be easy to handle and the label should show the information expected by buyers of the product. The manufacturer must also carefully choose a **brand name** for the product.

12.8.3 Pricing

A price for the product must be set which **covers** all costs of **production** and yet is **low** enough to attract consumers from other products.

12.8.4 Distribution

There are a number of **channels of distribution** available to manufacturers (see Unit 4). A choice may have to be made between, for example, selling through mail order, selling directly to retailers or operating through wholesalers. Involved in the activity of distribution is the choice of a method of transport. For example, should a manufacturer operate his own fleet of vehicles to deliver goods to buyers?

12.8.5 Advertising

See Units 12.1 to 12.7.

12.8.6 Sales promotion

As well as advertising firms use sales promotion to attract customers to their products. Methods of sales promotion include:

(a) price reductions on goods for a limited period. **Coupons** can also be sent to householders who can exchange them for cheaper goods at shops.

(b) free gifts can be given to consumers who buy particular products.

(c) loss-leaders can be used to encourage consumers to enter shops (see Unit 2.4).

(d) competitions. Consumers are encouraged to enter competitions run by manufacturers but the entries must be accompanied by labels from products.

(e) point of sale displays. Manufacturers can provide shops with special fittings on which to display goods.

(f) demonstrations. Retailers selling home computers, for example, can demonstrate how to use the computers.

(g) after-sales service. For technical products the existence of a good after-sales service might encourage customers to buy.

(h) guarantees. Many firms are now offering longer guarantees on the goods they sell.

(i) trading stamps. Retailers buy trading stamps from a trading stamp company and then distribute them to their customers in proportion to the value of the goods each customer has bought. When sufficient stamps have been collected customers can exchange the stamps for cash or for goods at the trading stamp company. The retailers hope that the offer of trading stamps will increase sales sufficiently to cover at least the costs of running the scheme. Most retailers, however, have now given up trading stamps and offer lower prices instead.

12.8.7 Market research

Market research is undertaken so that a firm can identify:

(a) the market for a product, that is, whether a product is **likely to sell** in sufficient quantities to make production profitable,

(b) the **appropriate** marketing activities to use if production did take place.

Fig. 12.2 shows some of the ways in which a potential manufacturer of home computers could use the information obtained from market research.

Information on	*To decide on*
total demand for home computers number of firms producing home computers	whether there is a market for the firm's home computer
for what activities is the computer likely to be used? the technical features of existing home computers	product development — what type of home computer to produce
should the computer be portable?	packaging
the incomes of likely purchasers the prices of existing home computers	pricing
would consumers need advice before buying?	distribution — mail order may not be suitable
the newspapers and magazines read by potential buyers	advertising — in which newspaper or magazine to advertise?
is after-sales service important?	sales promotion — after-sales service could be used to promote sales

Fig. 12.2 The need for market research

Market research can be carried out by:
(a) the manufacturer's own market research department
(b) a market research company
(c) an advertising agency
Whichever organization carries out the research the **methods of market research** available to them include:
(a) **test marketing** which involves trial selling of the product in a small geographical area.
(b) **field investigation** where market researchers, using **questionnaires,** stop consumers in the street, telephone them or go from door-to-door.
(c) **consumer panels** where a specially chosen group of consumers is asked to use the product and report on it.
(d) **investigation** into similar products already on the market. This is done in order to identify the good and bad points of such products
(e) research into **statistics** of, say, population trends or income levels.

13 Consumer protection

13.1 The Need for Consumer Protection

When consumers buy goods and services they can be exploited. For example:

1 goods bought on credit may be unfairly repossessed (Unit 11.2.)
2 advertisements can be misleading (Unit 12.5)
3 the incorrect weight or quantity might be given
4 goods can be incorrectly labelled
5 firms may act together to charge high prices

Consumer protection is therefore needed to help consumers obtain a **fair deal.** This help can come from the **Government,** from **industry-supported** organizations and from **independent** organizations.

13.2 Consumer Legislation

The main way in which the Government is involved in consumer protection is through legislation, that is, Acts of Parliament. Several of the major Acts are discussed in the following paragaphs.

13.2.1 The Sale of Goods Act 1979

Under this Act the seller of goods has three main obligations. The goods sold must be:

1 of **merchantable** quality i.e. they must work properly. A washing machine which stops working after a few days is not of merchantable quality.
2 **fit for the purpose made known by the customer to the seller.** If a consumer specifically asks a shopkeeper for a knife to cut leather, the knife sold must be a capable of performing that task.
3 **as described.** A dress described as red must not turn out to be blue.

If any of these obligations has not been met the consumer should complain to the shopkeeper. The shopkeeper is obliged to refund the cost of the goods bought by the consumer although the consumer can, instead, accept a replacement or a repair. The consumer does **not** have to accept a credit note and his rights are not affected by notices saying 'No refunds' which have no lawful effect.

13.2.2 The Supply of Goods and Services Act 1982

This Act extends the provision of the Sale of Goods Act 1979 to many **services.**

Both these Acts are part of **civil law** which means that the consumer can, if necessary, sue the shopkeeper for compensation if goods or services supplied are faulty. The **Small Claims Court** has been designed to help consumers in this respect. In most cases, however, shopkeepers are aware of their obligations and the consumer will be able to enforce his rights relatively easily.

Criminal law, in direct contrast with civil law, is not enforced by members of the public but by, amongst other bodies, Trading Standards Officers, Environmental Health Officers (Unit 13.3.) and the police. The Acts listed below are part of criminal law.

13.2.3 The Trade Descriptions Acts 1968 and 1972

Enforced by Trading Standards Officers these Acts make it an offence wrongly to describe goods and services whether in writing (including advertisements) or orally. For example:

1 a sweater described as 100% wool must be just that.
2 a retailer must not offer goods for sale at a reduced price unless either they were on offer at the old price for at least 28 consecutive days in the preceding six months, or the retailer clearly states that this is not the case.
3 goods carrying a UK trade mark must indicate their real country of origin if this was outside the United Kingdom.

13.2.4 The Weights and Measures Acts 1963, 1976 and 1979

These Acts require that:

1 most prepacked products should show the quantity of goods contained in a packet e.g. by weight, volume or number.

2 consumers should not be given short weight. Thus Trading Standards Officers inspect weighing machines to ensure that they are accurate.

13.2.5 The Food and Drugs Acts 1955 and 1976

It is an offence under these Acts to sell unfit food, to describe food falsely or to mislead consumers about the quality of food on sale. The Acts are enforced by Environmental Health Officers.

13.2.6 The Prices Act 1974

This Act, parts of which are enforced by Trading Standards Officers, require that prices should be clearly displayed and that the unit price (e.g. price per kilo) should be shown for goods such as prepacked meat which are sold by weight. Date marking of foodstuffs is also compulsory under this Act.

13.2.7 The Consumer Safety Act 1978

This Act ensures that goods are safe for consumers to use. For example, it is an offence to sell an oil-heater which is dangerous to use.

13.2.8 The Unsolicited Goods and Services Act 1971

It is an offence for a trader to demand payment for goods which have not been ordered under this Act. If a consumer is sent unordered goods and advises the supplier, the goods become the consumer's property, if not collected, after thirty days. If the supplier is not informed then ownership passes after six months.

A wide range of other legislation such as the Consumer Credit Act 1974 (see Unit 11.6), the Fair Trading Act 1973 and the Resale Prices Acts 1964 and 1976 (see Unit 13.4) aims to protect the consumer.

13.3 Trading Standards and Environmental Health Officers

Trading Standards (or Consumer Protection) Officers are employed by **local authorities** to **enforce** consumer legislation. They will regularly test weighing equipment in shops, and will take action on behalf of consumers who have been cheated, e.g. under the Trade Descriptions Acts (see Unit 13.2.3). Trading Standards Officers give **advice** to consumers by, for example, publishing consumer information and operating through the Consumer Advice Centres which are set up by local authorities.

Environmental Health Officers, who are also employed by local authorities, enforce consumer legislation concerned mainly with the cleanliness of shops where food is sold.

13.4 The Office of Fair Trading

The **Office of Fair Trading** (OFT) set up by the Fair Trading Act 1973 is a Government agency whose job it is to protect both consumers and businesses against unfair trading practices. The Director-General of Fair Trading helps consumers by:

1 publishing information so that consumers know their rights.

2 encouraging members of **trade associations** to draw up Codes of Practice (see Unit 13.6).

3 enforcing part of the Consumer Credit Act 1974 through, for example, the issue of licences (see Unit 11.6)

4 advising the Government about the changes needed in the laws relating to consumer protection.

The OFT cannot take up a consumer's complaint about unfair trading practices. This responsibility rests with the Trading Standards Officers or other organizations like the Citizens Advice Bureaux (see Unit 13.7.3).

The OFT also encourages competition between firms by, for example, monitoring **1** monopolies and mergers and **2** restrictive practices.

1 The OFT can recommend that a **monopoly** or **merger** be investigated by the **Monopolies and Mergers Commission** to see if a firm or firms are operating against the public interest. Any recommendation by this Commission is made to the **Government** which makes the final decision.

2 Groups of firms may jointly fix prices and avoid competition so that consumers may suffer by not having the benefit of lower prices. The actions of these firms are a form of **restrictive practice** which the OFT could ask the Restrictive Practices Court to investigate and make unlawful. Under the Resale Prices Acts 1964 and 1976, for example, a manufacturer is **not** allowed to practise **resale price maintenance** (RPM) where thé manufacturer would insist that all retailers should sell his product at a fixed price. For this reason manufacturers can generally only set **recommended retail prices** (RRP) for the goods they supply and it is up to individual retailers to decide whether these goods should be sold at a lower price to the public. There are, however, a few products for which RPM is still allowed e.g. books.

13.5 Other Government-Supported Organizations

The **National Consumer Council** was set up in 1975, and, although financed by the Government, acts independently of the Government. It tests products, publishes its recommendations and advises the Government on matters concerned with consumer protection.

The **Consumer** or **Consultative Councils** of the nationalized industries (see Unit 20.2) have been set up to protect the interests of consumers in their dealings with these industries. Each nationalized industry has a Consultative Council to which a consumer can complain if he thinks he has been unfairly treated.

13.6 Industry-Supported Organizations

Some forms of consumer protection are financed and run by the **industries** themselves to give confidence to consumers buying the goods and services of those industries. This often involves the establishment of **Codes of Practice** operated by **trade associations.** Thus travel agents who choose to be **members** of the Association of British Travel Agents agree to follow the standards of conduct set out in the Association's Code of Practice.

Examples of industry-supported organizations include:

1 The Association of British Travel Agents (ABTA) which operate a central fund to safeguard the holidays of customers who have booked with a member firm which has defaulted.

2 The British Insurance Brokers Association (see Unit 14.3) which deals with complaints about insurance **brokers** as opposed to insurance **companies.**

3 The Advertising Standards Authority's British Code of Advertising Practice (see Unit 12.5) which requires, for example, mail order traders to deliver most goods within 28 days or to inform the customer if they cannot do this.

4 Mail order associations. Most newspapers and magazines belong to associations which have mail order **protection schemes.** Under these schemes customers who have sent money to advertisers will have their money refunded if the advertiser goes bankrupt before the goods are received. These schemes do not, however, cover classified advertisements or firms which advertise in catalogues from which goods are ordered.

5 The **British Electrotechnical Approvals Board for Domestic Applicances** (BEAB). The BEAB tests domestic electrical appliances for safety. Those appliances which pass the test can carry the BEAB label (Fig. 13.1).

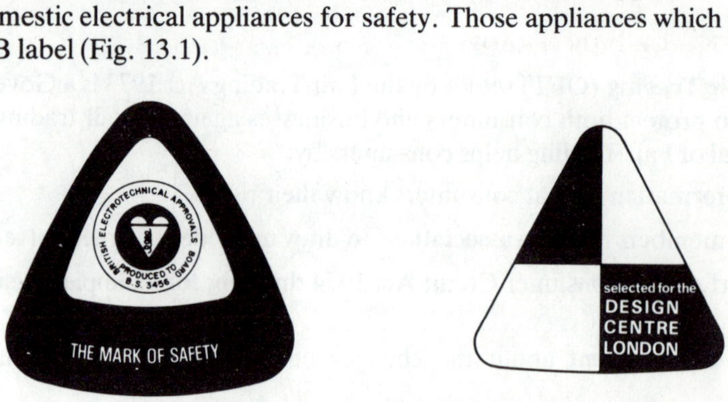

BEAB — Design Centre

Fig. 13.1 Consumer protection labels

6 The **Industrial Design Council** was set up to promote and improve the design and quality of British goods. Those goods of which it approves can carry the Design Centre label (Fig. 13.1).

13.7 Independent Organizations

There are consumer protection organizations which are **independent** of both Government and industry although some, for example the BSI and CAB, receive grants from Government.

13.7.1 The Consumers Association publishes the monthly magazine *'Which?'* which contains the results of surveys made on a varied range of products and services. Very often a **'best buy'** is selected. The Consumers Association is non-profit making and obtains finance from members, who pay subscriptions to receive the monthly magazine, and from the sale of its publications.

13.7.2 The British Standards Institution (BSI) issues the **Kitemark** (Fig. 13.2) for those goods which comply with the stringent standards it lays down. BSI inspectors regularly visit factories to ensure that these standards are being maintained.

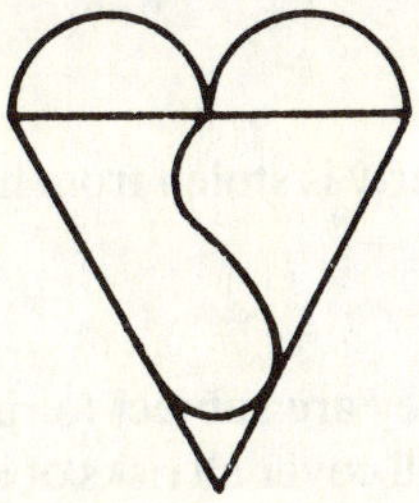

Fig. 13.2 The Kitemark

13.7.3 The Citizens Advice Bureaux (CAB) provide free confidential advice on a wide range of matters including consumer protection. They obtain finance from public donations and from grants made by local authorities. The Bureaux are staffed by volunteers.

13.7.4 The Automobile Association (AA), to which motorists pay subscriptions to join, provides a free breakdown service, legal help where necessary and test reports on cars. Garages and hotels which conform to certain standards can display an 'AA approved' sign.

14 Insurance

14.1 Introduction

Insurance allows individuals and firms to cover **risks** such as fire or theft by paying sums of money called **premiums** to **insurers** e.g. insurance companies (see Unit 14.16), Lloyd's underwriters (14.15). If a financial loss then occurs the insured can claim **compensation** from the insurer.

Insurance is, therefore, important to:

1 **Individuals,** because it allows cover to be obtained against the possibility that, for example, a house may get damaged as a result of fire.

2 **Firms,** because it allows them to reduce the risk of loss which inevitably occurs in business. Some risks cannot be insured but a large number can (see 14.13) and without insurance, it is likely that a number of firms would cease trading. Insurance is, therefore, an important **aid to trade.**

Insurance is also important to:

3 **The United Kingdom economy**

(a) The City of London is an important insurance centre which earns large sums of foreign currency by selling insurance services abroad. The United Kingdom **balance of payments** benefits from such **invisible exports** (see Unit 6.4).

(b) The insurers are major **institutional investors** who use part of their premium income to buy, for example, Government stock, ordinary shares and property. In the case of life assurance part of the interest, dividends and capital gains received from such **investment funds** is paid to policy holders who have with-profits policies (see Unit 14.14.) The **savings** of policyholders are therefore being channelled so that they can be used by others.

14.2 Kinds of Insurance

1 Fire

(a) Property. Buildings and their contents (furniture, stocks of goods etc) can be covered against fire together with any damage caused in putting out the fire e.g. water soiling stocks of goods. Loss as a result of **flooding, storm** and **earthquake** is also usually included in this kind of insurance.

(b) Consequential loss (or business interruption). When a fire occurs a firm may be unable to trade for a period of time. Consequential loss insurance covers any earnings lost and also the expenses which might still have to be paid (wages, rent etc) while the firm is closed because of the fire.

2 Burglary (or theft)

Compensation can be claimed if property is stolen from houses and business premises.

3 Goods in transit

When goods are being transported they are subject to risks such as fire, theft and damage. An **'all risks'** goods in transit insurance will cover all risks of loss or damage from the time the goods are placed on a vehicle until the time the goods are unloaded at the destination.

4 Fidelity guarantee

This covers loss resulting from the dishonesty of employees. It would, for example, cover the theft of cash by a wages clerk.

5 Plate glass

Plate glass windows are expensive to replace and shops, in particular, can take out insurance to cover damage caused to such windows.

6 Employers' liability

An employee may suffer injury or contract a disease while at work. For example, an employee may injure an arm because a machine has not been fitted with a guard. If the employer is found to be negligent then damages could be awarded against him in a court of law. Employers' liability insurance provides compensation to cover such damages and employers are now required, by law, to take out this kind of insurance.

7 Public liability

Damages can also be awarded against a firm if, as a result of the firm's negligence, a member of the public is injured e.g. a customer tripping over a loose carpet in a shop and breaking a leg. Public liability insurance covers this kind of risk. Such insurance can be extended to cover damage caused to consumers when they use a firm's products e.g. being burnt by a faulty hairdryer. This extension is called **product liability** insurance.

8 Credit (or bad debts)

When firms sell goods on credit there is the danger that money owed to them by customers will not be paid. Credit insurance covers any bad debts incurred in this way. A special form of credit insurance is provided by the Government-backed **Export Credits Guarantee Department** (see Unit 6.8).

9 Motor vehicle

Vehicles owned by persons and firms can be insured. There are three categories of motor vehicle insurance available:

(a) Third party. Third party insurance covers only damage caused **to others** (including passengers in the injured person's vehicle) or their property but does not cover damage caused to the insured's own vehicle.

(b) Third party, fire and theft. This is similar to third party insurance but is extended to cover **any** damage caused to the insured's own vehicle by fire and theft.

(c) Comprehensive. As its name suggests comprehensive insurance covers a wide range of risks and provides for compensation to be paid for damage caused, not only to others, but also to the insured's own vehicle. Comprehensive is the most expensive kind of vehicle insurance.

All motorists are required, by the **Road Traffic Act 1972,** to have insurance which covers, at least, liability for injuries caused to others (including passengers) in traffic accidents. Such cover is less than that provided by third party which includes, as well, liability for damage to other people's property.

10 Personal accident and sickness

This provides for compensation if a person dies or becomes partially or totally disabled as a result of an accident. Cover can also be provided for hospital expenses incurred as a result of illness; people going on holiday abroad are often advised to take out personal accident and sickness insurance for the duration of their holiday.

11 Marine and aviation

Ships, aeroplanes and their cargoes can be insured against a variety of risks (see Lloyd's of London, Unit 14.15).

12 Life assurance

See Unit 14.14.

13 National Insurance

See Unit 22.6.

14.3 Obtaining Information about Insurance

The **premiums** charged and the **cover** provided can vary considerably between insurance companies. It is important, therefore, that a person wishing to take out insurance obtains information from a number of companies so that the most suitable form of insurance can be chosen on the most favourable terms. Information can be obtained in a number of ways:

1 By directly contacting the **offices** of a number of different insurance companies such as the Prudential or Commercial Union.

2 By contacting **insurance agents** who can:
(a) be full-time employees of insurance companies who, for example, regularly visit homes to collect premiums.
(b) work on a part-time basis for one or more insurance companies and be engaged in other full-time occupations such as solicitors, bank managers and garage owners.

The **disadvantages** of these two methods of finding information are that:
(i) a number of offices or agents would have to be contacted so that a comparison could be made between insurance companies and this could be time-consuming;
(ii) the advice given by an office or an agent might not be impartial.

A better way, therefore, might be:

3 to contact an **insurance broker.** An insurance broker is **not** an employee of any insurance company. He is able to give information and impartial advice on a number of insurance companies. The broker's only reward is the **commission** paid by insurance companies for any business placed with them. Specific safeguards for those dealing with insurance brokers are that:
(a) insurance brokers must, by law, be registered with the **Insurance Brokers' Registration Council;**
(b) many brokers belong to the **British Insurance Brokers' Association** which helps its members provide a high level of service to clients.

14.4 The Insurance Prospectus

An insurance company provides information in the form of a prospectus for those wishing to take out insurance. A **prospectus** could include details of:

1 the **cover** provided i.e. what risks are included.

2 any cover which is specifically **excluded** i.e. the risks for which compensation will not be paid.

3 the **cost** of the insurance i.e. the premiums.

A simplified prospectus for personal accident insurance is shown in Fig. 14.1.

INSURANCE PROSPECTUS

Accident involving:	*Compensation paid*
Death	£1000
Loss of one or more limbs	£1000
Loss of sight of one or both eyes	£1000
Permanent total disablement	£1000

The main exclusions are:
Taking part in dangerous sports, flying other than as a passenger on a scheduled flight, accidents resulting from the use of drugs or alcohol, self-injury.

Cost of insurance	*Annual premium per £1000 insured*
Class 1 Professional, clerical, housewives	£2.50
Class 2 Shopkeepers, tradesmen superintending but not handling tools or machinery	£4.25
Class 3 Butchers, greengrocers and other tradesmen handling tools and machinery	£6.50
Class 4 Farmers, drivers and persons engaged with heavy machinery	£9.00

Fig. 14.1 An insurance prospectus

This prospectus shows that by paying a premium of £2.50 per year, a housewife would obtain compensation of £1000 if she lost the sight of an eye in an accident. If, however, the accident was a result of her taking part in a dangerous sport then no compensation would be paid.

14.5 The Proposal Form

Once a person has selected the insurance company with which he wishes to deal the company will first ask for a **proposal form** to be completed. A simplified version of a completed proposal form is given in Fig. 14.2 and it is based on the prospectus for personal accident insurance shown earlier in Fig. 14.1.

PROPOSAL FORM

PERSONAL ACCIDENT

	Name of persons	*Date of birth*	*Occupation*	*Height*	*Weight*	*Cover*
1.	John Davies	18.8.37	Butcher	5′ 11″	12st 4lb	£5000
2.						

In respect of the persons to be insured:
(a) are any already insured against accident? YES/NO
(b) do any have existing disability or illness? YES/NO
(c) do any work in conditions of physical hazard? YES/NO
If any of the answers given above are 'YES' please give full details below

....

....

DECLARATION
I declare that the information given in this proposal form is true and complete.

Signature John Davies Date 19.8.85

Fig. 14.2 A proposal form

The proposal form shows that John Davies, a butcher, wishes to take out personal accident insurance for £5000. When completing the proposal form the proposer (in this case John Davies) must remember two important principles of insurance which apply to **all** kinds of insurance: **1** utmost good faith and **2** insurable interest, both of which are discussed in Unit 14.6.

14.6 The Principles of Utmost Good Faith and Insurable Interest

14.6.1 Utmost good faith (uberrimma fides) means, quite simply, that a proposer must tell the truth when completing the proposal form. John Davies must, therefore, **disclose all information relevant to the risk being insured, whether it has been asked for or not.** This is because the information contained in the proposal form allows the insurance company to **estimate the risk involved** and then decide **whether to insure** John Davies and, if so, **what premium** he should be charged.

The higher the risk the greater will be the premium charged.

John Davies has applied for personal accident cover of £5000 (Fig. 14.2). The correct premium for him should be £32.50 per year (Fig. 14.1) because:

$$£1000 \text{ cover costs } £6.50$$
$$£5000 \text{ cover costs } 5 \times £6.50$$
$$= £32.50 \text{ per year}$$

If, on the proposal form, John Davies had said he was a shopkeeper, instead of a butcher, this would be a breach of utmost good faith. The insurance company would charge him a premium of only 5 × £4.25 = £21.25 per year (Fig. 14.1). Such a premium would be **too low,** compared with the risk involved, because butchers are **more likely** to be involved in personal accidents than are shopkeepers.

If an insurance company finds out that a proposal form has **not** been filled in correctly the insurance may be declared **void.** This means that the insurance company could refuse to pay any compensation in the event of a claim.

Utmost good faith must also be shown by the **insurance company.** The company should point out to the client:

1 the **main clauses** of the policy
2 any **exclusions**
3 any **unusual features** of the policy

14.6.2 Insurable interest means that a person can insure against those risks which will result in him suffering a financial loss if the risk occurs. Thus, John Davies can insure himself against personal accident because he would suffer a loss if he became disabled as the result of an accident. He cannot, however, insure his neighbour against personal accident.

In a similar way a person can insure his own house against fire but he cannot insure his neighbour's house unless, of course, he owns his neighbour's house!

14.7 The Cover Note and the Policy

Once an insurance company has agreed to insure a person the company will inform that person of the premium to be charged. When the first premium is paid **cover** begins i.e. the person is now insured. As evidence of this the insurance company sometimes issues a **cover note** which is a **temporary** document while the policy is being prepared. In the case of motor insurance a **certificate of insurance** is issued as evidence of cover in addition to the policy and any cover note.

The **policy** is a **contract of insurance** between the insurance company and the insured. It sets out precisely the terms under which the insurance company has agreed to cover the insured. The policy includes details of:

1 the risks to be covered
2 any risks **not** covered i.e. the exclusions
3 the amount of premium to be paid and the dates of such payment for policies where the premium does not change e.g. life assurance
4 the amount of **compensation** to be paid in the event of a loss
5 the method of claiming compensation
6 any **endorsements** which are **additions** to the policy e.g. if the insurance company has agreed to extend cover in return for an additional premium then this would be added to the policy in the form of an endorsement

The policy should not be confused with the insurance prospectus. The prospectus gives only an **outline** of the terms of insurance. The policy gives **full** details and it is the policy to which reference will be made by the insurer or the insured if a claim is made.

14.8 Payment of Premiums

It is important that premiums are paid on time otherwise cover will **lapse** i.e. the policyholder will no longer be insured. To avoid difficulties of this kind many insurance companies prefer policyholders to pay premiums by standing order or direct debit (see Unit 9.7). Nevertheless, cash would still be used by those without bank accounts or by those policyholders paying the insurance agents who regularly visit their homes. Insurance companies remind policyholders that premiums are due by sending them **renewal notices.** The companies, however, recognize that some policyholders may simply forget to pay their premiums on time. They, therefore, usually allow some **days of grace** e.g. if a premium is due on 1 April and 15 days of grace are allowed the policyholder would be covered until 16 April. If the premium had not been paid by then the policy would lapse.

14.9 Making a Claim and Indemnity

In the event of a loss the policyholder can obtain compensation from the insurance company by completing a **claim form** or **accident report form.** The information contained in these forms allows the insurance company to determine

1 whether the loss is **accidental** and has not been deliberately caused by the **policyholder.**
2 whether the loss is covered **under the terms of the policy**, that is, **proximate cause.**
3 the **amount** of compensation which should be paid.

In deciding the amount of compensation to be paid the insurance company will be guided by the principle of **indemnity** which requires that the policyholder should be placed in the **same financial position** that he was in before the risk occurred. The insured is, therefore, **not allowed to make a profit** out of a loss. Thus the owner of a ten year old car will, in the event of total loss, only receive the market value of an equivalent ten year old car. Where **under insurance** has occurred the insured cannot be **fully** indemnified and any compensation paid can only be up to the **maximum insured** (see Unit 14.11). For some claims insurance companies employ **assessors** or **loss adjusters** to decide on the correct amount of compensation to be paid.

Indemnity, together with **utmost good faith** and **insurable interest,** are the three principles of insurance.

Indemnity does **not** apply in the case of:

1 life assurance.
2 personal accident, where a lost limb cannot be replaced.
3 'new for old' policies. For buildings and contents insurance some insurance companies offer replacement as new cover. For a higher premium the policyholder will be able to replace, say, a three year old television set with a new television set of the same make. The insurance company will not make any deduction for depreciation.

14.10 Contribution and Subrogation

When paying compensation the insurance company could be guided by two extensions to the principle of indemnity called **contribution** and **subrogation.**

14.10.1 The contents of a person's home are worth £6000 and they are fully insured against theft with each of two insurance companies. If the insurance companies discover that this has been done they will share any claim between them. Thus in the event of total loss each insurance company will contribute £3000. The principle of **contribution** does not allow the insured to make a profit by insuring with more than one insurance company.

14.10.2 A motorist insures his car for £3000 and it is 'written off' in an accident. The insurance company pays compensation of £3000 and takes (**subrogates**) the scrap value of the car. If the insured received the scrap value in addition to full compensation he would make a profit which indemnity does not allow.

14.11 Under-Insurance and Over-Insurance

A householder is quoted an annual premium of £8 per £1000 to insure his house against fire. The true value of the house is £20 000 and, therefore, the 'correct' premium is £160 per year. The householder decides to insure the house for:

1 £30 000: this is **over-insurance.** In the event of total loss the insured will only receive £20 000.

If the insured value of £30 000 is paid a profit of £10 000 would be made which is not allowed under indemnity. The insured, therefore, gains no benefit from paying higher premiums.

2 £10 000: this is **under-insurance.**

(a) In the event of **total loss** i.e. £20 000 the insured will only receive £10 000. He has not paid the correct premium of £160 and is not fully insured.

(b) If, instead, damage of £5000 is caused to the house the insured will only receive compensation of £2500. He has insured his house for **half** its true value and only half of any damage, up to £10 000, would be paid. The scaling down of compensation arising from under-insurance is called **averaging.**

14.12 The Pooling of Risks

Insurance is based on the **pooling of risks** where policyholders pay premiums into a pool. The pool of money so created is then used to pay compensation to those who claim. This is sometimes described as the **fortunate helping the unfortunate,** where the many who do not suffer loss arising from the insured risk help the few who have to claim (Fig. 14.3).

Fig. 14.3 The pooling of risks

The money collected in premiums should be sufficient to:

1 pay **compensation**

2 cover the **administrative costs of** running the pool e.g. the wages of insurance company employees

3 leave some **profit** for the insurance company.

The insurer operating the pool, e.g. an insurance company will try to run a **separate pool** for each type of risk e.g. there will be one pool for fire insurance and a different one for burglary insurance. Ultimately, however, each of these pools does form part of a single large pool for **each** insurer.

Large industrial and commercial organizations often do not use insurance companies. Since their risks are sufficiently widespread they can run their own 'pools' just like insurance companies. This practice is called **'self-insurance'.**

14.13 Insurable and Uninsurable Risks

An insurance company must ensure that the premiums received from policyholders are sufficient to meet the various claims made on the pool. Insurance companies, therefore, employ **actuaries** to calculate the **correct premium** to be charged. The actuary looks at past records (**statistics**) of, say, fire claims and on the basis of these calculates the **probability** of the risk occurring in the future and the likely level of losses. The higher the probability the greater will be the premium charged. An actuary cannot, of course, predict which policyholder will suffer loss.

Past records form an essential part of insurance and a risk can only be insured if reliable statistics exist. This is what is meant by the **statistical basis of insurance.** Risks which can be insured are called **insurable risks.** (See Unit 14.2 which lists some insurable risks.)

Uninsurable risks, in contrast, are those risks which **cannot** be insured. Examples include:

1 the risk of a firm not being able to sell a new range of clothes. In this case past records give no guide to possible future losses. A premium cannot be reliably calculated and the risk cannot, therefore, be insured.

2 risks arising during war. Here the **unpredictability** and the likely compensation involved are so great that the insurance company is not prepared to offer cover. For this reason damage resulting from war is shown as an exclusion on household policies.

3 where there is **no insurable interest** and the insured would not suffer loss (see Unit 14.6).

14.14 Life Assurance

Insurance covers those risks from which losses **may** or **may not** occur, e.g. fire or theft. Assurance covers those risks which are **bound** to occur, e.g. death. Although death is certain there is still the uncertainty of knowing when death will occur and, for this reason, past records are used in life assurance to predict **average** life expectancy. As with insurance, statistics form the basis of assurance. Life assurance policies can be used:

1 to provide compensation on the policyholder's death
2 as a method of saving

The main kinds of life assurance policy are:

14.14.1 Whole life A person takes out a whole life policy for a sum assured of £20 000. He will continue paying premiums until he dies. On his death the assurance company will pay the dependants £20 000.

14.14.2 Term A businessman takes out a 25 year term policy on his partner for a sum assured of £20 000. He is able to do this because he has insurable interest in his partner's life for if the partner dies the business could suffer. If the partner dies within that period the businessman will receive £20 000. If the partner survives the period **no payment** will be made by the assurance company.

A term policy is often taken out by those with **mortgages** and the term chosen is the length of the mortgage. The policyholder then knows that if he dies before the mortgage is repaid the sum assured can be used to repay the mortgage.

14.14.3 Endowment An endowment policy is similar to a term policy but with the important difference that if the policyholder survives the period of assurance he will **receive the sum assured.** The endowment policy, therefore, provides a **means of saving** for the policyholder as well as providing cover in the event of his death.

An endowment policy is the **most expensive** type of life assurance policy because it provides the greatest benefits.

If an endowment policyholder wishes to stop paying premiums he can 'sell' back his policy to the life assurance company for a sum of money called the **surrender value.** Surrender values are usually low in the early period of a policy and it is to the policyholder's disadvantage to surrender his policy at this time.

14.14.4 Without profits or with profits Most life assurance policies can be taken out on a without profits or with profits basis. If the policy is **without** profits the **sum assured** at the start of the policy will be the **sum paid** on death or after an agreed number of years. If the policy is **with** profits the **sum assured** will have **bonuses** added to it which are based on the profitability of the **investment funds** operated by the assurance company (see Unit 14.1).

The policyholder is guaranteed the sum assured but will hope to receive a sum of money far greater than this. The policyholder must, therefore, choose an assurance company which he expects to be profitable.

The amount paid in **premiums** by those taking out life assurance cover will vary and will depend upon, for example:

1 the **sum assured**— the greater the sum the higher the premium.

2 the **type of policy**— an endowment policy is more expensive than a whole-life policy because the benefits are greater.

3 the **age of the policyholder**— a younger person pays less for life assurance than an older person because there is less risk of a young person dying.

4 the **sex of the policyholder**— a 30 year old man will pay more than a 30 year old woman for the same type of life assurance policy because the average life expectancy for females is higher than that for males.

5 the past and current **health of the policyholder**— those in poor health, if they can obtain assurance, will pay higher premiums because the risk of early death is greater.

14.15 Lloyd's of London

14.15.1 A market for insurance

Lloyd's of London is a market for insurance through which those who wish to **buy** insurance can contact those who **sell** insurance. The market is controlled by the **Corporation of Lloyd's** which does not itself transact insurance business but:

1 provides the facilities for arranging insurance e.g. by providing premises
2 establishes rules for the market
3 controls membership of the market

14.15.2 Members of the market

The members of the market are **brokers** and **underwriters** who pay annual subscriptions to the Corporation of Lloyd's.

Those wishing to buy insurance at Lloyd's of London can do so only through a **Lloyd's broker** who will act as an agent and receive **commission.**

Those selling insurance are grouped into over four hundred **syndicates.** Each syndicate is made up of a number of wealthy individuals, called **underwriters,** who are prepared to offer insurance cover. Each syndicate is then represented at Lloyd's of London by an **underwriting agent** or **professional underwriter.** It is the underwriting agent who accepts the risk on behalf of the syndicate. If the premiums collected by the underwriting agent are insufficient to cover the claims made on the syndicate the **personal wealth** of the underwriters can be used to meet any unpaid claims. For this reason the Corporation of Lloyd's insists that underwriters must:

1 provide evidence of considerable wealth;
2 deposit a large sum of money with the Corporation as a guarantee;
3 agree to regular audits of their personal wealth;
4 accept unlimited liability under which their personal assets can be claimed by creditors.

The major reason for these controls on underwriters is that **confidence** must be maintained in the market. If buyers of insurance felt that there was the risk that compensation would not be paid in the event of loss they would take their business elsewhere. The Corporation has, therefore, provided a further guarantee of the solvency of the market by establishing a **central fund** financed from levies on the premium income of syndicates. If a syndicate is unable to meet its legal liabilities then this central fund can be used to cover any shortfall.

14.15.3 Risks covered at Lloyd's of London

One important risk covered at Lloyd's of London is **marine** insurance. The main types of marine insurance are listed below.

1 Hull insurance covers damage to or loss of a ship. Where a number of ships are included under one policy it is called a **fleet** policy. Hull insurance is usually written on a **time** basis, for say, twelve months, irrespective of the number of journeys made within that period.

2 Cargo insurance covers damage to or loss of the goods being carried and can be on a **voyage** basis where the cargo is insured for a particular journey.

3 Shipowners' liability covers claims made on the shipowner arising from, for example, the death of passengers, damage caused to other ships or to docks.

4 Freight insurance. Freight refers to the amount charged by the shipping firm for **transporting** the cargo. If the freight is **not** prepaid then the shipping firm can take out freight insurance to cover non payment of freight charges when goods fail to be delivered. When the freight charge is prepaid it forms part of the value of the cargo insured by the owner.

In addition to marine insurance Lloyd's of London covers **aviation** insurance (with policies similar to those in marine) and most other risks covered by insurance companies (fire, theft etc) but **not** long-term life.

14.15.4 Taking out insurance at Lloyd's of London

A person or firm wishing to take out cover at Lloyd's of London must approach, not simply a broker, but a **Lloyd's broker.** The broker enters details of the cover required on a **slip** and then approaches a number of underwriting agents to obtain the best deal. An underwriting agent signifies his acceptance of the risk by initialling the slip. If the cover required is large an underwriting agent may be prepared to take only part of the risk, say a third, and he will indicate this on the slip together with the premium charged. The broker then takes the slip to other underwriting agents until the full risk is covered. The first underwriting agent to sign the slip is called the **'lead'** and the other underwriting agents involved on the slip quote the same rate of premium as the lead. Any subsequent claim will be shared by the syndicates in the proportions indicated on the slip.

This sharing of risks also occurs in **reinsurance** when one underwriting agent accepts the full risk immediately and then parts of the risk are covered by additional policies placed with other insurers.

14.15.5 Lloyd's List

Lloyd's List and Shipping Gazette is published daily by Lloyd's of London and gives details of the movement of shipping throughout the world. Lloyd's of London has agents in many countries who provide information for this List to be compiled. The agents also survey damage and settle claims on Lloyd's policies.

Lloyd's Register of Shipping gives details (name, weight, condition) of ships operating throughout the world. Regular surveys are made to ensure that ships conform to certain standards. Although Lloyd's Register is a valuable source of information for underwriting agents it is published by an organization which is independent of Lloyd's of London.

14.16 Insurance Legislation

Insurance companies fall into two categories:

1 the **proprietary** companies which are owned by shareholders who are entitled to profits made by the company, *and*

2 the **mutual** companies which have no shareholders and are owned by the policyholders themselves.

Because they are companies they are subject to the various **Companies Acts,** and specifically

1 the **Insurance Companies Acts** 1974, 1981 and 1982 which allow the Department of Trade and Industry to:

(a) inspect the books of insurance companies;
(b) require insurance companies to have a minimum amount of funds;
(c) restrict the types of risk which an insurance company can cover;
(d) approve changes in the directors and owners of large shareholdings in insurance companies;
(e) give authorization to new insurance companies before they can start business.

2 the **Policyholders Protection Act 1975** which allows levies to be made on insurance companies to compensate policyholders who have insured with an insurance company which fails.

15 Transport

15.1 The Importance of Transport

Transport is important to **firms** and is an essential **aid to trade** in the chain of distribution; it

1 brings raw materials and semi-finished goods to manufacturers
2 delivers finished goods to wholesalers and retailers
3 allows employees to reach places of work

An efficient transport system also benefits **consumers** in that:

1 they can obtain a variety of goods from all over the world;

2 by being able to sell throughout the world, firms can obtain larger markets which allows mass production and therefore cheaper prices;

3 countries, regions and firms are able to specialize and the consumer obtains cheaper and better quality goods.

15.2 Factors to Consider Before Deciding on a Form of Transport

A firm often has to choose between different forms (modes) of transport for delivering goods. Should goods be sent by road, rail, air or sea? When deciding on the best form of transport the firm should consider:

1 the **nature** of the goods. Are the goods **bulky** (large and difficult to carry e.g. grain), **heavy** (steel), **expensive** (gold), **fragile** (china) or **perishable** (fresh fruit)?

2 the **urgency** with which the goods are needed, e.g. medical supplies may have to be quickly delivered;

3 the **cost** of transport: air is usually more expensive than other forms of transport;

4 the **quantity** to be carried. If a larger quantity of goods has to be delivered then a whole lorry or ship may have to be hired;

5 the **destination.** Which forms of transport can best reach the destination?

6 the **distance** involved. It might be sensible to use road transport for **short** journeys. Using road **and** rail over short distances would involve a significant loss of time when the goods are being transferred between the different forms of transport.

15.3 Road Transport

Road transport is the major form of **inland** transport in the United Kingdom (see Fig. 15.1). The firms engaged in the road transport industry range from the large scale **road haulage** firms which deliver goods throughout the country to the much smaller **local** carriers which operate only in a small geographical area. There are, as well, traders and manufacturers who have their **own fleets** of vehicles (see Unit 15.3.1).

Total tonne-kilometres (thousand millions)

	1972	(%)	1977	(%)	1982	(%)
Road	87.5	(65.1)	98.0	(63.3)	92.0	(56.9)
Rail	21.0	(15.6)	20.1	(13.0)	15.9	(9.8)
Water (coastal and waterways)	22.5	(16.7)	27.9	(18.0)	44.4	(27.5)
Pipelines	3.5	(2.6)	8.8	(5.7)	9.3	(5.8)
	134.5	(100.0)	154.8	(100.0)	161.6	(100.0)

Source: Annual Abstract of Statistics

Fig. 15.1 Goods transport in Great Britain

Advantages of road transport

1 It is usually **cheaper** than other forms of transport especially over **short** distances (less than 200 miles).

2 It is usually **faster** over short distances.

3 It provides a door-to-door service where only one form of transport needs to be used. There is, therefore, **less handling** of goods which reduces the risks of theft and damage particularly when a firm's own vehicles are used (see Unit 15.3.1).

4 Road vehicles do not run to a fixed timetable which makes road transport more **flexible** than rail — vehicles can be sent from a depot at any time.

5 The road network in the United Kingdom is very extensive and most parts of the country can be reached. The building of **motorways** has also speeded up road haulage and reduced its costs.

Disadvantages of road transport

1 It is **slower** than rail over longer distances.

2 It is not suitable for carrying **bulk goods** over **long** distances e.g. carrying a large consignment of coal on a 300 mile journey.

3 Lorries and their loads cannot exceed a certain size and weight.

4 There could be congestion and delays particularly when operating in towns, or during 'holiday periods' on the road.

5 There could also be delays because of bad weather.

6 The cost of road transport could be high if there is no return load for the vehicle to carry.

7 Those living close to busy roads are troubled by noise and fumes. These examples of pollution are called social costs.

15.3.1 Own Fleet Operations

Several manufacturers, wholesalers and retailers prefer to operate their own fleets of vehicles instead using other firms to deliver goods for them. Such vehicles can be **owned, leased** (see Unit 11.4.2) or **hired** by the firms.

Advantages of own fleet operations

1 It could be **cheaper** than using transport firms.

2 The vehicles are always on hand and can, therefore, be sent out at short notice which ensures **quicker delivery.**

3 Own vehicles can carry **'free' advertising** for the firm.

4 The firm can employ its own drivers which **reduces the risks of theft and damage.**

Disadvantages of own fleet operations

1 **More capital** could be needed particularly if the vehicles are purchased outright.

2 If the fleet is not fully used it could be **more expensive** than using road transport firms.

3 **Additional costs** for servicing, employment of drivers, garaging and licensing the vehicles are created.

The alternative ways of transporting goods if a firm does not have its own fleet operation are:

1 employing **road haulage firms** to carry goods over long distances. One major road haulage firm is the privately-owned **National Freight Consortium** plc (formerly the government-owned National Freight Corporation) which owns British Road Services (BRS), National Carriers (NCL) and Pickfords;

2 employing **local carriers** to deliver goods over short distances.

15.4 Rail Transport

The publicly-owned **British Rail** is responsible for most rail transport in the United Kingdom.

Advantages of rail transport

1 Rail is faster than road for **long journeys** between main centres.

2 Goods trains are **cheaper** than road for sending **bulk** goods over **long** distances.

3 **Passenger** trains are suitable for carrying **small** quantities of **urgently needed** goods over **long** distances e.g. mail from London to Manchester and the **Red Star** service for carrying parcels between stations.

4 Rail services are less likely to be disrupted by poor weather conditions.

5 Rail is **safer** than road for carrying dangerous products e.g. nuclear waste.

6 Rail transport has specialist facilities for carrying certain goods e.g. oil by rail tanker and the Freightliner service (see below) for carrying containers.

Disadvantages of rail transport

1 Rail is **slower** than road over **short** distances.

2 Rail is **more expensive** than road over **short** distances.

3 Road vehicles are still needed at some stage (unless firms have their own **rail sidings**). Therefore rail can be **slower** over **long** distances for firms not near a railway.

4 The transfer of goods between road and rail increases costs and the risks of damage and theft.

5 Trains run to timetables and therefore do not possess the flexibility of road transport where own vehicles can be despatched at any time.

Recent improvements in rail freight services

In the last twenty years British Rail has tried to improve its freight services by:

1 closing many loss-making lines and stations and concentrating on the more profitable routes between cities;

2 using diesel and electric locomotives which give a faster service;

3 modernizing signalling and improving rail tracks;

4 introducing the Total Operations Processing System (TOPS) for controlling freight by computer;

5 developing new services such as:

(a) express parcel delivery by passenger train. For example:

(i) The **Red Star** service guarantees **same-day** delivery but the parcel has to be taken to the station of departure and then collected at the station of destination.

(ii) The **Night Star** service guarantees delivery on the **following day** to the door of the addressee.

(b) Freightliner which is a **container** service operating between major terminals. (The use of containers in transport is described in Unit 15.10.)

The **advantages** of the Freightliner service are:

(i) it is a **fast** door-to-door service

(ii) it runs to a guaranteed **timetable**

(iii) large quantities can be carried by a single train e.g. some firms will hire a whole train to carry their goods

(iv) space can be reserved

(v) it is **safe** because containers are sealed.

15.5 Sea Transport

There are many types of vessels used in **sea transport** the most important of which are discussed below.

1 Cargo liners run on **fixed** routes to **fixed** timetables. They carry mixed cargoes although some are specialized e.g. refrigerated liners and container liners. Some also carry a few passengers. Their owners belong to **shipping conferences** e.g. the Far East Shipping Conference which decide freight charges and the frequency of journeys for certain routes.
The **advantages** to an exporter of using a cargo liner.
(a) The exporter knows, in advance, the times of departure and arrival of cargo liners, and
(b) can tell customers when to expect delivery of the goods.
(c) The cost of transport can be calculated in advance because the freight charges are published.
(d) An exporter can send:
(i) small quantities of goods which would **not** fill the hold of a ship e.g. mail, spare parts not needed urgently, *or*
(ii) goods which need careful handling e.g. cars, fruits.

2 Tramps do **not** have set routes or set timetables and generally do not carry passengers. They usually carry bulk cargoes e.g. coal, grain and timber. Tramps are **chartered** (hired) at **freight markets** e.g. the Baltic Exchange for a specific journey (**voyage charter**) or for a specific period (**time charter**). Freight charges for tramps vary and depend on the demand for and supply of shipping space.
The **advantages** to an exporter of using a tramp.
(a) The departure times of tramps are not fixed and can therefore be arranged to suit exporters.
(b) Tramps can be used to deliver goods to ports not visited by conference liners.
(c) An exporter can use a tramp for:
(i) bulk goods which can fill the hold of a ship, *and*
(ii) which do **not** need careful handling e.g. coal.

3 Bulk carriers carry a specific type of bulk cargo e.g. coal, grain, and ore. **Tankers** are also types of bulk carrier and are used for carrying gases, oil and other liquids.

4 Container ships are specially built to carry containers (see Unit 15.10) in their holds or on deck. Delivery by container ship is usually fast because containers can be quickly transferred on and off ships.

5 Ferries, including **hovercraft,** are used for carrying passengers, goods and vehicles. Many ferries provide Roll-On/Roll-Off facilities (see Unit 15.10).

6 Coastal vessels are generally used as an alternative to inland transport and carry bulk cargoes e.g. coal around the coastline of the United Kingdom. Coastal vessels are of small size and can, therefore, dock at the smaller ports.

It should be noted that the classification of vessels used above can and does involve some overlapping. For example, a container ship running to a fixed timetable and a fixed route is operating as a cargo liner. An oil tanker used on a time charter could be operating as a tramp.

15.6 Seaports

An efficient port system is essential for the smooth flow of imports and exports into and out of the country. The ports in the United Kingdom, which are run by port authorities e.g. the Port of London Authority, should provide some, though not necessarily all, of the following facilities.
1 Deep water to take larger vessels
2 Shelter for vessels by building, for example, sea walls
3 A clear channel to the port achieved, for example, by dredging and by using pilots and buoys
4 Supplies of coal, oil, food, water, electricity and so on for ships calling at the port
5 Wharves and cranes for loading and unloading cargo
6 Roll-On/Roll-Off facilities
7 Commercial premises such as warehouses and refrigerated stores
8 Government offices for immigration and customs control e.g. the supervision of bonded warehouses
9 Repair facilities, such as dry docks
10 Good communications, such as road and rail links, with the rest of the country

15.7 Canals

The canal system in the United Kingdom is largely under the control of the British Waterways Board which has made a number of improvements to the canal network. Nevertheless, canal transport now accounts for only a very small proportion of inland transport in the United Kingdom.

Advantages of canal transport

1 Canal transport is **cheap** and
2 provides a **smooth passage** for fragile goods e.g. china.
3 Canals are particularly suitable for **bulk cargoes** e.g. coal, iron ore.

Disadvantages of canal transport

1 Transport by canal is **slow.**
2 Only parts of the United Kingdom can be reached by canal.
3 Other forms of transport are also usually needed.
4 The water may freeze in winter.

15.8 Air Transport

The major British airline is the government-owned British Airways although there are a number of smaller independent operators. The major airlines throughout the world belong to the **International Air Transport Association** (IATA) which sets passenger and freight charges for scheduled air services. In this respect IATA acts very much like a shipping conference (see Unit 15.5). Instead of using the timetabled air services exporters can charter planes at air freight markets e.g. the Baltic Exchange.

The **advantages** to an exporter of using air transport.

1 Air is **fast** over **long distances** and would, therefore, be used for sending:
(a) medical supplies for emergencies
(b) perishables e.g. fresh flowers from Jersey to London
(c) spare parts to replace a broken machine. The extra cost of sending spare parts by air is covered from the profits made by the machine which is quickly repaired

2 Goods sent by air are under closer supervision and there is **less risk of theft or damage.** Air is, therefore, particularly suitable for **high value low bulk** goods e.g. diamonds which can bear the high cost of transport.

3 The exporter does not have to hold large stocks of goods in many countries because supplies can be quickly sent to many destinations. This results in **lower warehousing costs** and a **reduction** in the **costs** of **holding stocks.**

The **disadvantages** to an exporter of using air transport.

1 Air transport is **expensive** particularly for heavy goods.
2 Air transport has **limited** weight and size capacity.
3 **Long** road journeys could be needed to **complete** the journey in areas where there are few airports.
4 Even where there are many airports additional transport needed from airports could significantly **increase** the time taken for delivery.
5 **Bad weather** may restrict flights.

15.9 Pipelines

Pipelines are used to carry liquids and gases over short and long distances. Examples of pipelines include those linking oilfields in the North Sea to refineries on the mainland and the natural gas grid which carries gas to people's homes.

Advantages of pipelines

1 Pipelines are a **safe** form of transport with little risk of theft or damage.
2 They are **cheap** to run with low costs of maintenance.
3 They provide a **quick** form of transport.

Disadvantages of pipelines

1 They are very **expensive** to build.
2 If one part of the pipeline is damaged then the whole pipeline cannot be used.
3 Only **limited** types of goods can be carried by pipeline.

15.10 Containers

A major development in transport has been the introduction of containers. Containers are large metal boxes of **standard** sizes which are filled with goods at, for example, the manufacturer's warehouse. The containers are then sealed and are not opened until they reach the destination. Containers are used in road, rail, sea and, to a limited extent, in air transport. They carry goods which are not large or bulky e.g. clothes, television sets.

Advantages of using containers

1 Increased speed of transport

(a) Containers can be **quickly transferred** between different forms of transport using specialized machinery e.g. straddle cranes. The goods themselves are not taken out of the containers.

(b) Lorries, carrying containers, can drive directly on to a ship without the containers being unloaded. This is one application of the **Roll-On/Roll/Off** system (RO/RO) used, for example, on cross-channel ferries. (RO/RO is a term which covers any form of transport where the cargo is driven on and then driven off a ship. It is not necessarily a container system.)

(c) The **TIR** system (see 15.11) allows increased speed through customs.

2 Reduced cost of transport

Although more expensive equipment has to be used there is an overall reduction in cost because fewer men are needed to handle goods. The quicker **turn-round** of vehicles also reduces costs.

3 Increased **safety**

There is less risk of theft or damage because the containers are sealed. This also reduces insurance costs.

4 Storage

Containers, which can be **stacked,** reduce the need for warehousing.

5 Specialized containers

Some containers are **refrigerated** and are suitable for perishables, e.g. meat.

Special provision is now being made by different forms of transport to carry containers e.g. purpose-built vehicles (road), the Freightliner service (rail), container ships and container ports (sea) and wider-bodied aircraft for carrying smaller containers (air). Often containers have to be transferred between different forms of transport and this has created the need for a more **integrated** transport system.

15.11 Transport Internationale Routier (TIR)

The TIR system operates in **international road** transport although sea transport may be involved at some stage. It works in the following way.

1 Goods are packed in a container in the country of departure.

2 The Customs authorities of that country inspect the container and provide a certificate of contents.

3 The container is then sealed.

4 When the vehicle carrying the container passes through intermediate countries the goods are not inspected provided the seal has not been broken.

5 When the goods reach the country of destination the seals are broken and the Customs authorities of that country inspect the goods and charge any import duties.

6 Duties are not charged when the goods pass through intermediate countries.

The TIR system is faster and cheaper because vehicles are not delayed by border checks.

15.12 Government Controls on Transport

The Government is directly involved in the transport system of the United Kingdom through its ownership of organizations such as British Rail, British Airways, the British Waterways Board and some port authorities. The actions of the Government, often through legislation, also affect many other parts of the transport system.

1 Manufacturers have to produce vehicles which conform to safety and pollution standards.

2 Drivers of vehicles are tested, licensed and subject to many laws such as those relating to the wearing of safety belts or the number of hours which a commercial vehicle driver is allowed to work.

3 The vehicles are also tested and licensed.

4 The Department of Transport has overall responsibility for roads in the United Kingdom.

5 Ships registered in the United Kingdom are inspected by Department of Trade and Industry officials to check seaworthiness.

6 The Government-controlled Civil Aviation Authority is responsible for supervising civil aviation in the United Kingdom by, for example, enforcing safety standards for aircraft.

16 Communications

16.1 The Meaning of Communications

In its widest sense **communications** is concerned with the **transmission of information** and the **transfer of goods and other items** such as cash. Communications can occur:

1 within firms e.g. the branch manager of a chain store who posts to head office weekly sales figures or who telephones a regional depot to enquire about the non-delivery of goods.

2 between firms e.g. a manufacturer who transports goods to a wholesaler.

3 between firms and the public e.g. a manufacturer who advertises a new product for sale.

4 between members of the public e.g. word of mouth publicity about a new product or a person who posts a letter containing cash to a friend.

The **advertising** and **transport** aspects of communications are covered elsewhere in this book in Units 12 and 15. This unit deals with the narrower definition of communications which covers primarily postal and telecommunication services. Even here, however, transport can still be important e.g. in the transfer of letters by road, rail, sea and air.

16.2 Postal Services

The **Post Office,** which is **government-owned,** is responsible for the provision of postal services in the United Kingdom although it also has a number of banking functions such as the National Savings Bank (see Unit 10.5) and National Girobank (see Unit 10.3). The Post Office does not have a complete monopoly of postal services and faces competition from other public corporations, e.g. British Rail, and private operators, e.g. Securicor, in the delivery of parcels and urgent mail. Listed below are the main postal services of the Post Office. Up-to-date details of all Post Office services can be found in the **Post Office Guide.**

1 Letter post Letters and postcards can be sent to inland addresses using **first class** or **second class** post. This is called the **two-tier** system. First class is quicker but is more expensive. **Postal codes** are used for inland mail to make sorting and therefore delivery quicker. Airmail is quicker than seamail for sending letters and postcards overseas, but is more expensive.

2 Parcel post Parcel post can be used for sending packages up to a certain size and weight to inland and overseas destinations. The **Postage Forward Parcel Service** allows a parcel to be sent and payment for the delivery of the package to be made by the addressee (the person receiving the package).

3 Express services Urgent delivery of a letter or parcel can be made by, for example,

(a) Expresspost: despatch riders (couriers) are used for collection and delivery and same day delivery can often be made. Over longer distances this service can use Inter-City passenger trains.

(b) Datapost: A package can be handed in at any post office displaying the 'DATAPOST HERE' sign. **Datapost Inland** travels separately from ordinary mail with a money-back guarantee of **overnight delivery.** Firms sending packages on a regular basis can arrange Datapost **contracts** where collection is made by the Post Office at the firms' premises. **Datapost International** provides a speedy and reliable service for overseas packages.

4 Certificate of posting For a small fee any post office can provide the sender with proof that a letter or package has been posted. The letter or package **must be handed in** at a post office and **not** posted in a letter box.

5 Recorded delivery Recorded delivery not only provides proof of posting but proof of delivery because the addressee has to sign for the letter or package. If any loss occurs compensation is low. The service is therefore used for sending **non-valuable** items which require proof of delivery, e.g. a court summons!

6 Registered post Registered post is similar to recorded delivery but provides **more compensation** if a loss occurs. It is, therefore, used for sending **valuable** items through the post. Specially made registered envelopes can be bought at post offices and these **must** be used when money is sent. A summary of these last three services is shown in Fig. 16.1 which lists them in order of cost — registered post being the most expensive.

Name of Service	*Proof of posting*	*Proof of delivery*	*Compensation if lost*	*Use*
Certificate of posting	Yes	No	No	When proof of posting only is required
Recorded delivery	Yes	Yes	Limited	For important but non-valuable items
Registered post	Yes	Yes	Can be large	For cash and valuable items

Fig. 16.1 Post Office services which give proof of posting and proof of delivery

7 Business reply service This service uses special envelopes of standard sizes which allow customers to write to firms without paying any postage e.g. sending for a mail order catalogue.

8 Freepost Freepost is similar to the business reply service except that special envelopes are not issued. Instead the word 'Freepost' is included in the address of the firm. Freepost can only be used for second class mail.

For both services a firm must first obtain a licence from the Post Office by paying a deposit, to cover likely postal charges for a month. It is the firm and not the customer which pays the Post Office for the postage.

9 Cash on delivery (COD) Mail order firms use the COD service to deliver goods to customers. The postman collects payment from the customer before handing over any goods.

10 Post restante A letter can be addressed to a post office marked 'Post restante'. The addressee will then collect the letter from that post office. This service is useful for sales representatives who are continually moving from town to town.

11 Franking machines It can be very time-consuming for some firms to place stamps on the many letters they post. Firms, therefore, use franking machines which place on letters the amounts of postage paid. The machine keeps a record of the amount spent on postage. Stamps are **not** used. Franking machines can be hired from the Post Office or from private suppliers who have to be Post Office-approved.

16.3 Telecommunications

Telecommunications services in the United Kingdom are mainly run by **British Telecom** which was government-owned but is now a public limited company.

1 Telephone The telephone allows firms to contact quickly other firms at home or abroad. The advantage to a firm, of using the telephone is that an **immediate answer** to any question is possible. The disadvantage is that **no written record** is provided.
Users of the telephone can benefit from:

(a) subscriber trunk dialling (STD) and International Direct Dialling (IDD) which allow telephone calls to be made to home and foreign numbers respectively without using the services of the operator.

(b) telephone credit cards A salesman could use his company's telephone credit card to make operator-connected calls on credit and his employer will settle with British Telecom at a later date.

(c) directories which list the telephone numbers of subscribers. For example, *'Yellow Pages'* is a classified directory which lists firms by the nature of the goods or services they provide. Thus cash and carry wholesalers are grouped together.

(d) Freefone A firm can have a 'Freefone' number so that it pays for any Freefone calls received from, for example, customers or agents. Freefone calls are made through the operator.

(e) various other services such as:

(i) **radiopaging** where a subscriber carries a bleeper which indicates when he is wanted,

(ii) **radiophone** which allows a call to be made from a vehicle to any telephone in the United Kingdom,

(iii) information services e.g. Stock Exchange news and the correct time can be obtained by dialling the appropriate number.

2 Telex A firm wishing to use the telex system can rent a **teleprinter** (a combination of typewriter and telephone) from British Telecom. The firm is also given its own individual telex number. To send a message the firm must first dial the telex number of the addressee and then type the message using the teleprinter. The message is automatically transferred and printed on the addressee's teleprinter.
The **advantages** of using telex are that
(a) it is **quick,**
(b) it provides a **written record,**
(c) the teleprinter can receive messages **without an operator** being present and is thus particularly useful to international firms operating in different time zones.

3 Telemessage Telemessage has replaced the inland telegram. British Telecom accepts telemessages by telephone or telex and the message is delivered by first class post on the following day. **International telegrams,** however, are still in existence.

4 Confravision Confravision is a British Telecom service which links individuals or groups of people in different cities by sound and vision. Using Confravision could be cheaper and quicker for a firm than having to assemble staff in one location.

5 Facsimile reproduction (Fax) **Intelpost,** which is run by the Post Office, offers high speed transmission of black and white facsimiles (i.e. exact copies) of documents and drawings. The original can be collected by messenger or taken to any post office displaying the Intelpost sign. At the destination post office the facsimile can be collected or delivered by messenger or first class post. Firms throughout the United Kingdom with their own facsimile equipment can also use Intelpost to reach those without such equipment.

A similar service called **Bureaufax** is operated by British Telecom.

6 Videotex Videotex (sometimes called **Teletex**) refers to any **computer-based system** which allows text to be received and displayed on a screen. Where text is transmitted by **television signal** it is called **teletext** e.g. the Ceefax and Oracle systems of BBC and ITV. Where **telephone lines** are used for transmission it is called **Viewdata** e.g. British Telecom's Prestel service. Teletext and Viewdata are, therefore, two forms of Videotex.

Teletext is not as powerful a system as Viewdata because it is a **one-way** system where information only is received. Viewdata is a **two-way** system. For example, by using a special keyboard which is provided a Prestel user can enquire about the cost of a holiday. The information is then displayed on a television screen and the holiday can be immediately booked using the same system.

Viewdata, in particular, has enormous potential. British Telecom, through its **Datel** service, allows electronic data to be transmitted between different locations. With suitable equipment a firm could run an electronic mail system between a network of offices which would reduce the need for letter post.

7 Radio and television These provide other means of communications by broadcasting, for example, weather reports, news and so on. The development of **satellites** allows television signals to be quickly transmitted around the world and the use of **cables** means that more information can be transmitted.

17 Business accounts

17.1 The Need for Accounts

A firm needs to keep a detailed and accurate record of, for example

1 the value of **assets** i.e. items owned by the firm,
2 the value of **liabilities** i.e. amounts owed by the firm to others,
3 **changes** in assets and liabilities,
4 the value of **sales,**
5 the value of **purchases.**

Such a system of **accounts** is essential if the firm is to calculate and then make available to owners/shareholders details of the value of the firm and the profits made.

In addition the Government requires firms to keep proper accounts:

1 so that tax can be assessed e.g. income tax, corporation tax, value added tax (see Unit 22).
2 to meet the provisions of the Companies Act 1980 which requires that a copy of a company's accounts must be filed (see Unit 18.6).

17.2 The Balance Sheet and Forms of Capital

The **balance sheet** of a firm lists the assets and the liabilities of that firm at a **particular date** (Fig. 17.1).

Balance Sheet of Firm X
as at 31.12.85

LIABILITIES	£	ASSETS		£
Capital owned	4600	*Fixed assets*		
		Land	4000	
		Machinery	2000	6000
Long-term liabilities				
10 year loan	4000			
		Current assets		
		Bank	2000	
		Debtors	1000	
Current liabilities		Stock	600	
Creditors	1200	Cash	200	3800
Total	9800	*Total*		9800

Fig. 17.1 A balance sheet

Assets can be divided into:

1 **fixed** assets whose values do **not** change from day to day e.g. land, machinery;
2 **current** assets whose values **do** change from day to day e.g. bank, debtors (money owed to the firm) and stocks of goods.

The external liabilities of a firm are the amounts owed by the firm to others and can be divided into:

1 **fixed** or **long-term** liabilities which have to be repaid over a number of years e.g. a 10 year loan.
2 **current** liabilities which are **short term** and have to be repaid in less than a year e.g. creditors (money owed by the firm to suppliers).

By drawing up a balance sheet the firm is able to calculate:

1 **capital owned** which is a measure of the value or **net worth** of a business and is given by assets minus external liabilities.

In Fig. 17.1 capital owned = £9800 − £5200 = £4600. Capital owned appears as a liability in the balance sheet because it is an internal liability, being the amount owed by the firm to its owners.

2 capital employed which is a measure of the assets which are being used in the business. Two measures of capital employed can be used—
(a) gross capital employed = total assets = £9800
(b) net capital employed = total assets minus current liabilities = £9800 − £1200 = £8600
3 circulating capital which is measured by the sum of current assets viz. £3800. It is called circulating capital because the current assets are always changing their form (Fig. 17.2).

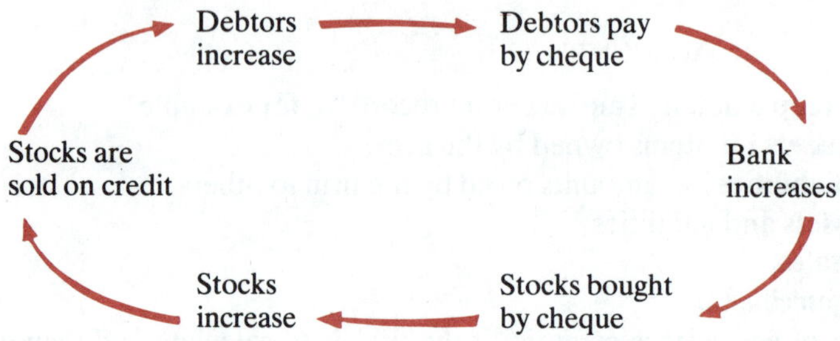

Fig. 17.2 Circulating capital

4 working capital which equals current assets minus current liabilities, e.g. in Fig. 17.1 working capital = £3800 − £1200 = £2600
A firm must have sufficient working capital to meet its day to day expenditure, e.g. the payments of wages, advertising, creditors and to buy new stock. Sometimes working capital is a misleading measure of the ability of a firm to meet its immediate debts and
5 liquid capital is used instead. Liquid capital refers to those assets such as cash and bank, or any assets which can quickly be converted into cash.

In Fig. 17.3, therefore, working capital of £6000 − £4000 = £2000 seems adequate.

Current liabilities	£	*Current assets*	£
Creditors	4000	Debtors	2400
		Stock	2500
		Bank	1100
			6000

Fig. 17.3 Current assets/liabilities

However a large part of current assets is made up of debtors who may not pay or who may pay late and stock which may be difficult to sell. The liquid capital is only £1100 which is not enough to pay creditors if claims become due.

17.3 Turnover and Rate of Turnover

Turnover is the value of **net** sales (sales minus returns) in a given period of time
Rate of turnover (or **rate of stockturn**) is a measure of how **quickly** goods are sold in a given period of time which is usually a year. The rate of turnover can be measured in two different ways.

1 $\dfrac{\text{Value of net sales}}{\text{Average stock at selling price}}$ *or* **2** $\dfrac{\text{Cost of goods sold}}{\text{Average stock at cost price}}$

Thus, using measure 1, if
turnover = £10 000 per year and
average stock at selling price = £1000 $\left(\text{calculated by } \dfrac{\text{opening stock + closing stock}}{2}\right)$
then the rate of turnover = $\dfrac{10\,000}{1000}$ = 10 times per year

The rate of turnover expected will vary from firm to firm. Thus for very expensive items, e.g. high quality furniture, the rate of turnover will be low because these goods sell slowly and remain in stock for a long time. For perishables, e.g. fresh fruit and newspapers the rate of turnover will be very high because a shop has to sell such goods quickly as they will not last.

17.4 Gross Profit and Net Profit

1 The **gross** profit of a firm is given by **net sales minus cost of goods sold.** Thus if goods costing £6000 are sold for £8000 the gross profit is £2000. In this example the gross profit mark-up is

33⅓% $\left(\frac{2000}{6000} \times \frac{100}{1}\right)$ because the cost of goods has been increased by 33⅓% to give the selling price.

For the same example the gross profit **margin** is 25% $\left(\frac{2000}{8000} \times \frac{100}{1}\right)$ because the gross profit represents 25% of net sales. Mark-up is, therefore, based on cost price and margin on selling price.

2 The **net** profit of a firm is given by **gross profit minus expenses (overheads)** incurred in running the business. Thus if gross profit is £2000 and the expenses of rent, rates, wages, insurance, heating, lighting and depreciation equal £1500 the net profit is £500.

If the firm is unsuccessful then gross losses and net losses could occur.

17.5 Measures of Profitability

Figures of gross and net profit on their own give little indication of the **profitability** of a firm because no information is provided about the relative size of a firm. To overcome this difficulty the following measures of profitability can be used.

1 $\frac{\text{Net (or gross) profit}}{\text{Turnover}}$ **2** $\frac{\text{Net (or gross) profit}}{\text{Capital employed}}$

Thus in Fig. 17.4, firm A has a higher level of profit than firm B. However, firm B has a higher level of profitability for both measures of profitability.

	Firm A	*Firm B*
Net profit	£50m	£1m
Capital employed	£500m	£5m
Rate of return on capital employed	10%	20%
Turnover	£1000m	£10m
Rate of return on turnover	5%	10%

Fig. 17.4 Profit and profitability

Such calculations of **rates of return** on turnover and capital employed give some indication of the efficiency of a firm. Thus a rate of return on capital employed of only 5% is unsatisfactory because a much higher rate of return (rate of interest) can be obtained by purchasing risk-free Government stock.

17.6 Methods of Increasing Net Profit

Net profit is more important than gross profit because it is the **'final'** profit of a firm which becomes liable to income tax or corporation tax (see Unit 22.2). The profit remaining after tax then becomes available for ploughing back into the business, e.g. by buying new machinery, and for distribution to owners/shareholders.

Net profit can be increased by **1** increasing turnover, **2** reducing cost of goods sold, **3** reducing expenses.

1 Increasing turnover might be achieved by:
(a) lowering prices and hoping that the extra demand created more than covers the fall in price,
(b) increasing prices hoping that consumers will still buy at the higher prices,
(c) more advertising,
(d) sales promotion e.g. competitions, free gifts,
(e) selling loss-leaders (see Unit 2.4),
(f) allowing credit,
(g) stocking goods which are more likely to sell.

It should be noted that any of these policies could alter expenses which would, in turn, affect net profit. Thus if advertising is increased then this will increase expenses. Although turnover and gross profit may rise net profit will fall if the increase in expenses is greater than the increase in gross profit.

2 Reducing cost of goods sold could be achieved by:
(a) buying in greater bulk at lower prices,
(b) switching to a cheaper supplier.

If the firm maintains turnover but is able to reduce the cost of goods sold then gross profit will increase. Whether net profit also increases depends upon the change in expenses. For example, the extra cost of warehousing goods bought in bulk may outweigh the lower cost of such goods and net profit will fall.

3 Reducing expenses could be achieved by:

(a) reducing advertising; in this case, however, net profit could fall if turnover falls because of the reduction in advertising,

(b) reducing the number of employees e.g. a wholesaler could switch to a cash and carry system,

(c) reducing the level of services provided e.g. a retailer may no longer provide a free delivery service to homes.

18 Private sector firms

18.1 The Private and Public Sectors

Private sector firms are those firms which are **not** owned by the State. Examples of business organizations in private ownership are sole traders, partnerships, private companies, public companies and co-operatives. (Co-operatives as a form of business organization are discussed in Unit 2.3). Public sector firms, in contrast, are owned by the State e.g. public corporations such as British Rail (see Unit 20). The United Kingdom economy is a **mixed economy** because it contains both private sector and public sector firms.

18.2 The Importance of Capital

The form a business takes partly depends upon its need for **fixed capital** i.e. **long-term** finance for the purchase of fixed assets such as land and machinery. Thus a firm set up to manufacture chemicals may be organized as a public company because it needs to raise large amounts of fixed capital from shareholders. A small corner shop, on the other hand, needs only a small amount of fixed capital and can be run by a sole trader or partnership. The other kind of capital needed by all firms is **circulating** capital (see Unit 17.2) to meet day-to-day expenses such as the payment of wages and the purchase of stock. Circulating capital is financed by **shorter-term** loans such as overdrafts from the clearing banks or suppliers willing to sell on credit (trade credit).

18.3 The Sole Trader

The main feature of a sole trader is that **one** person owns the business although others may be employed in the business.

Advantages of sole trading

The sole trader:

1 is able more easily to control the business because it is small and the owner can quickly discover the needs of customers and problems of staff.

2 obtains the benefits of independence by not having to consult others and quicker decisions can then be made.

3 keeps any profits and does not have to share them with others: this a direct reward for working hard and showing initiative.

4 can easily set up the business because:

(a) little capital is required, *and*

(b) there are fewer legal formalities compared with other forms of business.

Disadvantages of sole trading

The sole trader:

1 has **unlimited liability** which means that, in the event of bankruptcy, the sole trader's personal assets (car, house etc) can be claimed by creditors.

2 has limited capital which makes it difficult to expand.

3 suffers from lack of continuity. If the sole trader becomes seriously ill or dies the business may have to close.

4 bears the full responsibility of running the business and may not have the skill or experience to cope with all aspects of the business.

5 may make wrong decisions because he does not have to consult others.

Sources of fixed capital

1 The personal savings of the sole trader
2 Loans from banks (overdrafts are used to finance circulating capital)
3 Mortgages from building societies (see Unit 11.5)
4 Ploughed-back profits i.e. profits made by the sole trader which are used in the business
5 Finance houses provide hire purchase (see Unit 11.2) and leasing facilities (see Unit 11.4.2)
6 Loans and grants from government which are designed to help small firms

Sole trading occurs where the amounts of capital needed are small and is found mainly in the provision of services rather than in the production of goods e.g. small shops, hairdressing, house decorating.

18.4 Partnership

The Partnership Act 1890 allows between **two** and **twenty** persons to run a business as a partnership although firms of solicitors, accountants and stockbrokers are allowed to exceed the maximum number of twenty. Each partner may sign the partnership **Deed of Agreement** which gives the following details.

1 The amount of capital contributed by each partner
2 The rate of interest to be paid on such capital
3 The salaries to be paid to partners
4 How profits are to be allocated between the partners

If there is no Deed of Agreement or there is a Deed but it does not cover the point in dispute then the Partnership Act 1890 states that:

1 profits must be shared equally between the partners,
2 partners cannot claim salaries or interest on capital,
3 disagreements must be settled by a majority vote although all partners must agree if there is to be a change in the nature of the partnership.

Under the Partnership Act 1890 **ordinary** partnerships carry **unlimited liability** for all partners. The Partnership Act 1907, however, introduced the **limited** partnership which allows **limited liability** for those partners who are **limited** partners. This means that their personal assets cannot be claimed by creditors if the limited partnership becomes bankrupt. Limited partnerships must be registered with the Registrar of Companies and the limited partners cannot take part in the management of the partnership. They are, therefore, **sleeping** partners. One further important provision is that a limited partnership must have at least one general partner who has unlimited liability.

Advantages of partnership

1 More capital may be available compared with a sole trader.

2 The partnership can make use of the individual skills of the partners e.g. in a building firm one partner can specialize in plumbing and another in electrical work.

3 Partners can consult each other and correct decisions are more likely to be made.

4 There is a greater continuity compared with a sole trader. If one partner dies the partnership is automatically dissolved but the remaining partners can then draw up a new Deed of Agreement.

5 There is limited liability for limited partners.

Disadvantages of partnership

1 Ordinary partners have unlimited liability.

2 The membership of a partnership is limited which could make it difficult to raise large sums of capital.

3 There could be disagreements between partners.

4 Each partner is legally responsible for the actions of the other partners. Thus if the actions of one partner result in a large loss for the partnership each partner must suffer part of that loss in the proportions set out in the Deed of Agreement.

5 Partnerships can be slow to give major decisions if each partner first has to be consulted.
6 In a small partnership the death of one partner could make it difficult to continue the business because that partner might be difficult to replace.

Sources of fixed capital
These are similar to those for sole traders.
1 The personal savings of the partners
2 Loans from banks
3 Mortgages from building societies
4 Ploughed-back profits
5 Hire purchase and leasing
6 Government grants

Partnerships are common for firms of accountants, lawyers, solicitors and doctors where services are provided rather than goods being manufactured. The capital provided for such firms is not so much in the form of money as in professional skill. Partnerships have, however, declined in importance because of the growth of private limited companies (see Unit 18.6).

18.5 Incorporated and Unincorporated Businesses

Sole traders and partnerships are examples of unincorporated businesses. The features of such organizations are that:
1 they have **no separate legal existence.** For example a sole trader must sign any contract for the firm in his **own name** and he cannot use the name of the firm.
2 the owners are therefore fully responsible for a firm's debts.
3 the owners, except for limited partners, have **unlimited** liability.
4 no special registration is needed to set up the business apart from the registration of **limited partnerships** with the **Registrar of Companies.**

Companies are examples of **incorporated** businesses. The features of such organizations are that:
1 each has a separate legal existence.
2 it is the firm itself, and not the owners, which can enter into contracts in its own name. As a result it is the firm which can sue and be sued.
3 the owners can have limited liability.
4 registration is required and companies have to register with the Registrar of Companies.

18.6 Public Limited and Private Limited Companies

Any **two or more** persons may form a **public** or **private company.** The general characteristics of all companies are:
1 the company has a **separate legal existence** from its shareholders (see Unit 18.5).
2 all shareholders, apart from those of unlimited private companies, have **limited** liability, that is, the most they can lose is the amount paid for their shares. The shareholders cannot be sued for any remaining debts of the business.
3 shares are sold to raise finance.
4 the shareholders are the **owners** of the company.
5 the shareholders elect a **Board of Directors,** usually at annual general meetings, to run the company on their behalf.
6 profits are distributed to shareholders in the form of **dividends.**
7 the company is subject to the requirements of the various **Companies Acts** e.g.:
(a) the minimum number of directors and of shareholders is stipulated
(b) companies must be registered (see Unit 18.8.) and the annual accounts of most must be filed with the Registrar of Companies.

18.6.1 Public limited companies

The Companies Acts state that a public limited company:
1 after its name must use 'public limited company' or 'plc'
2 must have a minimum of **two directors**
3 must have a minimum of **two shareholders** with **no upper limit** placed on the number of shareholders
4 must have a minimum nominal share capital of £50 000
5 must have a **trading certificate** (see Unit 18.8).

In addition the shares of a public limited company:
6 can be sold to any member of the public
7 are freely transferable

Advantages of public limited companies

1 Capital is easy to raise because:
(a) shareholders have limited liability,
(b) members of the public can be invited to buy shares,
(c) the shares of public limited companies can be quoted on a Stock Exchange (see Unit 19.3). This helps the sale of shares because shareholders know that any shares bought can be sold at a later date on the Exchange.

2 The company is therefore able to operate on a large scale and obtain the benefits of economies of scale (see Unit 1.5).

3 There is continuity because any changes in directors or shareholders do not affect the company as a separate legal entity.

4 The money received from the sale of shares remains permanently with the company. When shareholders sell the company's shares it is to others and not to the company and the capital of the company remains unchanged.

Disadvantages of public limited companies

1 The formation of the public limited company is costly in time and money because of the many documents which have to be submitted to the Registrar of Companies (see Unit 18.8).

2 The annual accounts of public limited companies have to be filed with the Registrar of Companies and are thus open to inspection by anyone.

3 A public limited company can be subject to take-over if another company or person obtains 51% of the voting shares.

4 For large public limited companies the firm may become too large for efficient management and decision-making could be slow.

5 There is a divorce between ownership and control. The shareholders own the company but it is controlled by the managers and the interests of these two groups may be quite different e.g. a manager may wish to preserve his job while the shareholder may want maximum profit.

18.6.2. Private limited companies

The Companies Act 1980 states that any company which is **not** a public limited company must be a **private** limited or unlimited company. A private limited company:
1 must use 'limited' or 'ltd' after its name.
2 may have one or more directors.
3 must have a minimum of two shareholders with no upper limit.
4 does **not** need a trading certificate (see Unit 18.8).
5 is not required to have a minimum share capital.
In addition:
6 The shares of the company cannot be offered to the general public and cannot, therefore, be quoted on a stock exchange.

The Companies Acts no longer place restrictions on the rights of shareholders in private limited companies to transfer their shares although, in practice, many private limited companies include such restrictions in their Articles of Association (see Unit 18.8).

Many former partnerships prefer to operate as private limited companies and the advantages and disadvantages of such a conversion are now considered.

Advantages of private limited companies compared with partnerships

1 All shareholders have limited liability while ordinary partners have unlimited liability.

2 In a private limited company the maximum number of shareholders is unlimited which makes it easier to raise capital. In most partnerships the maximum number of partners allowed is twenty.

3 There is greater continuity because the company, unlike the partnership, has a separate legal existence.

4 If a firm wishes to grow so that it eventually becomes a public company quoted on a stock exchange then a number of years of trading as a company is required beforehand (see Unit 19.4).

Disadvantages of private limited companies compared with partnerships

1 Companies, unlike most partnerships, have to be registered.

2 The accounts of limited companies, unlike those of ordinary partnerships, are not private because they have to be filed with the Registrar of Companies.

18.7 Sources of Fixed Capital for Companies

Companies raise long-term finance by:

1 Issuing debentures
2 Issuing shares
3 Using ploughed-back profits
4 Borrowing from banks
5 Using hire-purchase and leasing facilities
6 Receiving loans and grants from government

1 The main features of **debentures** (or **loan stock**) are that the debenture holder:

(a) has given a **loan** to the company;
(b) is a **creditor,** and not a part owner, of the company;
(c) receives a **fixed rate of interest** which **must** be paid even if the company has made a loss;
(d) is paid interest or capital **before any shareholder**;
(e) will usually be **repaid the amount lent** at some specified future date, e.g. Debenture 1998-2003 will be repaid at some time in those years;
(f) has the right to **sell specified assets** of the company *if* the company is **unable** to repay, providing the debenture is **secured. Unsecured stock** gives the creditor no such right;
(g) can sell **quoted** debentures at any time on a stock exchange.

2 The **shares** issued by companies are of various kinds according to the **risks** involved for the shareholder (Fig. 18.1). Thus **ordinary shares (equities)** carry the greatest risks because they are the last to be paid, but they give the benefits of voting rights and a dividend which is generally linked to the level of profits of the company.

<table>
<tr><th>Name of share</th><th>Dividend</th><th>Voting rights</th><th>Order of dividend payment and possible capital repayment</th></tr>
<tr><td>Ordinary (equities)</td><td>varies and is based on profit</td><td>generally one vote for each share held</td><td>last to be paid</td></tr>
<tr><td>Preference</td><td>fixed but dividend is lost if insufficient profits are made</td><td rowspan="2">fewer than ordinary shares or sometimes none</td><td rowspan="2">before ordinary shares but after debentures</td></tr>
<tr><td>Cumulative preference</td><td>fixed but dividends unpaid in one year or years are paid when enough profits are made</td></tr>
</table>

Fig. 18.1 The main types of share

The types of share not shown in Fig. 18.1 are the less important participating preference, redeemable preference and deferred shares. **Participating preference** shareholders not only receive a fixed dividend but are also paid an additional dividend when profit is large enough. **Redeemable preference** shares can be bought back (or redeemed) by the company issuing the shares at a specified future date. **Deferred** shares offer high voting rights to holders but dividends are usually paid after those of ordinary and preference shareholders. The way in which interest and dividend payments are calculated is shown, in a simplified form, in Fig. 18.2.

3 Ploughed-back profits (retained earnings) i.e. **undistributed profits** are an important source of funds for many firms.

4 Loans from banks provide another means of raising fixed capital for companies. These can be obtained from the clearing banks or from more specialist institutions such as Finance for Industry (FFI).

5 Long-term finance is needed to buy fixed assets such as machinery. An alternative to outright purchase is hire purchase (see Unit 11.2) or leasing (see Unit 11.4.2) and the use of such methods reduces a firm's need for long-term finance from other sources.

Year		*1*	*2*	*3*	*4*	
Profit before interest paid on debentures		£600	£1000	£30	£800	
Payments on						
£500 6% Debentures		£30	£30	£30	£30	(a)
2000 5% (£1) Cum pref shares		£100	£100	owed £100	£200	(b)
1000 5% (£1) Pref shares		£50	£50	—	£50	(c)
6000 (50p) Ordinary shares	Div.	10%	20%		5%	(d)
		£300	£600	—	£150	
Ploughed-back profits		£120	£220	—	£370	(e)
		£600	£1000	£30	£800	

Notes:

(a) Debenture holders receive interest of £300 (6% of £500)

(b) Cumulative preference shareholders receive a fixed dividend of 5 pence per share (5% of £1). The payment missed in *Year 3* is paid in *Year 4*

(c) The preference shareholders lose the dividend not paid in Year 3

(d) The ordinary share dividend varies. In *Year 4,* for example, the dividend is 2½p per share (5% of 50p)

(e) Ploughed-back profit is the amount kept by the firm for use in the business

Fig. 18.2 The distribution of profits

6 Both central and local **government** provide **loans** and **grants** to firms which move, for example, into areas of high unemployment such as development areas or enterprise zones.

18.8 The Registration of Limited Companies

Any two or more persons may form a private or public limited company by delivering the following five documents to the Registrar of Companies.

1 Memorandum of Association This governs the **'external'** relationship of the company i.e. with the outside world and consists of the following clauses:
(a) the name of the company, followed by
(b) 'public limited company' (or 'plc') or for a private limited company 'limited' (or 'ltd'),
(c) the country in which the company is registered i.e. England, Wales, Scotland or N. Ireland,
(d) the objects of the company i.e. the reasons for which the company has been formed, e.g. to manufacture chemicals,
(e) a statement that the members (owners) of the company have limited liability,
(f) the share capital of the company e.g. the company wishes to issue a maximum of 500 000 ordinary shares of £1 each,
(g) an association clause signed by at least two members of the company to show that they have paid for a stated number of shares.

2 Articles of Association govern the **'internal'** relationship of the company with its members. They are signed by the members who signed the association clause of the Memorandum. The Articles contain the rules relating to:
(a) the voting rights of members e.g. one vote for each ordinary share held,
(b) methods of electing directors,
(c) the number of directors,
(d) procedures for calling meetings of shareholders.

3 Statement of Capital This statement contains the information already given in the 'share capital' clause of the Memorandum and is used for tax purposes.

4 Statement of Names of Directors and Situation of Registered Office The full names of directors and the address of the registered office must be shown.

5 Statutory Declaration This is a declaration that all the requirements of the Companies Acts in respect of registration have been complied with.

Once the Registrar of Companies is satisfied with the five documents listed above he will issue a **certificate of incorporation.** The firm now legally exists as a private or public limited company. The public limited company must however sell shares to the public to obtain capital. One method of issuing shares is by way of a prospectus (see Unit 19.1) and a copy of the prospectus must be sent to the Registrar. Once the Registrar is satisfied that the **public** limited company has sufficient capital he will issue a **trading certificate**. The public limited company can then start trading.

The **private** company can start trading when it has ensured that sufficient capital has been raised from the private sale of shares and it does not require any further document to be issued by the Registrar.

19 The issue of shares and the Stock Exchange

19.1 The Issue of Shares

Public limited companies can sell shares by using:

1 a prospectus
2 an offer for sale
3 a placing
4 a rights issue

1 A prospectus is an advertisement placed in newspapers e.g. the *Financial Times,* inviting the public to buy the newly offered shares of the company. Included in the prospectus are:

(a) a statement that a request has been made for permission for the shares to be quoted on the Stock Exchange
(b) the authorized and issued share capital of the company (see Unit 19.2)
(c) the number of shares to be sold
(d) the price of each share
(e) the profit record of the company
(f) the future plans of the company
(g) an application form for those wishing to buy shares
(h) the closing date for application

The drawing up of a prospectus is a specialist task and companies normally use the expertise of an **issuing house** to handle the entire sale by prospectus. Merchant banks, clearing banks and stockbrokers can act as issuing houses in return for a commission.

It would be very unusual for the number of shares applied for to be exactly equal to the number of shares on offer and Fig. 19.1 illustrates what is likely to happen in practice.

Issue of 2 million Ordinary Shares at £1.50 each	*Application for*
	1.5 million shares — UNDERSUBSCRIBED
	or
	5 million shares — OVERSUBSCRIBED

Fig. 19.1 Over- and undersubscription for a fixed price issue

If too **few** shares are applied for **(undersubscription)** each applicant receives the number of shares requested. The issuing house, is however, left with half a million unsold shares (Fig. 19.1) and these are bought by **underwriters** (usually merchant banks) who have agreed, beforehand, to take up any unsold shares at a previously agreed price. A minimum sum of money is, therefore, guaranteed from the issue of shares.

If too **many** shares are applied for (**oversubscription**) each applicant will only obtain a fraction of the shares requested. If an issue is heavily oversubscribed some applicants may not receive any shares.

To reduce the problems of over- and undersubscription some issues do **not** set a **fixed issue price** for the shares (£1.50 in Fig. 19.1). Instead an issue by **tender** is used where the issuing house asks applicants to state the price at which they are prepared to buy the shares subject to a stated minimum price. Thus, in Fig. 19.2, the issue has been popular and the issue price of £2.30, which is above the minimum tender price of £2.00, is the highest price at which all shares will be sold. All tenders at or above this price will receive in full the shares applied for at the issue price of £2.30.

Issue of		*Applications for*		*Sale of*
3 million shares at a minimum tender price of £2.00	→	8 million shares at prices of £2.00 and above	→	3 million shares at an issue price of £2.30

Fig. 19.2 Issue of shares by tender

2 Offer for sale In this case all the new shares are sold to an issuing house and the company immediately receives a fixed sum of money from the sale. The issuing house then offers the shares for sale to the public in a similar way to the sale by prospectus.

3 Placing Where an issue is small an issuing house may sell (place) the new shares with its own clients.

4 Rights Issue A company can raise additional finance by selling new shares to existing shareholders at a favourable price. For example, ordinary shareholders could be given the right to buy one new ordinary share for every five ordinary shares held at a price of £2.00 each, which compares with a market price of £2.30 for the existing ordinary shares.

19.2 Authorized and Issued Share Capital

When issuing new shares a company cannot exceed its authorized share capital. In Fig. 19.3 the company can only issue a maximum of five million £1 ordinary shares because this is the authorized capital quoted in the memorandum of association (see Unit 18.8). It has already issued four million £1 ordinary shares and can only issue a further one million shares. If it wants to exceed this figure the company must call a meeting of shareholders for permission to increase the authorized capital and application must also be made to the Registrar of Companies.

Authorized share capital	5 million (£1) Ordinary shares	£5m
Issued share capital	4 million (£1) Ordinary shares	£4m
Called-up share capital	4 million (£1) Ordinary shares at 75p each	£3m

Fig. 19.3 Authorized, issued and called-up capital

Sometimes a company issues shares but calls for only **part** of the amount payable on each share. Thus, in Fig. 19.3, if the company demands from shareholders payment of 75 pence for every £1 share held, the called-up capital will be £3m. The £1m which can be demanded at any future date is the **uncalled** capital. When the full price of each share is eventually paid the share is **fully paid-up** and no further claims can be made on shareholders.

19.3 Unquoted and Quoted Companies

All private limited companies and some public limited companies are **unquoted** companies because the shares of the companies are not allowed to be dealt in on a stock exchange. Quoted or listed companies, in contrast, are public limited companies whose shares can be bought and sold on a stock exchange.

19.4 The London Stock Exchange

The major stock exchange in the United Kingdom is the London Stock Exchange which together with a number of smaller **provincial** exchanges, e.g. in Manchester, form the **Stock Exchange of**

Great Britain and Ireland. The London Stock Exchange is a market for second-hand securities which is governed by the Council of the Stock Exchange.

A market for second-hand securities

A company sells **new** shares by prospectus or offer for sale etc and the buyers of the shares become the **first** owners of the shares. When these shares are subsequently sold on the Stock Exchange they are no longer new but **second-hand.** The Stock Exchange is, therefore, a market for second-hand securities. The **securities** bought and sold on the Exchange are the **debentures and shares** (ordinary, preference etc) of quoted public limited companies and **gilt-edged stock** issued by the Government (see Unit 21.4).

One recent development has been the establishment by the London Stock Exchange of a separate **Unlisted Securities Market** (USM). The rules for admission to the USM are much less rigorous than admission to a full Stock Exchange listing and, for this reason, smaller companies have been attracted to the new market in order to raise finance.

The Council of the Stock Exchange

The Council is elected from among the members of the Stock Exchange and has the authority:

1 to control the **admission** of new members,

2 to set rules of **conduct** for the Exchange,

3 to **discipline** and sometimes expel (**hammer**) members who break the rules,

4 through its **Quotation Committee** to allow the shares of companies to be traded on the Exchange,

5 to maintain a **compensation fund** to recompense investors should a member of the Exchange fail to meet its obligations.

To obtain a quotation on the London Stock Exchange a public limited company must **apply** to the Stock Exchange for **'permission to deal in and for quotation for'** a stated number of shares. The application, which is normally handled by the company's merchant bank or stockbroker, is dealt with by the **Stock Exchange Quotation Committee** which makes a detailed investigation of the company. The Committee considers:

1 the profits record of the company; to be quoted on the main Stock Exchange requires at least a **five** year and for the USM at least a **three** year trading record,

2 the number and type of shares to be quoted; to be quoted on the main Stock Exchange requires at least **25%** of the equity to be made available to the public while the USM requires only **10%,**

3 the directors of the company, e.g. have they a criminal record?

Once the application has been granted the shares of the company can be bought and sold on the Stock Exchange and their price published in the **Daily Official List.**

A public limited company may seek a Stock Exchange quotation because:

1 it is easier to sell new shares to shareholders if they know that there is a ready market for the shares. As a result the company is able to raise finance more easily.

2 the market price of the share is likely to increase because of the wider market now created.

3 it allows existing shareholders, possibly the directors, to sell their shares more easily.

19.5 Brokers and Jobbers

The **members** of the London Stock Exchange are either stockbrokers or stockjobbers. To become a member a person must

1 obtain approval from the Council of the Exchange,

2 have passed a qualifying examination,

3 pay an entry fee followed by annual subscriptions.

The work of the **broker** is to act as an **agent** for those wishing to buy and sell securities. The reward of the broker is **commision** which is based on the value of the deal.

The work of the **jobber** is to act as a **trader** (wholesaler) in securities and the jobber's reward is **profit.**

The rôles of these two types of member can be understood by reference to Fig. 19.4.

A stockbroker must always be used as an **intermediary** when individuals or firms wish to trade in securities on the London Stock Exchange. In Fig. 19.4 the buyer has instructed a broker to buy five hundred ordinary shares of Company X. The broker approaches the jobbers who specialize in the shares of Company X but **does not state whether he is buying or selling.** Each

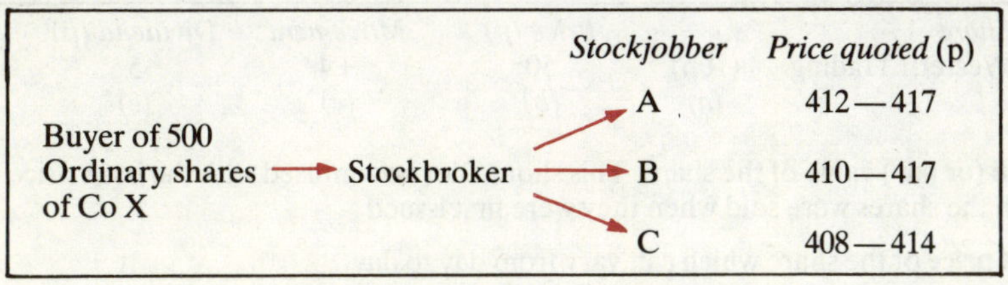

Fig. 19.4 The broker and jobber

jobber quotes two prices; 412 pence per share is the price at which jobber A is prepared to **buy** the shares of Company X and 417 pence per share is the price at which he is prepared to **sell** such shares. The broker strikes the deal (called a **bargain**) with jobber C because his selling price of 414 pence is the lowest.

The broker's reward is the commission received for arranging the purchase of shares. The jobber's reward is the difference between the buying and selling prices. If the jobber is able to buy at 408 pence and sell at 414 pence he makes a profit of 6 pence per share. This difference is known as the **jobber's turn.**

At present there is a clear distinction between the work of a broker and jobber, and a broker cannot also act as a jobber. It is likely, however, that the two rôles will be merged and this will bring the Stock Exchange of Great Britain and Ireland into line with the stock exchanges in the rest of the world.

19.6 Speculators on the Stock Exchange

To understand how speculators can operate on the London Stock Exchange it is necessary to look briefly at the Stock Exchange calendar. The Stock Exchange year is divided into a series of two (or occasionally three) weekly **accounts.** Settlement for deals which have taken place in a particular account must be made by **settlement day** which falls ten days after the end of an account. The settlement day for an account which runs from 1 March to 12 March is, therefore, 22 March and shares bought on any day during that account must be paid for on 22 March.

There are three types of **speculator** on the London Stock Exchange:

1 The bull
2 The bear
3 The stag

1 The bull buys shares and hopes to sell the same shares, **before the end of the account,** at a profit. Thus if he can buy shares for £5000 on 1 March and then sell the shares for £6000 on 10 March he has made a profit of £1000. The profit has been made without parting with any money because the purchase of and subsequent sale of the same shares are settled on the same day (22 March). Bulls profit when share prices are **rising.**

2 The bear sells shares he does not possess and hopes to **buy** the same shares at a lower price, **before the end of the account,** in order to fulfil his contract. Thus if he can sell shares on 4 March for £10 000 and then buy the same shares on 13 March for £8000 he has made a profit of £2000. Once again the two contracts are settled on 22 March. Bears profit when share prices are **falling.**

3 The stag specializes in the purchase of new shares. Suppose a company issues shares by prospectus at a fixed price of £1.50. The stag applies for some shares and is allotted 1000. When the shares are first quoted on the Stock Exchange they reach a market price of £1.80. The stag then sells the shares and makes a **profit** of £300 less expenses. If the market price had been below the issue price then the stag would have made a **loss** on the sale.

It is the nature of speculation that losses can occur for the speculator if prices move in the opposite direction to those expected by the bull, bear or stag.

It should also be noted that any individual or firm can be a speculator in securities and can, **at the same time,** be a bull for one share and a bear for a **different** share.

19.7 Share Price, Dividend and Yield

Many newspapers quote stock exchange prices and a typical entry, with an explanation of the prices quoted, is given in Fig. 19.5.

Newspapers also refer to the **Financial Times Industrial Ordinary Share Index** (FT Index). The FT Index measures the movement in the the share prices of **thirty** leading UK companies. The companies included in the Index are a representative selection of **blue-chip** (that is large and well-known) companies. The criticism of this Index is that it is too narrow because only thirty

High	*Low*	*Share*		*Price (p)*	*Movement*	*Dividend (p)*	*Yield*
70	28	Western Trading	(10p)	50	+4	5	10%
	(d)		*(a)*	*(b)*	*(c)*	*(e)*	*(f)*

(a) is the **nominal** (or **par**) value of the share. This should not be confused with the issue price which is the price at which the shares were sold when they were first issued

(b) is the **market price** of the share which can vary from day to day

(c) shows the change on the previous day's price, in this case a gain of 4p

(d) represents the highest and lowest market prices of the share for a given period

(e) is the **dividend** paid on each share. Very often a company declares a dividend as a percentage of the nominal value of the share. In this case the dividend is 50% because 50% of 10p = 5p

(f) is the **yield** which represents the dividend paid per share as a percentage of the share's market price.

Thus $\frac{5p}{50p} \times \frac{100}{1} = 10\%$

Fig. 19.5 Prices quoted in a newspaper

companies are included. For this reason the **Financial Times Stock Exchange 100 Share Index** was introduced in 1984. This new Index calculates, every minute, the movement in share prices of 100 leading UK companies.

19.8 The Importance of a Stock Exchange

1 Although the Stock Exchange is a **secondary** market which only deals in second-hand securities, its existence helps the **primary** (or **new issue**) market. Investors are more likely to buy new shares if they know that there is an easy means of selling them at a later date.

2 As a result companies and the Government find it **easier to raise finance.**

3 Prices established on the Stock Exchange allow a **means of valuing securities.** This is necessary:

(a) for the purpose of take-over bids,

(b) so that companies can correctly price new issues of shares by referring to existing issues,

(c) so that the shareholdings of individuals can be valued for tax purposes e.g. for Capital Transfer Tax (see Unit 22.2).

4 The Stock Exchange gives **savers** the opportunity, through buying shares, of **participating in the profits of UK industry.** The savings of individuals are also used by the **financial institutions** (insurance companies, pension funds etc) to purchase securities on the Exchange.

19.9 Other Terms used on the Stock Exchange

The following terms are also used on the Stock Exchange.

Ariel	Automated Real-Time Investments Exchange Ltd is a computerized transfer system for large quantities of shares and provides an alternative to the Stock Exchange for buying and selling securities
Bearish market	When share prices in general are falling
Bullish market	When share prices in general are rising
Contract Note	This is sent from the broker to the client and gives details of the securities that have been bought or sold and their prices
Dividend — interim and final	Payments to ordinary shareholders are normally made twice a year and consist of an interim and a final dividend
Insider dealing	This refers to investors who deal in securities using privileged information obtained from within (inside) a company
Middle price	The jobber quotes two prices for a share. The middle price is the middle of these two values
Scrip Issue	When existing shareholders receive additional shares in proportion to their shareholdings. No extra finance is raised by the company
Share Certificate	This is issued by the company or its agent and shows ownership of shares
Share register	This is kept by the company or its agent and lists the names and addresses of shareholders together with the number of shares held by each one. An up to date share register is important for the correct payment of dividends
Take-over Panel	The City Panel on Take-overs and Mergers was established to ensure that certain rules are followed during take-overs and mergers
Talisman	The Stock Exchange's computerized settlement system
Transfer Form	The form signed by the seller of a security instructing the company to take his name from the register and substitute that of the buyer

20 Public enterprise

20.1 The Public Sector

The **public sector,** in contrast to the **private sector,** covers all those activities for which **government** has some direct responsibility. In the United Kingdom the public sector spending of **central government, local authorities, public corporations** and **other forms of public ownership** accounts for about **50%** of total United Kingdom output.

Part of public sector spending is on activities such as defence, education and the National Health Service which are mainly financed from taxation. Other public sector activities such as the provision of gas, electricity and rail transport are sold, in the **market place,** at a **price,** and often with the aim of making some **profit.** This second type of public sector activity is called **public enterprise.** The major differences between public enterprise and private enterprise are given in Fig. 20.1.

	Public enterprise	*Private enterprise*
owned by	the state (central government) and local authorities	individuals and groups of individuals
financed by	where necessary taxation	sole traders, partners and shareholders
motive	to make some profit *or* to break even *or* to provide a service which may have to run at a loss	the major motive is to make profit

Fig. 20.1 Differences between public enterprise and private enterprise

20.2 Public Corporations

When an industry is **nationalized** the companies in that industry are taken over by the State (central government). Government Stock is usually given as **compensation** to shareholders for their shares held in the companies. The nationalized industry so created is run as a **public corporation** e.g. the National Coal Board, the British Gas Corporation, the Central Electricity Generating Board and area distribution Boards, British Steel, British Rail, the Post Office, the Bank of England and the British Broadcasting Corporation.

Main features of a public corporation

1 It is set up by an **Act of Parliament.**

2 It is a **corporate** body with a separate legal existence (see Unit 18.5).

3 It is run by a **Board** appointed by a Government Minister e.g. the Secretary of State for Transport appoints the Board for British Rail.

4 The **Government** makes the **policy decisions** for the public corporation e.g. whether to reduce the railway network. The **day-to-day control** of the corporation, however, is left to the Board and managers.

5 The Government sets **financial targets** for the corporation e.g. an industry might be expected to achieve a rate of return on capital employed of 10% (see Unit 17.5). The Government can also decide on the size of any price increase for the goods or services produced by the corporation.

6 The Government Minister can be questioned about the corporation in Parliament and the **Select Committee on Nationalized Industries** also investigates and reports on the activities of these industries.

7 The public corporation can have a Consumers (or Consultative) Council to protect the interest of consumers (see Unit 13.5).

Public corporations are financed by:

1 grants from the Treasury which have to be raised from general taxation,

2 borrowing from the Treasury which, in turn, has to borrow by issuing gilt-edged stock,
3 the issue of the corporation stock in foreign capital markets, e.g. the Electricity industry borrowing in West Germany,
4 ploughed-back profits from the sale of the corporation's goods or services.

The profits of public corporations can be used to:
1 pay interest on capital borrowed,
2 repay the capital borrowed,
3 plough back into the industry,
4 keep down the prices of the goods or services produced by the corporation,
5 raise the wages of the corporation's work-force,
6 subsidize other government activities.

The public corporation is the principal way in which central government runs State-owned industry. Other ways in which the State is involved include:
1 the operation of **Government Trading Departments** e.g. the Department of Trade and Industry controls the Royal Mint and the Export Credits Guarantee Department
2 the **ownership** of **shares of public limited companies** e.g. Government shareholdings in British Leyland and British Petroleum

When an industry is privatized (or denationalized) the reverse of nationalization takes place and the public corporation is returned to the private sector. Thus the National Freight Corporation was sold to its employees to form the National Freight Consortium p.l.c. and British Telecom became a public limited company in November 1984.

20.3 Local Authority Undertakings

Local authority (or **municipal**) undertakings are the responsibility of local, rather than central, government. Some of these undertakings can be regarded as public enterprise e.g. the provision of bus services, car parks and recreation facilities when prices are charged. Other services are **not** part of public enterprise because prices are not charged for the service e.g. full-time education for persons under nineteen years of age.

Daily control of a local authority enterprise is exercised by the **managers** (employees) of the enterprise while **policy decisions** for the enterprise are made by **elected councillors.**

Local authority enterprises are financed by:
1 grants from local authorities which have to be raised from, for example, rates and the Rate Support Grant (see Unit 22.9);
2 borrowing from the local authority which, in turn, might have to borrow (see Unit 22.9);
3 ploughed-back profits from the sale of the undertaking's goods or services.

20.4 Arguments in Favour of Public Enterprise

1 The complete ownership of an industry makes it easier to achieve economies of scale i.e. the industry is able to operate on a larger scale with a lowering of costs (see Unit 1.5).
2 Complete ownership also avoids unnecessary duplication of capital investment. For example if more than one firm was responsible for the provision of electricity to a particular area additional cabling would be required.
3 In capital intensive industries private owners may not have the resources necessary for large-scale investment, e.g. the large sums of money needed to develop a new coalfield may have to come from the Government.
4 Some industries are too important to be left in private hands e.g. coal, electricity, nuclear energy.
5 When certain services are essential but unprofitable they should be provided by the State e.g. railway services to rural communities.
6 The Government may wish to take over a firm which is operating against the public interest, e.g. a monopoly which is charging high prices.
7 With a large public sector the Government can more easily control economic activity. For example, if it is necessary to reduce total spending in the economy the Government could reduce public sector spending.

20.5 Arguments Against Public Enterprise

1 The public enterprise may become too large to be efficiently managed. Decision-making processes may be slow and diseconomies of scale can result (see Unit 1.5).

2 Many public corporations are monopolies which face little competition. There is, therefore, no incentive to improve.

3 The lack of a profit motive in the provision of public services could result in a waste of funds.

4 The Government, for political reasons, may interfere too much in the operation of public enterprise which could result in a conflict between the Board and the Minister.

5 The Minister may not have sufficient expert knowledge to make the correct policy decisions for the enterprise.

21 Income and saving

21.1 Gross and Net Wages

The **gross wage** of an employee is the wage (or salary) received **before** any deductions are made. **Net wage** (or **take-home pay**) is **after** deductions have been made, **at source,** by the employer. Examples of deductions include:

1 national insurance (see Unit 22.6);

2 income tax (see Unit 22.2) collected under Pay As You Earn (PAYE);

3 superannuation which is a contribution to the employer's pension scheme;

4 trade union contributions. Employees can ask for contributions to be subtracted from pay packets.

Details of earnings and deductions are given to an employee in the form of a **payslip.** A simplified payslip is shown in Fig. 21.1.

The net wage of an employee can be paid by **cash, cheque** or **credit transfer** to an employee's bank or building society account.

Employee's name A. J. SMITH	*(a)* Works No. 873 482	*(b)* NI No. ZT 48 27 33 B	*(c)* Tax Code 236 L	*(d)* Date June 1985

(e) Basic Pay £430	*(f)* Overtime £30	*(g)* Total Gross Pay £460

(h) NI £28	*(i)* Tax £80	*(j)* Supern. £16	*(k)* Trade Union £2	*(l)* Total Deductions £126	*(m)* Net Pay £334

(a) Firms often give employees individual reference numbers

(b) Each employee has a National Insurance (NI) number

(c) The Tax Code, issued by the Inland Revenue, tells the employer the amount of income tax to be deducted

(d) This payslip is for the month of June 1985

(e) Basic pay is the pay for a normal working week of, say, 38 hours

(f) Payment for any hours worked above the 38 hours per week is overtime payment

(g) = *(e)* + *(f)*

(l) = *(h)* + *(i)* + *(j)* + *(k)*

(m) = *(g)* − *(l)*

Fig. 21.1 A payslip

21.2 A Family Budget

A **family** (or personal) **budget** is a list of planned and possible **future income** and **spending.**

The **income** of an average family consists of:

1 the net wages of members of the family

2 any state benefits received e.g. child benefit

3 interest received from, say, building society accounts or similar income from other forms of saving

The **spending** of the family is on:

1 necessities such as food, clothing, heating and transport

2 items for which payment has already been agreed e.g. interest on a mortgage, hire purchase repayments

3 avoidable expenses such as payments for holidays and entertainment

Fig. 21.2 gives two examples of family budgets.

Planned annual income		*Planned annual spending*	*Planned annual saving*
Family A	£8000	£7000	£1000
Family B	£8000	£9600	−£1600

Fig. 21.2 Family budgets

Family A expects to be able to **save** £1000. This amount of saving is, of course, only planned and **not certain.** If there are unexpected expenses then the amount actually saved would be less. Family B expects to **overspend** by £1600 and this could perhaps be avoided if they:

1 tried to increase their income e.g. by working overtime

2 reduced planned spending by cutting down on non-essentials

3 were able to draw on past savings

4 were able to borrow; the family should remember, however, that they would have to pay interest on and would eventually have to repay the amount borrowed.

21.3 Reasons for Saving

People might wish to save in order to:

1 be able **to buy expensive items** e.g. to pay for a holiday.

2 receive **extra income** from those savings e.g.

(a) interest from a building society or bank deposit account,

(b) a dividend from the ownership of shares,

(c) a capital gain from buying shares at a low price and selling them at a higher price.

3 provide a **fund** of money for use in an emergency e.g. in case of unemployment or the illness/death of the main wage-earner.

4 obtain the funds to start a business, e.g. personal savings are an important **source of finance** for sole traders.

5 accumulate funds for **retirement** e.g. by taking out endowment assurance (see Unit 14.14.3).

21.4 Methods of Saving

1 A wide range of very safe methods of saving is provided by the Government through the network of post offices. When savers use these methods of saving they are lending money to the Government. Examples of these methods are listed below:

(a) The National Savings Bank offers ordinary and investment accounts and a Save As You Earn (SAYE) scheme. A saver joining the SAYE scheme agrees to make monthly contributions over a five-year period. The savings are **index-linked** which means that their value increases in line with the Index of Retail Prices and is, therefore, inflation-proofed.

(b) National Savings Certificates are a **medium**-term method of saving; they carry a fixed rate of interest and some Certificates are index-linked.

(c) Premium bonds do not give the saver a rate of interest. Instead the holder of a premium bond has the chance of winning a cash prize in the weekly and monthly draws of premium bond numbers.

(d) National Girobank deposit accounts. For further details see Unit 10.3.2.

(e) Gilt-edged stock The Government borrows by issuing its own stock which usually carries a fixed rate of interest. The stock will be repaid at some date in the future although stocks such as Consols are never repaid. A saver can buy or sell most of the issues of gilt-edged stock through the Post Office. Gilts are also traded on the Stock Exchange so a saver could, instead, buy and sell through a stockbroker.

2 Local authorities borrow from savers by accepting short-term deposits. They also issue local authority bonds (stock) which carry a fixed rate of interest and run for a fixed period of time. Some of these bonds can be bought and sold on the Stock Exchange. Local authority bonds are virtually as safe as central Government stock.

3 Building society accounts Building societies offer a wide range of accounts which vary in, for example, the notice required for withdrawal, the rate of interest given and the minimum deposit required.

The most popular form of account is the **ordinary share account** which requires little or no notice of withdrawal. The holders of ordinary share accounts are the **owners** of the building societies which are non-profit making organizations and which must register with the **Registrar of Friendly Societies.** The basic function of building societies is, of course, to borrow from the public and then lend by way of mortgages to those who wish to buy property.

Building societies are popular with savers because:

1 they give a better rate of interest than, for example, clearing bank deposit accounts,
2 they are open at convenient times including Saturday mornings,
3 there are many branches throughout the country,
4 depositors obtain preferential treatment for mortgages.

4 The clearing banks (see Unit 9.1), including the Trustee Savings Banks (see Unit 10.4), offer deposit or investment accounts.

5 The shares and debentures of public limited companies, particularly those which are quoted on the Stock Exchange. The saver hopes to benefit from a capital gain (profit) when the security is sold, and interest from debentures and dividends from shares. Shares are, however, a particularly risky method of saving because the share price of the company may fall. If the company becomes insolvent the shares may even become worthless.

6 Unit trusts A saver with a small sum of money will be able to buy the ordinary shares of only a few companies. If these companies collapse the savings are likely to be completely lost. An indirect and safer way of buying ordinary shares is through a unit trust. A unit trust is run by professional managers, e.g. M and G Group, Save and Prosper Group, who attract funds by selling 'units' to many savers. With this large sum of money the managers can buy shares in many companies on behalf of unit holders. The individual unit holder or saver, therefore, has a very small investment in many companies. Units can be bought from and sold to the unit trust managers at any time. The prices of units in different trusts, which are published in many

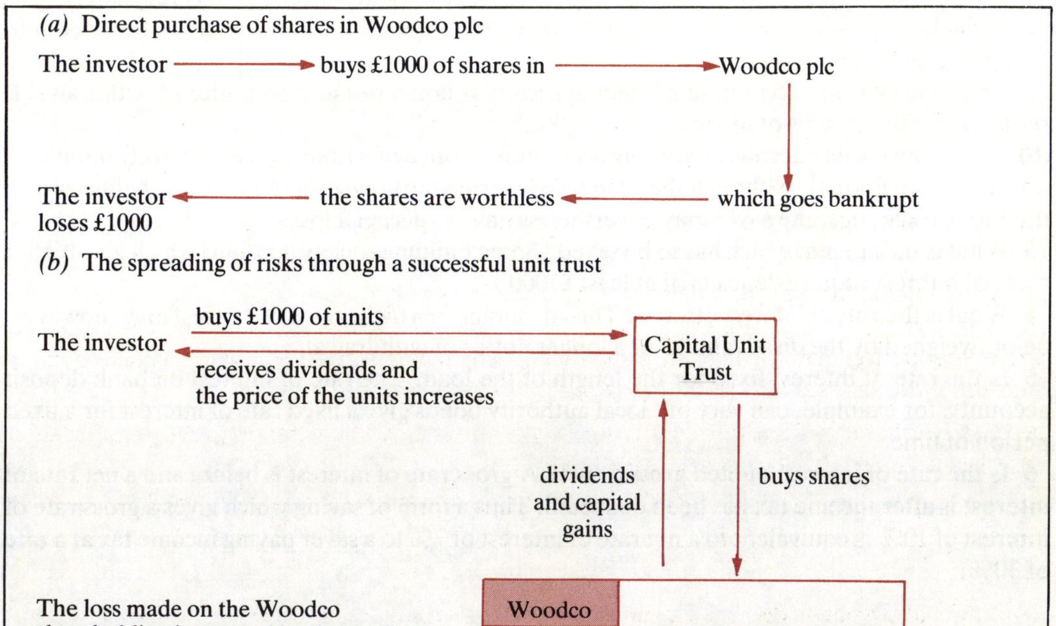

Fig. 21.3 The spreading of risks through a unit trust

newspapers, rise or fall in line with the prices of and dividends paid on the shares which have been purchased for the particular unit trust fund.

The **advantages** to a saver of buying units in a unit trust include the following:

1 the saver's risk is spread because it is linked to the fortunes of many companies (Fig. 21.3).

2 the trust is run by professional managers who have more expertise than individual savers.

3 unit trusts have separate funds specializing in particular securities e.g. Japanese shares, gold mining shares, gilt-edged stock and the saver can, therefore, choose a particular sector.

4 the purchase of units can be linked to an endowment assurance policy (see Unit 14.14.3).

5 An investment trust, e.g. Baillie Gifford Technology plc is similar to a unit trust because it buys securities in a range of public companies. It differs from a unit trust, however, because it raises money from savers, not by sellings units, but from the sale of shares which might be issued, for example, by prospectus (see Unit 19.1). The shares of investment trusts are quoted on the Stock Exchange in the same way as the shares of public limited companies.

6 Finance houses e.g. United Dominions Trust, offer a number of accounts which give a higher rate of interest than, for example, clearing bank deposit accounts because they are:

(a) more risky for the saver because the funds are, for example, used for hire purchase lending,

(b) usually longer-term,

(c) for a given period, and withdrawal is not usually possible until the end of that period.

7 Life assurance policies An endowment policy (see Unit 14.14.3) is a long-term method of saving.

8 Property The most important form of saving undertaken by many people is the purchase of a house or flat. If property is bought on, for example, a 100% mortgage over 25 years, then after that period of time the mortgage-holder will have saved an amount equal to the value of the property.

9 Other methods used are collecting antiques, postage stamps, gold coins, oil paintings or any asset which is likely to increase in value. If the increase in value is greater than the rate of inflation then the real value of savings has increased.

21.5 Factors to Consider when Deciding Where to Place Savings

Unit 21.4 shows the wide range of methods of savings available to those with **unspent income.** In deciding which form of saving to choose the saver should ask the following questions.

1 Is the form of saving **safe**? (For example, lending to the UK Government is very safe.)

2 Is the form of saving **liquid** or **illiquid?** An asset is liquid if it can be quickly converted into money **without great loss:**

(a) an ordinary share account in a building society is liquid because no notice of withdrawal is required for small sums of money,

(b) a building society account requiring six month's notice of withdrawal is relatively illiquid,

(c) shares are illiquid. Although they can be converted fairly easily into money by being sold on the Stock Exchange, the saver may nevertheless have to accept a loss.

3 What is the **amount** which has to be saved? Some building society accounts which give higher rates of interest require deposits of at least £1000.

4 What is the **rate of interest** offered? The advantage of a higher rate of interest may, however, be outweighed by the disadvantage of a longer notice of withdrawal.

5 Is the rate of interest **fixed** for the length of the loan? The rate of interest on bank deposit accounts, for example, can vary but local authority bonds give a fixed rate of interest for a fixed period of time.

6 Is the rate of interest quoted **gross** or **net?** A gross rate of interest is **before** and a net rate of interest is **after** income tax has been deducted. Thus a form of saving which gives a gross rate of interest of 10% is equivalent to a net rate of interest of 7% to a saver paying income tax at a rate of 30%.

22 Government spending and income

22.1 Central Government Spending and Income

The major items of central government **spending** are on:

1 social security
2 defence
3 the National Health Service
4 education
5 the Rate Support Grant—grants by central government to local authorities
6 interest on the National Debt. The **National Debt** is the amount borrowed by the Government as a result of issuing gilt-edged stock, National Savings Certificates and so on. Interest has to be paid on such borrowing.

To **finance** its spending the Government:

1 levies taxes:
(a) direct taxes on income and capital (see Unit 22.2) are collected by the Inland Revenue;
(b) indirect taxes on expenditure (see Unit 22.3) are collected by HM Customs and Excise.
2 receives **National Insurance Contributions** from employers and employees (see Unit 22.6).
3 borrows where Government spending is **greater** than Government income:
(a) the Government borrows in the **short-term** by selling **three month Treasury Bills;**
(b) the principal form of **long-term** borrowing is the issue of **gilt-edged stock.**

The amounts raised in taxation in the United Kingdom for 1982 are shown in Fig. 22.1.

	£m	(%)
Taxes on incomes and capital	40 300	(34.2)
Taxes on expenditure	47 082	(39.9)
National Insurance and other contributions	18 069	(15.3)
Miscellaneous receipts e.g. rent, interest and dividends	12 557	(10.6)
	118 008	(100.0)

Source: Annual Abstract of Statistics

Fig. 22.1 United Kingdom central government receipts (1982)

22.2 Taxes on Income and Capital

1 Income tax is paid by individuals and **unincorporated businesses**. The amount of income tax paid by an individual is based on the individual's **taxable income** while for a firm it is based on **taxable profits.**

The taxable income of an individual is given by **gross income minus allowances.** The taxable income is then subject to **tax rates** which, in the United Kingdom, increase in stages as taxable income increases. Most income tax payers in the United Kingdom pay tax at the **standard** (or **basic**) rate of tax of 30% while those with higher taxable incomes can pay up to a rate of 60%. An example of the calculation of income tax, using the tax rates and allowances for 1984/5, is shown in Fig. 22.2.

For employed persons income tax is collected under the **Pay As You Earn** (PAYE) system where the **employer** deducts the income tax, **at source,** before paying the **net wage** to the employee.

Income tax payers can also obtain **tax relief** on the **interest paid on mortgages** and also for **premiums paid on life assurance policies** taken out **before mid-March 1984.** Building societies and other providers of mortgages and life assurances companies allow such relief at source for mortgage and policyholders. Thus in the case of a mortgage a standard rate tax payer who should

Allowances		*Taxable income (£)*	*Tax rate (%)*
Married man	£3115	1—15 400	30
Single person *or* married woman	£2005	15 401—18 200	40
Superannuation	in full	18 201—23 100	45
Expenses paid		23 101—30 600	50
in connection with		30 601—38 100	55
employment	can be allowed	over 38 100	60

A married man has an annual income of £26 100 and pays superannuation of £1035 per year. He pays a subscription of £150 per year to a professional association which HM Inspector of Taxes has agreed is a necessary expense in relation to his employment

Calculation of taxable income

Income		= £26 100
Less allowances		
Married man	£3115	
Superannuation	£1035	
Expenses	£150	£4300
Taxable income		£21 800

Calculation of tax paid

Taxable income		*Rate*		*Tax paid*
£15 400	at	30%	=	£4620
£2800	at	40%	=	£1120
£3600	at	45%	=	£1620
£21 800		Tax paid	=	£7360

Fig. 22.2 Calculation of income tax for 1984/5

pay interest of £3000 per year obtains tax relief of £900 (30% of £3000) and pays £2100 per year to the building society.

2 Corporation tax is paid by **incorporated businesses** e.g. companies on their **profits** (income) after allowances have been made for items such as depreciation on machinery and interest on borrowing. In the budget of March 1984 it was announced that companies will be able to claim fewer expenses to offset against profits. To compensate for this effective increase in their corporation tax liability, the rate of corporation tax will be progressively reduced from 50% in 1984/5 to 35% by 1986/7. At the same time the rate of corporation tax paid by **smaller** companies was also reduced from 38% in 1983/4 to 30% in 1984/5.

3 Capital gains tax may have to be paid when assets are sold at a profit. Thus a saver who makes a capital gain of £8000 as a result of buying and selling shares may have to pay capital gains tax on the profit.

4 Capital transfer tax may have to be paid when assets are transferred from one person to another. Thus if a father dies and leaves £100 000 to his daughter capital transfer tax may have to paid.

22.3 Taxes on Expenditure

Expenditure taxes are placed on **goods** and **services** and are collected by **HM Customs and Excise.** Such taxes may be **ad valorem** or **specific.** Ad valorem taxes are quoted as a **percentage** of the price of a product e.g. a tax of 15%. Specific taxes quoted in **unit terms** e.g. a tax of £1.50 per litre of wine.

1 Value Added Tax (VAT) Value added tax of 15% must be paid on a wide range of goods and services. The tax is based on the **'value added'** by a firm and is collected at each stage of the production process. Fig. 22.3 gives an illustration of how VAT is calculated for an imaginary rate of 10%.

There are certain categories of goods and services which are

(a) zero rated Firms do **not** pay VAT on zero-rated goods they sell e.g. children's clothes and newspapers and any VAT already paid on inputs bought (raw materials and other supplies) **can be reclaimed,** *or*

	Cost of input	+	*VAT on input*	*Price of output*	+	*VAT on output*	*Net amount paid to HM Customs & Excise*	*Value added which is 10% of*
Extractive industry	0		0	50		5	5	50
sells to								
Manufacturer	50		5	80		8	3	30
sells to								
Retailer	80		8	100		10	2	20
Consumer	pays £110 which includes VAT of						10	100

The value added at any stage of the production process is the difference between the price paid for inputs and the price received from the sale of outputs. Thus, and ignoring VAT, if a manufacturer buys raw materials and other supplies for £50 and converts the materials into finished goods which are sold for £80 then the value added by the manufacturer is £30 (£80 minus £50).

Assume now that VAT is levied at 10% so that the manufacturer has to pay VAT of £3 (10% of £30). The tax is administered in the following way.

In the table the manufacturer buys inputs from extractive industry for £55 which includes VAT of £5 that has already been paid by extractive industry to HM Customs and Excise. The manufacturer then sells his output to the retailer for £88. Included in the £88 is VAT of £8 that is now owed to HM Customs and Excise. The manufacturer can, however, reclaim VAT of £5 which he has already paid on his input making a net VAT payment of £3.

Similar calculations are made at each stage of the production process so that the £10 in VAT which is eventually received by HM Customs and Excise is 10% of the value of total output.

Fig. 22.3 Calculation of VAT for a rate of 10%

(b) exempt. Firms do **not** pay VAT on exempt goods and services they provide e.g. insurance and health services, but VAT already paid on inputs **cannot be reclaimed.**

2 Excise duties are specific taxes levied on certain classes of goods e.g. tobacco, alcohol, petroleum products, whether they have been **home-produced** or **imported,** but only when they are consumed in the United Kingdom. When home-produced goods are exported **no** duties or taxes are levied. Thus a UK manufacturer selling whisky to the USA pays no UK duty on the whisky.

3 Vehicle excise duties Motorists must pay for **road fund licences** for vehicles which are used on United Kingdom roads.

4 Customs duties or **tariffs** are levied on imports which enter the United Kingdom from countries **outside** the EEC. Trade between the EEC countries is free of customs duties. All EEC countries charge the same customs duties on non-EEC goods (the **Common External Tariff**) and the revenue raised from such duties is payable to the EEC to finance its own expenditure.

22.4 Direct and Indirect Taxation

Taxes on income and capital are examples of **direct** taxation because the burden of the tax is directly borne by the person or firm on whom the tax is levied. Taxes on expenditure are **indirect** taxes because those responsible for paying the tax are able to pass some or all of the tax on to the final consumer who then, indirectly, pays the tax e.g. VAT (Fig. 22.3).

22.5 Progressive, Proportional and Regressive Taxation

Income	*Tax paid*	*(%)*	*Tax paid*	*(%)*	*Tax paid*	*(%)*
£50	£2	(4)	£2	(4)	£2	(4)
£100	£10	(10)	£4	(4)	£3	(3)
£200	£40	(20)	£8	(4)	£4	(2)
	progressive		proportional		regressive	

Fig. 22.4 Progressive, proportional and regressive taxation

Fig. 22.4 shows that for a **progressive** tax system those on higher incomes pay a **higher percentage** of their income in tax. An example of such a system is income tax where tax rates rise as taxable income increases (Fig. 22.2). A **proportional** tax occurs when the percentage paid in tax remains **constant.** A **regressive** tax is where the percentage paid in tax **falls** as income rises. Thus a £5 duty on a bottle of whisky is regressive because it represents 10% of the income of a consumer earning £50 per week but only 5% for a consumer earning £100 per week.

22.6 National Insurance Contributions

National Insurance contributions are **compulsory** for all employers and employees and they are, in effect, a form of tax. The amount of contributions is linked to the earnings of the employee and is paid into the **National Insurance Fund.** The Fund is then used to pay State benefits such as:

1 unemployment benefit
2 sickness benefit
3 retirement pensions

The National Insurance Fund may not have sufficient income from National Insurance contributions to finance its total expenditure. The Government, therefore, meets any deficiency out of general taxation.

22.7 The Reasons for Taxation

Taxes are levied by UK central government for the following reasons.

1 Revenue is raised to finance **Government spending** on defence, education and so on. Customs duties, however, are levied to raise revenue for the EEC.

2 Taxation redistributes income from rich to poor. A progressive tax system taxes those on higher incomes more heavily and such revenue can also be used to give benefits to those on low incomes.

3 Taxes discourage consumption of particular commodities e.g. high excise duties on tobacco.

4 UK industries are protected from foreign competition e.g. customs duties on goods entering the UK from non-EEC countries.

5 The amount of spending in an economy is **controlled.** If too much spending in an economy causes inflation the Government can increase taxation to reduce consumers' ability to spend.

22.8 The Budget

The Government draws up a budget each year which is an estimate of **Government spending** and **income** for the coming financial year. In drawing up the budget the Chancellor of the Exchequer has to decide:

1 the amounts to be allocated to different forms of government **expenditure** e.g. how much is to be spent on defence?

2 how much **revenue** has to be raised from taxation in general and how much should be raised from different taxes e.g. should more indirect taxation be used?

3 the amount which the Government has to **borrow** when Government expenditure is likely to be **greater** than Government revenue (called a **budget deficit**). When there is a **budget surplus** and Government expenditure is less than Government revenue borrowing is **not** required.

22.9 Local Authority Spending and Income

The major items of local authority spending are:

1 education
2 law and order
3 social services
4 housing
5 interest on borrowing

To finance such spending local authorities receive income from:

1 rates (see Unit 22.10),

2 the **Rate Support Grant** (RSG) which is a grant from central government. This grant is either:

(a) specific, when it can only be used for a particular kind of expenditure, e.g. housing, *or*

(b) general when it can be used for any kind of expenditure,

3 rents from council houses and other property,

4 the **profits** of local authority undertakings e.g. bus services.

If local authority spending is greater than income then the local authority will have to **borrow** by, for example:

1 accepting **short-term deposits** from savers
2 issuing its own **stock**

3 obtaining funds from the **Public Works Loans Board** which provides loans to local authorities for capital projects e.g. building roads (but not the costs of maintaining them as that falls under current expenditure).

22.10 Local Authority Rates

Rates are paid by **occupiers of property** (householders and businesses) and the amount paid is determined by **1** the **rateable value** of the property, and **2** the **rate charged** by the local authority.

Thus if the rateable value of a property is £500 and the rate charged is 60 pence in the pound the amount paid in rates is 500 × 60p = £300

1 The **rateable value** of a property is an estimate of the annual rent that might be charged on the property if it was let. Thus if a house with a rateable value of £300 is extended to include two further bedrooms its rateable value will rise.

2 The rate in the pound charged by a local authority usually varies from year to year and will depend upon the amount of revenue the local authority needs to raise from property in its area in order to fund its spending.

The system of local authority rates has been criticized for the following reasons.:

1 The rates paid by a householder need not reflect the householder's **ability to pay.**

	Annual income	*Annual rates*	*Proportion of income paid in rates*
Household *A*	£10 000	£400	4%
Household *B*	£4000	£400	10%

Fig. 22.5 Rates and the ability to pay

Thus, in Fig. 22.5, households *A* and *B* live in equally rated homes yet, in proportion to its income, household *B* faces a far greater rates burden since it represents 10% of its income compared with household *A*'s payment of 4% of its income. This burden on household *B* would be reduced, however, if it was able to obtain a rates rebate.

2 The rates pay for services within a local authority area which may be used by those living in another local authority area.

3 Rates are levied on industrial and commercial property and the burden of such fixed costs, which are **unrelated to the profits** of businesses, may discourage the businesses from expanding.

The alternatives to rates could be a local income tax, a local expenditure tax or increased grants from central government. It is unlikely, however, that the rating system will be changed in the near future.

Part III
Self-test units

There is a self-test unit for each of the core units contained in Part II. The main type of test used is sentence completion where you have to select the correct word(s) from those given in the box within the self-test unit. **A word cannot be chosen more than once.** Before attempting a self-test unit work through the relevant core unit.

Answers to the questions in this section are given on pp. 128 to 131.

tertiary	specialization	acceptability
assemble	money	double coincidence of wants
manufacturing	buying and selling	aids to trade
producers	banking	interdependence
money	luxuries	transport
trade	subsistence	producer
mass production	production	chain of production
convert	necessities	direct services
consumers	economies of scale	extractive

Unit 1 Production

1 In which branch of production would each of the workers in **(a)** to **(j)** and firms in **(k)** to **(p)** be placed? Select your answer from:
extractive, manufacturing, constructive, commerce (trade), commerce (aids to trade) and direct service.
(a) a fisherman **(b)** a computer assembler **(c)** a steelworker **(d)** an insurance clerk **(e)** a hairdresser **(f)** a shop assistant **(g)** a worker on an oil rig **(h)** a worker in an oil refinery **(i)** a lorry driver **(j)** a refuse collector **(k)** the National Coal Board **(l)** Sainsbury's **(m)** British Leyland **(n)** Lloyds Bank **(o)** Wimpey Homes **(p)** British Rail

2 For **(a)** to **(f)** state the type of take-over which is taking place. Select your answer from: horizontal, vertical (forward), vertical (backward), diversification.

(a) one hotel taking over another hotel
(b) a bank taking over a property company
(c) an oil company taking over a number of petrol stations
(d) a retailer of clothes taking over a maker of clothes
(e) a wholesaler of groceries taking over a supermarket
(f) a manufacturer of chocolates taking over a manufacturer of soft drinks

3 In **(a)** to **(x)** find the correct word(s) to complete each sentence.

(a) Those who provide goods and services are called ________.
(b) Those who buy goods and services are called ________.
(c) Food, drink, clothing and shelter are examples of ________.
(d) Those goods which are not essential are called ________.
(e) Industry, commerce and direct services make up ________.
(f) Industry can be divided into extractive, constructive and ________.
(g) Workers who take raw materials from the land and the sea are called ________ workers.
(h) Manufacturers ________ raw materials into finished products.
(i) Constructive workers ________ components into products ready for use.
(j) Commerce is made up of ________ and ________.
(k) Trade is the ________ of goods.
(l) Two examples of ancillaries to trade are ________ and ________.
(m) Dentists and doctors are examples of ________ workers.
(n) Commerce and direct services make up ________ industry.
(o) A ________ shows the links between the different stages of production.
(p) When different stages of production rely on each other it is called ________.

(q) Goods used by firms to make other goods are called _________ goods.

(r) When production occurs on a large scale it is called _________. Such production allows firms to obtain the benefits of _________.

(s) Another name for the division of labour is _________.

(t) An economy in which people grow and make everything they need for themselves is called a _________ economy.

(u) In a barter economy goods are exchanged but no _________ is involved.

(v) One of the problems of a barter economy is the need for _________.

(w) All modern economies are _________ economies in which there is considerable specialization and exchange.

(x) The most important attribute of money is _________.

Unit 2 Retailing

1 Complete the following table

	Number of branches	*Prices (high or low)*	*Responsibility for buying goods rests with*	*Suppliers are usually*
Unit shops				
Department stores				
Multiples				

2 In **(a)** to **(u)** find the correct word(s) to complete each sentence.

(a) Retailers sell to the _________ and buy from _________ and _________.

(b) Unit shops are sometimes called _________ retailers and many of these shops are located near _________.

(c) Prices are usually _________ in unit shops because the shops can only buy in _________ bulk from _________.

(d) Multiples or _________ stores can be divided into _________ and _________.

(e) All the major decisions concerning a chain store are taken by _________.

(f) Department stores are located in _________ and sell a _________ range of goods.

(g) Responsibility for ordering goods for each department in a department store rests with the _________ but in a _________ department store this is often done, instead, by head office.

(h) Mail order firms often employ _________ to collect orders and _________ will then be used which give illustrations and details of the goods for sale.

(i) When goods are bought by mail order customers do not visit _________.

(j) Retail co-operative societies differ from other types of retailing because _________ are distributed to customers in the form of _________ stamps. These stamps can be exchanged for _________ or _________ or added to the customers' _________ in the society.

(k) Hypermarkets are located on the _________ of towns because they need large amounts of _________.

(l) Hypermarkets sell at _________ prices and try to attract those customers owning _________.

(m) A specialist retailer selling only the more popular brands of goods and employing a minimum standard of display is called a _________.

(n) One form of retailing where goods are brought to the customers' homes is a _________.

(o) _________ is when goods are sold using coin-operated machines.

(p) Supermarkets, superstores and hypermarkets sell goods using _________ although there is usually a _________ for selling cigarettes.

(q) Self-service stores try to increase sales by using _________ and by encouraging _________ buying.

(r) In a local market a customer may not pay the first price asked by a stallholder because _________ takes place.

(s) An area set aside for shops and from which traffic is excluded is a shopping _________.

(t) _________ is where a retailer agrees to rent the name and methods of selling of an established firm.

(u) Information about a product is contained in _________ which are printed on the labels of many grocery items.

manufacturers	mobile shop	dividend
chain	bar codes	shops
city centres	self-service	specialist
franchising	buyer	land
wholesalers	homes	wide
cars	variety	independent
loss-leaders	cash	agents
precinct	low	public
catalogues	bargaining	discount store
head office	share capital	counter service
high	wholesalers	impulse
profits	multiple	small
edges	goods	automatic vending

Unit 3 Wholesaling

1 In **(a)** to **(l)** find the correct word(s) to complete each sentence.

(a) Wholesalers buy _________ from manufacturers.

(b) The wholesaler _________ goods from a number of manufacturers which gives the retailer a better _________ of goods.

(c) The wholesaler breaks bulk by buying in _________ quantities and selling in _________ quantities.

(d) The wholesaler can even out price fluctuations by _________ goods from the warehouse when the prices of these goods are about to rise.

(e) _________ retailers do not buy from wholesalers but buy directly from manufacturers.

(f) Goods which are unsuitable for distribution via a wholesaler are _________.

(g) When a manufacturer sells to the public without using a wholesaler or retailer it is known as _________.

(h) Spar, V.G. and Mace are examples of _________.

(i) A wholesale warehouse should be located close to _________.

(j) The departments in a warehouse which deal with the ordering of goods are the _________ departments.

(k) The Co-operative Wholesale Society is involved in the manufacture of and _________ of goods to _________.

(l) _________ wholesalers provide no credit and no delivery.

voluntary chains	selection	finished goods
small	stocks	large
commodity	releasing	cash and carry
perishables	retail co-operative societies	distribution
retail outlets	direct dealing	large

Unit 4 Channels of distribution

1 In **(a)** to **(p)** find the correct word(s) to complete each sentence.

(a) A channel of distribution shows the way in which food, for example, moves from _________ to _________.

(b) New Covent Garden is a wholesale food market which deals in _________. Other examples are _________ (meat) and _________ (fish).

(c) A _________ is a statutory organization which can compel producers to sell all their output to it.

(d) One major advantage of a marketing board, to farmers, is that _________ are often guaranteed.

(e) Raw materials are sold on commodity _________.

(f) The raw material which is traded on the Baltic Exchange is _________.

(g) Raw materials which have to be sampled are sold by _________ e.g. _________.

(h) Raw materials which can be accurately graded are sold by _________ e.g. _________.

(i) Diamonds have to be sold by _________ because they vary so much in _________.

(j) An agreement to take delivery of a raw material in six months time but at a price agreed to-day is called a _________ contract. Such contracts are only possible for raw materials which can be accurately _________.

(k) Contracts signed for immediate delivery are called _________ contracts.

(l) Changes in the prices of raw materials encourage _________ to operate in the hope of making a _________.

(m) When manufacturers sign spot contracts, at the same time they usually also sign _________ contracts.

(n) Ring trading is used at the _________.

(o) Buyers and sellers are able to contact each other at _________.

(p) The development of _________ has enabled international markets to be established.

prices	profits	market
speculators	hedging	communications
quality	graded	spot
consumers	inspection	fruit and vegetables
Smithfield	marketing board	exchanges
grain	description	tea
auction	Billingsgate	farmers
futures	cocoa	London Metal Exchange

2 Look at the table of prices for cocoa and then answer the questions listed below. Ignore any dealing expenses.

Immediate delivery	£1300 per tonne
3 months delivery	£1350 per tonne
6 months delivery	£1400 per tonne

Prices of cocoa on 1 September

(a) What is the spot price of cocoa on 1 September?

(b) What is the cost of buying 1000 tonnes of cocoa for immediate delivery?

(c) On 1 September a manufacturer signs a contract for 500 tonnes of cocoa to be delivered in six month's time. Work out the total cost of this contract.

(d) In six months the spot price of cocoa is £1300 per tonne. How much could the manufacturer, referred to in **(c)**, have gained by not dealing in futures and by buying only spot cocoa?

(e) In spite of the loss on the futures contract, why would a manufacturer continue to deal on a futures basis?

Unit 5 The middlemen of trade

1 In **(a)** to **(i)** find the correct word(s) to complete each sentence.

(a) The middlemen of trade deal in _________, _________ and _________.

(b) A middleman acting on his own account is _________ and his reward is _________.

(c) A middleman acting for others is _________ and his reward is _________.

(d) Wholesalers and retailers are examples of middlemen because they are intermediaries between _________ and _________.

(e) Brokers do not _________ the goods in which they deal nor do they arrange contracts in their own _________. Their rôle is to bring _________ and _________ together.

(f) The factor is only concerned with _________ goods and, unlike a broker, does _________ the goods in which he deals.

(g) Del credere agents earn extra _________ as a reward for guaranteeing that _________ will be made.

(h) Merchants buy and sell on their _________. Their reward is _________.

(i) Export houses can act as either _________ or _________.

buyers	manufacturers	foodstuffs
name	commission	own account
raw materials	an agent	manufactured goods
a principal	possess	profit
commission	selling	sellers
final consumers	possess	payment
profit	principals	agents

Unit 6 Foreign trade

1 For each of the following transactions state where and how it is recorded in the UK balance of payments. Choose from:

visible export, visible import, invisible export, invisible import, capital inflow, capital outflow

(a) The UK sells oil to Holland.

(b) A UK citizen takes a cruise on a foreign passenger liner.

(c) An American insurance company buys shares in a UK company on the London Stock Exchange.

(d) A UK firm receives dividends from foreign shareholdings.

(e) The UK buys watches from Japan.

(f) UK citizens buy property in the South of France.

2 Complete the missing figures in the following table; (a) has already been completed.

	(a)	(b)	(c)	(d)	(e)
Visible exports	£800	£800	£400	£900	£422
Visible imports	£600	£200	£700	£800	?
Balance of trade	+£200	?	?	?	−£6
Invisible exports	£650	£300	£100	£200	?
Invisible imports	£1000	£280	£120	£380	£218
Invisible balance	−£350	?	?	?	+£68
Balance on current account	−£150	?	?	?	?

3 In **(a)** to **(r)** find the correct word(s) to complete each sentence.

(a) International specialization occurs when _________ concentrate on the production of particular goods and services.

(b) Specialization results in _________ being created which have to be _________.

(c) _________ means that countries should concentrate on producing those goods and services at which they are most efficient.

(d) International trade is important to the UK because some _________ do not naturally occur in the UK.

(e) Visibles is the trade in _________ but invisibles is the trade in _________.

(f) Another name for the visible balance is the _________.

(g) If the balance of trade has a deficit of £100m and the invisible balance has a surplus of £140m then the current account balance will have a _________ of £40m.

(h) Three of the UK's major invisible exports are _________, _________ and _________.

(i) The UK's visible exports and imports are mainly _________ goods and _________ goods.

(j) When the UK joined the EEC her pattern of trade moved away from the _________ and towards the _________.

(k) The units of currency of West Germany and Japan are the _________ and the _________ respectively.

(l) The Export Credits Guarantee Department provides _________ for exporters. It also guarantees export finance which makes it easier for the exporter to _________ from banks.

(m) A government organization which provides information for exporters is the _________.

(n) Two non-government organizations which can help exporters are _________ and _________.

(o) HM Customs and Excise control _________ warehouses.

(p) Another name for a tariff is an _________.

(q) A complete ban on trade with certain countries is an _________.

(r) The duty paid by non-member countries when selling goods to EEC countries is the _________.

exchanged	surpluses	common external tariff
embargo	goods	chambers of commerce
BOTB	insurance	services
mark	finished	yen
Commonwealth	borrow	Common Market
banking	credit insurance	semi-finished
balance of trade	trade associations	tourism
raw materials	bonded	surplus
countries	import duty	comparative advantage

Unit 7 Business documents used in home trade

1 (a) Calculate the total cost of the following goods if 20% trade discount is allowed

5 typewriters at £800 each
10 filing cabinets at £100 each

(b) Two typewriters are now returned as damaged and are not replaced.
(i) Name the document which the supplier will issue
(ii) Calculate the final amount shown on this document
(c) How much does the customer finally owe as a result of the transactions described in question 1?
(d) If the customer is now given a 5% cash discount calculate the amount which he will pay if he makes full settlement.

2 In **(a)** to **(r)** find the correct word(s) to complete each sentence.
(a) Business documents are essential because they provide _________ records of transactions between firms.
(b) The letter of _________ is sent by a customer to a supplier asking for details of goods available.
(c) A supplier might send a _________ to a customer who has asked for the prices of the supplier's goods.
(d) The disadvantage of using catalogues is that they are _________ to produce. For this reason separate _________ are often used which are cheaper to reprint.
(e) Detailed descriptions of goods by customers are unnecessary when catalogue _________ are used.
(f) Orders placed by telephone must usually be confirmed in _________.
(g) A document issued by the transport firm which carries the supplier's goods is the _________.
(h) An advice note informs customers that goods have been _________.
(i) Trade discount is given to _________ and not to the _________.
(j) _________ discounts encourage customers to buy in greater bulk.
(k) A supplier can increase the prices of goods to customers by _________ trade discount.
(l) _________ means that full costs of delivery are met by the supplier.
(m) The document which gives full details of the goods sent to a customer is the _________.
(n) _________ is given to encourage prompt payment.
(o) A debit note is used to correct _________ on the invoice.
(p) _________ are usually printed in red and are issued, for example, when a customer has returned _________.
(q) A _________ gives a summary of the transactions between a supplier and a customer in a given period of time.
(r) Receipts have become less important because most payments between traders are made by _________.

an undercharge	cash discount	credit notes
price lists	invoice	writing
public	lowering	quantity
consignment note	quotation	inquiry
written	traders	numbers
expensive	statement of account	carriage paid
cheque	despatched	packing cases

Unit 8 Business documents used in foreign trade

1 In **(a)** to **(u)** find the correct word(s) to complete each sentence.
(a) Orders for goods in foreign trade are sometimes called _________.
(b) When goods are delivered by an exporter to a port the port authority will issue _________.
(c) The freight note is prepared by _________ and gives the cost of _________ the goods.
(d) The bill of lading is provided by the shipping company but is completed by _________.
(e) Bills of lading are prepared, at least, in sets of _________.
(f) If the ship's master receives goods which are damaged he will issue a _________ bill of lading.
(g) The bill of lading is a _________ because it allows ownership of goods to be claimed.
(h) Full details of the transaction between an exporter and importer is shown in _________.
(i) Before goods are allowed into some countries _________ must be first obtained.
(j) In air transport the bill of lading is replaced by the air _________.
(k) Proof that a product has been manufactured in a certain country is given in _________.
(l) A bill of exchange is sent from the exporter to the importer so that the importer can _________ it.

(m) When a bank __________ a bill of exchange it buys the bill from the exporter.

(n) When a bill of exchange is supported by, for example, a bill of lading, insurance policy and export invoice it is called a __________ bill of exchange.

(o) One basic problem of the bill of exchange is that the importer may not __________ the bill.

(p) Documentary letters of credit are __________ than documentary bills of exchange because a __________ guarantees payment for the exporter.

(q) The two banks involved in arranging a documentary credit are the __________ bank and the __________ bank.

(r) Irrevocable documentary credits can only be __________ with the permission of the exporter.

(s) The safest form of documentary credit is the __________ credit.

(t) A __________ allows a bank to sell a firm's goods to settle a debt owed to the bank.

(u) The development of __________ has meant that funds can be quickly transferred between countries.

safer	advising	cancelled
the exporter	the shipping company	a dock receipt
an import licence	accept	documentary
confirmed	indents	documents of title
dirty	three	waybill
shipping	the export invoice	bank
discounts	honour	letter of hypothecation
issuing	communications	the certificate of origin

Unit 9 Banking: the commercial banks

1 (a) J. Smith, who banks at Lloyds Bank, Birmingham, sends a cheque to D. Wilson who banks at Barclays Bank, Manchester. Draw a diagram to illustrate how this cheque is cleared.

(b) If, instead, D. Wilson banked at Lloyds Bank, Manchester, what difference would it make to the answer to **1(a)**?

2 Draw up a bank statement of account for:
1 May Opening balance £83.46 2 May Received salary (BGC) £137.42 3 May Paid by cheque (462) £288.38 10 May Paid by cheque (463) £110.37 21 May SO payment £8.46 1 June Received salary (BGC) £419.27

3 In **(a)** to **(s)** find the correct word(s) to complete each sentence.

(a) Most payments from a current account are made using __________.

(b) The disadvantages of a current account are that no __________ is earned and __________ may have to be paid.

(c) Deposit accounts are used for __________ and withdrawals from this type of account requires __________.

(d) A __________ account spreads the cost of bills throughout the year.

(e) The person who writes a cheque is the __________ and the person receiving payment is the __________.

(f) An __________ cheque can be cashed over the counter at the __________.

(g) __________ cheques must be paid into a bank account.

(h) A special crossing on a cheque requires the name of a __________ to be written within the crossing.

(i) The __________ can order the drawee to pay someone else by __________ an order cheque.

(j) Bearer cheques are rarely used because they are __________.

(k) A __________ cheque is more than six months old.

(l) Wages can be paid by employers using the bank __________ credit system.

(m) A method of bank borrowing in which interest is charged only on the amount actually used is the __________.

stale	overdraft	cash dispenser
standing order	credit cards	charges
savings	unsafe	payee
drawer	budget	drawee bank
payee	cheques	payee
interest	notice	open
bank	crossed	giro
security	endorsing	cheque guarantee card

(n) Banks often require __________ from a borrower which can be sold if the debt is not repaid.
(o) Regular payments of a fixed amount from a current account can best be made using a __________.
(p) With direct debit the __________ requests payment.
(q) Shops are more willing to accept cheques if a __________ is also presented.
(r) A method of obtaining cash from a bank when it is closed is by using a __________.
(s) Barclaycard and Access are examples of __________.

Unit 10 Other kinds of bank and methods of payment

1 In **(a)** to **(j)** find the correct word(s) to complete each sentence
(a) The name of the central bank in the United Kingdom is __________.
(b) The __________ manufactures coins.
(c) The accounts held by the clearing banks at the Bank of England are used to settle debts between banks which result from __________.
(d) The Bank of England pays interest to those who have bought __________.
(e) Larger firms employ merchant banks when they want to issue __________ or when they want to __________ from organizations overseas.
(f) Trustee Savings Banks provide services for __________ rather than for __________.
(g) The National Girobank is operated through __________.
(h) Transfers between Girobank accounts are quick because accounts are held at a single __________.
(i) Payment by Girobank account holders to those who do not possess Girobank accounts can be made using __________.
(j) The Post Office charges __________ on postal orders.

Government stock	poundage	computer centre
the Bank of England	the clearing of cheques	firms
Girocheques	individuals	borrow
shares	post offices	Royal Mint

Unit 11 Buying and selling on credit

1 The cash price of a television set is £500. A customer buys this set on hire purchase and pays a 20% deposit followed by 20 monthly instalments of £30.
(a) Calculate the total HP price.
(b) The customer pays four instalments and then wants to return the set. Can he do this? Give reasons for your answer.
(c) He carries on paying instalments but after eight instalments fails to pay anything further. What can the finance company do?
2 Attempt question 1 again but assume that the television set has been bought under a credit sale agreement instead of hire purchase.
3 In **(a)** to **(o)** find the correct word(s) to complete each sentence.
(a) When goods are bought on hire purchase they become the property of the buyer after payment of the __________.
(b) When credit agreements are signed off trade premises a __________ period is allowed.
(c) Goods sold on hire purchase usually have a good __________ value.
(d) A shop budget account is also known as __________.
(e) Vouchers of various values which can be used to buy goods at certain shops are called __________.
(f) A major provider of funds for credit selling is the __________.
(g) An arrangement whereby a firm can rent equipment for a given number of years is known as __________.
(h) A __________ will take over the debts owing to a firm.
(i) Building societies lend by means of __________ where property is given as __________ for loans.
(j) The true rate of interest is also known as the __________.
(k) Under the Consumer Credit Act 1974 a consumer is allowed a __________ if early settlement of a debt is made.
(l) Liability for faulty goods sold on credit rests with the __________ and __________ of credit.

(m) A credit reference agency keeps lists of those who have _________ on credit agreements.

(n) One disadvantage to a consumer of buying on credit is that he might buy more than he can _________.

(o) Firms choose to sell on credit because the _________ from extra sales are greater than the _________ of arranging the credit.

costs	leasing	resale
mortgages	providers	arrangers
trading checks	profits	final instalment
cooling-off	afford	financial factor
rebate	APR	defaulted
revolving credit	finance house	security

Unit 12 Advertising and marketing

1 In **(a)** to **(o)** find the correct word(s) to complete each sentence.

(a) Competitive or _________ advertising encourages consumers to buy products.

(b) Competitive advertising makes use of _________ names.

(c) An advertisement which gives details of a new bus timetable is described as _________.

(d) Newspapers and television are examples of advertising _________.

(e) A magazine directed at those in particular businesses or occupations is called a _________.

(f) Ambition and romance are examples of advertising _________.

(g) The _________ for a product is those people who might be willing to buy the product.

(h) A manufacturer will carry out _________ to discover the type of product customers want.

(i) The trial selling of a product in a small geographical area is called _________.

(j) Firms often employ specialists called _________ to conduct advertising campaigns for them.

(k) The IBA supervises advertising on _________.

(l) Complaints about advertisements in newspapers can be made to the _________.

(m) By allowing mass production to take place advertising keeps the prices of goods _________.

(n) One disadvantage of advertising is that consumers are tempted to buy goods they cannot _________.

(o) Competitions and the offer of free gifts are examples of _________.

radio and television	ASA	low
potential market	sales promotion	media
brand	test marketing	trade journal
informative	devices	market research
advertising agencies	afford	persuasive

Unit 13 Consumer protection

1 In **(a)** to **(k)** find the correct word(s) to complete each sentence.

(a) The Sale of Goods Act 1979 states that goods should be of _________ quality. This Act is part of _________ law and action against a trader can only be taken by a _________.

(b) A shopkeeper who states that a nylon jumper is 100% wool can be prosecuted under the _________.

(c) Under the _________ inspectors visit garages to check that petrol pumps are giving the correct volume of petrol.

(d) Goods which have been supplied but not ordered are called _________ goods.

(e) _________ employ Trading Standards Officers who can prosecute, under _________ law, shopkeepers who trade illegally.

(f) The main government agency concerned with consumer protection is the _________.

consultative councils	Weights and Measures Act	civil
consumer	resale price maintenance	criminal
merchantable	unsolicited	Consumers Association
Trade Descriptions Act	Codes of Practice	recommended retail prices
local authorities	Office of Fair Trading	BSI

(g) If a supplier is able to dictate to a shopkeeper the price at which a product is sold it is called ________. This practice is now illegal for most products and all suppliers can now do is to set ________.

(h) The nationalized industries have ________ to protect the interests of consumers.
(i) Consumers can benefit from the ________ run by trade associations.
(j) The ________ publishes the magazine *Which?*
(k) The Kitemark is issued by the ________.

Unit 14 Insurance

1 Name the kind of insurance which a supermarket would take out to cover each of the following:
(a) a shop window being broken
(b) a cashier stealing money
(c) a customer being injured in the shop
(d) a reduction in profit because of a fire
(e) risks, such as theft and damage, to goods while being delivered to the shop
(f) an employee being injured in the shop
(g) the minimum motor vehicle insurance required by law

2 For each of the following, state whether the insurance premium paid by a motorist is likely to increase or decrease. The motorist:
(a) is now able to park his car in a garage
(b) buys a more powerful car
(c) agrees to accept an excess of £100. (This means he agrees to pay the first £100 of any damage)
(d) changes from comprehensive to third party insurance
(e) does not claim from the insurance company for a number of years and is given a No-Claims bonus of 60%
(f) wants to allow a learner driver to use his car
(g) is convicted of a serious motoring offence
(h) moves his home from Oxford to London

3

Contents insurance
Premium (in £) for every £100 insured

Insurance company	*Area* *A*	*B*	*C*
X	1.00	2.00	3.00
Y	1.20	2.30	3.50
Z	1.10	2.60	3.40

Work out the premium for:

	Insurance company	*Area*	*Value of contents*
(a)	X	A	£700
(b)	X	C	£600
(c)	Y	B	£400
(d)	Z	A	£200
(e)	X	B	£250

4 In **(a)** to **(r)** find the correct word(s) to complete each sentence.
(a) A ________ is an intermediary between those wishing to take out insurance and insurance companies.
(b) Regular payments to insurance companies are called ________.
(c) A ________ must first be completed when taking out insurance.
(d) The principle of ________ means that full and accurate information must be given when taking out insurance.
(e) If a person has insurable interest it means that the risk insured can cause the person to suffer ________.
(f) The ________ is a contract of insurance.

(g) __________ means that a profit must not be made out of a loss.

(h) An insurance company can employ a __________ to assess the amount of compensation to be paid.

(i) Insuring an article for less than it is worth is called __________.

(j) Insurance can be described as the __________ of risks.

(k) __________ calculate premiums for insurance companies.

(l) Insurable risks are those risks for which there are __________.

(m) __________ means that a claim is bound to arise.

(n) __________ policies provide a sum of money for the assured, if he survives the period of assurance.

(o) Lloyd's of London is a __________ for insurance.

(p) A group of underwriters is called a __________.

(q) One important kind of insurance taken out at Lloyd's of London is __________ insurance.

(r) Members of syndicates have __________ which means that their personal assets can be claimed to meet debts.

reliable statistics	market	unlimited liability
indemnity	pooling	assurance
proposal form	broker	utmost good faith
under-insurance	marine	loss adjuster
premiums	policy	financial loss
endowment	syndicate	actuaries

Unit 15 Transport

1 In **(a)** to **(r)** find the correct word(s) to complete each sentence.

(a) Road transport is faster over __________ distances.

(b) If road only is used for delivering goods there is __________ handling which reduces the risks of __________ and __________.

(c) One disadvantage of road transport is that vehicles cannot exceed a certain __________.

(d) Rail transport is faster over __________ distances.

(e) Urgently needed goods can be sent by __________ train.

(f) The __________ service of British Rail is a container service which runs to a fixed __________.

(g) Rail transport is the only form of transport that needs to be used if firms have their own __________.

(h) Cargo liners run on set __________ to set timetables.

(i) The cost of carrying sea freight on some cargo routes is set by __________.

(j) Cargo liners are used when the exporter has to send a __________ quantity of goods which need careful __________.

(k) Tramps are used for carrying __________ cargoes and are __________ for a particular period or __________.

(l) Seaports are run by __________.

(m) The disadvantages of canals are that they are __________ and that their network is __________.

(n) Air transport is used for __________ value __________ bulk goods.

(o) Liquids and gases can be transported by __________ or in __________.

(p) The __________ system allows vehicles with their loads to be transported by ship.

(q) Container transport is safe because the containers are __________.

(r) The __________ system allows lorries to travel across borders with the minimum of checks by Customs.

Freightliner	routes	bulk
small	limited	low
tankers	TIR	theft
damage	short	high
slow	rail sidings	handling
shipping conferences	long	Roll-On/Roll-Off
voyage	port authorities	timetable
less	passenger	chartered
weight	pipeline	sealed

Unit 16 Communications

1 In **(a)** to **(r)** find the correct word(s) to complete each sentence.

(a) The transfer of information is called ________.

(b) In the United Kingdom ________ is in charge of postal services and ________ is in charge of telecommunications.

(c) ________ mail is sent to addresses within the United Kingdom.

(d) Second class post is used because it is ________.

(e) Datapost is used for ________ deliveries.

(f) A ________ only gives proof of posting and not proof of ________.

(g) Proof of delivery for non-valuable letters is best provided by ________.

(h) The Post Office service which provides most compensation if a package is lost is ________.

(i) A mail order firm can encourage a customer to reply by enclosing a ________ or by using a ________ address.

(j) With ________ the addressee collects the letter from a post office.

(k) The use of ________ means that firms do not have to place postage stamps on letters.

(l) ________ allows telephone calls to be made without using the operator.

(m) ________ allows a customer to ring a firm without paying the cost of the call.

(n) ________ give telephone numbers of businesses only.

(o) One advantage, to a firm, of using telex instead of the telephone is that telex provides a ________.

(p) An urgent message to a person who does not possess a telephone can be made using a ________.

(q) The Viewdata service which allows a customer to order goods from his own home is called ________.

(r) The ________ service of British Telecom links studios in different cities by sound and by vision.

telemessage	STD	Prestel
cheap	recorded delivery	British Telecom
registered post	freepost	franking machines
the Post Office	Yellow Pages	certificate of posting
urgent	Inland	business reply envelope
delivery	post restante	Freefone
written record	communications	Confravision

Unit 17 Business accounts

1 The table below lists all the assets and liabilities of a firm at a particular date

	£		£
Capital owned	?	Bank	8000
Creditors	400	Machinery	4000
5 year loan	3000	Debtors	500
		Stock	2000
		Buildings	6000

State the value of:

(a) fixed assets

(b) current assets

(c) capital owned

(d) net capital employed

(e) working capital

2 In **(a)** to **(i)** find the correct word(s) to complete each sentence.

(a) The ________ lists the assets and liabilities of a firm at a particular date.

(b) An overdraft is an example of a ________ liability.

(c) Capital which is continually changing its form is known as ________ capital.

(d) The value of net sales is called ________.

(e) ________ is a measure of how quickly goods are sold.

(f) Gross profit = sales minus ________.

(g) Gross profit minus expenses = ________.

(h) Profit as a percentage of selling price is known as ________.

(i) The rate of return on capital employed is a measure of ________.

turnover	cost of goods sold	circulating
profit margin	balance sheet	profitability
current	stockturn	net profit

Unit 18 Private sector firms

1 Fill in the missing figures for the following table which shows the distribution of profits for a company.

Year	*1*	*2*	*3*	*4*
Profit before interest on debentures	£1450	£80	£1000	£4450
Payments on				
£1000 8% Debentures				
5000 10% (50p) Cum. Pref. shares				
4000 3% (£1) Pref. shares				
10 000 (10p) Ordinary shares				
Ploughed-back profits				
	═══	═══	═══	═══

Dividend paid on ordinary shares: *Year 1* 40%, *Year 3* 20%, *Year 4* 100%

2 In **(a)** to **(q)** find the correct word(s) to complete each sentence.

(a) A public limited company is part of the _________ sector because it is not owned by the State.

(b) _________ means that personal assets can be claimed by creditors in the event of the bankruptcy of the firm.

(c) In the absence of a _________ profits of partnerships must be shared equally between partners.

(d) A _________ partner takes no active part in the running of the partnership.

(e) Firms which do not have a separate legal existence are referred to as _________ bodies.

(f) _________ are the owners of companies and receive part of the profits by way of _________.

(g) The word 'limited' in the name of a company means that the owners have limited _________.

(h) The shares of a _________ are freely transferable.

(i) One disadvantage of limited companies is that their annual accounts have to be filed with the _________.

(j) Debenture holders are _________ of a company.

(k) The dividend paid on _________ shares varies with the profits of a company.

(l) Dividends not paid in any year on _________ shares are paid once the company makes sufficient profit.

(m) Another name for retained earnings is _________.

(n) The _________ contains the 'external rules' of a company.

(o) Procedures for calling meetings of shareholders are contained in the _________.

(p) A firm becomes a company once the Registrar of Companies has issued a _________.

(q) A _________ is issued once the Registrar of Companies is satisfied that a public limited company has raised sufficient capital.

Registrar of Companies	sleeping	trading certificate
shareholders	articles of association	ploughed-back profit
deed of agreement	cumulative preference	certificate of incorporation
memorandum of association	unincorporated	unlimited liability
private	dividends	public limited company
creditors	liability	ordinary

Unit 19 The issue of shares and the Stock Exchange

1 In **(a)** to **(o)** find the correct word(s) to complete each sentence.

(a) An issue by _________ and an offer for sale both use advertisements inviting the public to buy shares.

(b) _________ usually handle the sales of new shares for companies.

(c) When an issue is undersubscribed unsold shares are often bought by _________.

(d) A method of issue in which investors are asked to state the price at which they are prepared to buy shares is called a sale by _________.

(e) The sale of new shares to existing shareholders, often at a favourable price, is a _________ issue.

(f) The issued share capital cannot exceed the _________ share capital.

(g) The shares of _________ public companies are not traded on the Stock Exchange.

(h) A stock exchange is a market for _________ securities.

(i) The two types of member of the London Stock Exchange are brokers and _________.

(j) Those wishing to buy or sell shares on the London Stock Exchange must first contact a _________.

(k) A deal on the London Stock Exchange is called a _________.

(l) A _________ can profit when share prices are falling.

(m) The yield of a share is the dividend paid as a percentage of the share's _________.

(n) _________ shares are the shares of large well-known companies.

(o) The new issue market is a _________ market.

second-hand	broker	primary
unquoted	rights	issuing houses
authorized	prospectus	underwriters
jobbers	tender	bear
market price	bargain	blue-chip

Unit 20 Public enterprise

1 In **(a)** to **(h)** find the correct word(s) to complete each sentence.

(a) Firms owned by the State are part of the _________ sector.

(b) Public sector firms which charge prices and attempt to make some profit are part of public _________.

(c) The compulsory purchase of private firms by the State is called _________.

(d) The large public enterprises in the United Kingdom are organized as _________.

(e) The Government Minister in charge of a public corporation is not concerned with the _________ but with the _________ of the corporation.

(f) _________ has ultimate control over the activities of public corporations.

(g) The reverse of nationalization is called _________.

(h) Policy decisions for local authority enterprises are made by _________.

enterprise	day to day operation	Parliament
nationalization	privatization	public
policy decisions	public corporations	councillors

Unit 21 Income and saving

1 In **(a)** to **(l)** find the correct word(s) to complete each sentence.

(a) A person's take-home pay is also called _________ income.

(b) _________ is a regular contribution made by an employee to a firm's pension scheme.

(c) A _________ lists likely future income and spending.

(d) A _________ asset can be quickly converted into money without very great loss.

(e) The _________ rate of interest is the rate of interest before income tax has been deducted.

(f) If savings are _________, it means that the value of such savings increase in line with inflation.

(g) The ownership of _________ gives a saver the chance to win cash prizes.

(h) _________ stock is issued by the UK government in order to raise funds.

(i) _________ have to register with the Registrar of Friendly Societies.

(j) Unit trusts allow savers to have an indirect stake in the _________ of public limited companies.

budget	index-linked	gilt-edged
premium bonds	endowment	superannuation
net	liquid	gross
ordinary shares	inflation	building societies

(k) The ________ policies of life assurance companies provide a means of saving.
(l) If the value of savings has risen by more than the rate of ________, then the real value of savings has also risen.

Unit 22 Government spending and income

1

Allowances		*Taxable Income*	*Tax Rate* (%)
Married man	£3000	£1—£10 000	30
Single person	£2200	£10 000—£15 000	40
Superannuation	in full	£15 001 and above	50

Using the allowances and tax rates listed above work out
(i) the taxable income *and*
(ii) the income tax paid for
(a) a single person earning £20 000 per year and paying superannuation of £1800 per year
(b) a married man earning £6400 per year and paying superannuation of £300 per year
(c) a single person earning £7200 per year and paying no superannuation

2 In **(a)** to **(r)** find the correct word(s) to complete each sentence.
(a) The amount owed by the Government is called the ________.
(b) Taxes on income and capital are collected by the ________.
(c) Most taxpayers pay tax at the ________ rate of income tax.
(d) The tax levied on the profits of companies is ________ tax.
(e) Profits from the sale of shares by an individual may be liable to ________ tax.
(f) Taxes on spending are collected by ________.
(g) A percentage tax is called an ________ tax.
(h) Under ________ certain goods and services are zero-rated or exempt.
(i) Taxes levied on both home produced and imported goods are called ________.
(j) There are no ________ imposed on goods which move between EEC countries.
(k) Taxes on expenditure are called ________ taxes.
(l) Income tax is ________ because those on higher incomes pay a greater percentage of their income in tax.
(m) If there is too much spending in an economy the Government could ________ taxation.
(n) Unemployment benefit is paid from the ________.
(o) An estimate of future Government income and spending is called a ________.
(p) Rates are levied by ________.
(q) The amount in rates paid by householder is dependent on the ________ of his property and the rate in the pound charged by the local authority.
(r) Central Government helps to finance part of local authority spending through the ________.

rateable value	customs duties	budget
National Insurance Fund	progressive	capital gains
corporation	Inland Revenue	indirect
HM Customs and Excise	Rate Support Grant	VAT
National Debt	ad valorem	basic
excise duties	local authorities	increase

Answers to self-test units

Unit 1

1 **(a)** extractive **(b)** constructive **(c)** manufacturing **(d)** commerce (aids to trade) **(e)** direct service **(f)** commerce (trade) **(g)** extractive **(h)** manufacturing **(i)** commerce (aids to trade) **(j)** direct service **(k)** extractive **(l)** commerce (trade) **(m)** constructive **(n)** commerce (aids to trade) **(o)** constructive **(p)** commerce (aids to trade) or direct service

2 **(a)** horizontal **(b)** diversification **(c)** vertical (forward) **(d)** vertical (backward) **(e)** vertical (forward) **(f)** diversification

3 **(a)** producers **(b)** consumers **(c)** necessities **(d)** luxuries **(e)** production **(f)** manufacturing **(g)** extractive **(h)** convert **(i)** assemble **(j)** trade, aids to trade **(k)** buying and selling **(l)** banking, transport **(m)** direct service **(n)** tertiary **(o)** chain of production **(p)** interdependence **(q)** producer **(r)** mass production, economies of scale **(s)** specialization **(t)** subsistence **(u)** money **(v)** double coincidence of wants **(w)** money **(x)** acceptability

Unit 2

1

	Number of branches	*Prices (high or low)*	*Responsibility for buying goods rests with*	*Suppliers are usually*
Unit shops	1-9	high	owner	wholesalers
Department stores	any number	high	buyer or head office	manufacturers
Multiples	at least 10	low	head office	manufacturers

2 **(a)** public, wholesalers, manufacturers **(b)** independent, homes **(c)** high, small wholesalers **(d)** chain, variety, specialist **(e)** head office **(f)** city centres, wide **(g)** buyer, multiple **(h)** agents, catalogues **(i)** shops **(j)** profits, dividend, cash, goods, share capital **(k)** edges, land **(l)** low, cars **(m)** discount store **(n)** mobile shop **(o)** automatic vending **(p)** self-service, counter service **(q)** loss-leaders, impulse **(r)** bargaining **(s)** precinct **(t)** franchising **(u)** bar codes

Unit 3

1 **(a)** finished goods **(b)** stocks, selection **(c)** large, small **(d)** releasing **(e)** large **(f)** perishables **(g)** direct dealing **(h)** voluntary chains **(i)** retail outlets **(j)** commodity **(k)** distribution, retail co-operative societies **(l)** cash and carry

Unit 4

1 **(a)** farmers, consumers **(b)** fruit and vegetables, Smithfield, Billingsgate **(c)** marketing board **(d)** prices **(e)** exchanges **(f)** grain **(g)** auction, tea **(h)** description, cocoa **(i)** inspection, quality **(j)** futures, graded **(k)** spot **(l)** speculators, profit **(m)** hedging **(n)** London Metal Exchange **(o)** market **(p)** communications

2 **(a)** £1300 per tonne **(b)** £1 300 000 **(c)** £700 000 **(d)** £50 000 **(e)** He is guaranteed delivery at a fixed price

Unit 5

1 **(a)** raw materials, foodstuffs, manufactured goods **(b)** a principal, profit **(c)** an agent, commission **(d)** manufacturers, final consumers **(e)** possess, name, buyers, sellers **(f)** selling, possess **(g)** commission, payment **(h)** own account, profit **(i)** principals, agents

Unit 6

1 **(a)** visible export **(b)** invisible import **(c)** capital inflow **(d)** invisible export **(e)** visible import **(f)** capital outflow

2 **(b)** +£600, +£20, +£620 **(c)** −£300, −£20, −£320 **(d)** +£100, −£180, −£80 **(d)** £428, £286, +£62

3 **(a)** countries **(b)** surpluses, exchanged **(c)** comparative advantage **(d)** raw materials **(e)** goods, services **(f)** balance of trade **(g)** surplus **(h)** banking, tourism, insurance **(i)** finished, semi-finished **(j)** Commonwealth, Common Market **(k)** mark, yen **(l)** credit insurance, borrow **(m)** BOTB **(n)** trade associations, chambers of commerce **(o)** bonded **(p)** import duty **(q)** embargo **(r)** common external tariff

Unit 7

1 **(a)** £4000 **(b)** *(i)* credit note *(ii)* £1280 **(c)** £2720 **(d)** £2584

2 **(a)** written **(b)** inquiry **(c)** quotation **(d)** expensive, price lists **(e)** numbers **(f)** writing **(g)** consignment note **(h)** despatched **(i)** traders, public **(j)** quantity **(k)** lowering **(l)** carriage paid **(m)** invoice **(n)** cash discount **(o)** an undercharge **(p)** credit notes, packing cases **(q)** statement of account **(r)** cheque

Unit 8

1 **(a)** indents **(b)** a dock receipt **(c)** the shipping company, shipping **(d)** the exporter **(e)** three **(f)** dirty **(g)** document of title **(h)** the export invoice **(i)** an import licence **(j)** waybill **(k)** the certificate of origin **(l)** accept **(m)** discounts **(n)** documentary **(o)** honour **(p)** safer, bank **(q)** issuing, advising **(r)** cancelled **(s)** confirmed **(t)** letter of hypothecation **(u)** communications

Unit 9

1 **(a)**

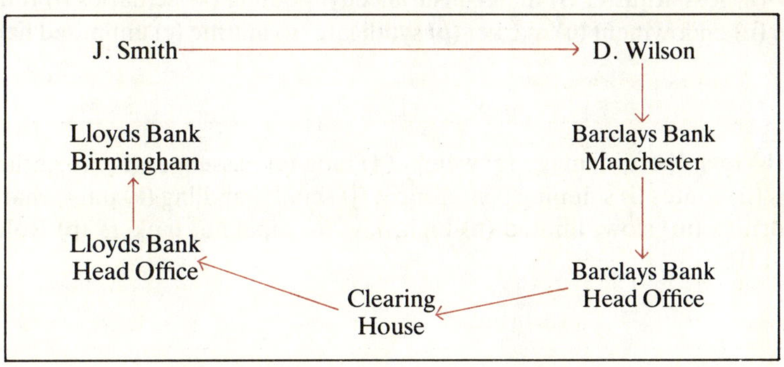

(b) The cheque would not enter general clearing but would be cleared internally

2

Date	*Details*	*Payments*	*Receipts*	*Balance*
May 1				83.46
2	BGC		137.42	220.88
3	462	288.38		6.75 OD
10	463	110.37		177.87 OD
21	SO	8.46		186.33 OD
June 1	BGC		419.27	232.94

3 **(a)** cheques **(b)** interest, charges **(c)** savings, notice **(d)** budget **(e)** drawer, payee **(f)** open, drawee bank **(g)** crossed **(h)** bank **(i)** payee, endorsing **(j)** unsafe **(k)** stale **(l)** giro **(m)** overdraft **(n)** security **(o)** standing order **(p)** payee **(q)** cheque guarantee card **(r)** cash dispenser **(s)** credit cards

Unit 10

1 **(a)** the Bank of England **(b)** Royal Mint **(c)** the clearing of cheques **(d)** Government stock **(e)** shares, borrow **(f)** individuals, firms **(g)** post offices **(h)** computer centre **(i)** Girocheques **(j)** poundage

Unit 11

1 **(a)** £700 **(b)** Yes, but he has to pay an extra £130 to bring his payments up to half the HP price **(c)** The television set can be repossessed but a court order will be needed because one third or more of the HP price has been paid

2 **(a)** £700 **(b)** He cannot cancel the agreement and return the television set **(c)** The finance company cannot repossess and can sue only for what is owing

3 **(a)** final instalment **(b)** cooling-off **(c)** resale **(d)** revolving credit **(e)** trading checks **(f)** finance house **(g)** leasing **(h)** financial factor **(i)** mortgages, security **(j)** APR **(k)** rebate **(l)** arrangers, providers **(m)** defaulted **(n)** afford **(o)** profits, costs

Unit 12

1 **(a)** persuasive **(b)** brand **(c)** informative **(d)** media **(e)** trade journal **(f)** devices **(g)** potential market **(h)** market research **(i)** test marketing **(j)** advertising agencies **(k)** radio and television **(l)** ASA **(m)** low **(n)** afford **(o)** sales promotion

Unit 13

1 **(a)** merchantable, civil **(b)** Trade Descriptions Act **(c)** Weights and Measures Act **(d)** unsolicited **(e)** local authorities, criminal **(f)** Office of Fair Trading **(g)** resale price maintenance, recommended retail prices **(h)** consultative councils **(i)** Codes of Practice **(j)** Consumers Association **(k)** BSI

Unit 14

1 **(a)** plate glass **(b)** fidelity guarantee **(c)** public liability **(d)** consequential loss **(e)** goods in transit **(f)** employers' liability **(g)** Act only

2 **(a)** increase **(b)** increase **(c)** decrease **(d)** decrease **(e)** decrease **(f)** increase **(g)** increase **(h)** increase

3 **(a)** £7 **(b)** £18 **(c)** £9.20 **(d)** £2.20 **(e)** £5

4 **(a)** broker **(b)** premiums **(c)** proposal form **(d)** utmost good faith **(e)** financial loss **(f)** policy **(g)** indemnity **(h)** loss adjuster **(i)** under-insurance **(j)** pooling **(k)** actuaries **(l)** reliable statistics **(m)** assurance **(n)** endowment **(o)** market **(p)** syndicate **(q)** marine **(r)** unlimited liability

Unit 15

1 **(a)** short **(b)** less, theft, damage **(c)** weight **(d)** long **(e)** passenger **(f)** Freightliner, timetable **(g)** rail sidings **(h)** routes **(i)** shipping conferences **(j)** small, handling **(k)** bulk, chartered, voyage **(l)** port authorities **(m)** slow, limited **(n)** high, low **(o)** pipeline, tankers **(p)** Roll-On/Roll-Off **(q)** sealed **(r)** TIR

Unit 16

1 **(a)** communications **(b)** the Post Office, British Telecom **(c)** inland **(d)** cheap **(e)** urgent **(f)** certificate of posting, delivery **(g)** recorded delivery **(h)** registered post **(i)** business reply envelope, Freepost **(j)** post restante **(k)** franking machines **(l)** STD **(m)** Freefone **(n)** Yellow Pages **(o)** written record **(p)** telemessage **(q)** Prestel **(r)** Confravision

Unit 17

1 **(a)** £10 000 **(b)** £10 500 **(c)** £17 100 **(d)** £20 100 **(e)** £10 100

2 **(a)** balance sheet **(b)** current **(c)** circulating **(d)** turnover **(e)** stockturn **(f)** cost of goods sold **(g)** net profit **(h)** profit margin **(i)** profitability

Unit 18

1

Year	*1*	*2*	*3*	*4*
Debentures	£80	£80	£80	£80
Cum. Pref. shares	£250	—	£500	£250
Pref. shares	£120	—	£120	£120
Ordinary shares	£400	—	£200	£1000
Ploughed-back profits	£600	—	£100	£3000

2 **(a)** private **(b)** unlimited liability **(c)** deed of agreement **(d)** sleeping **(e)** unincorporated **(f)** shareholders' dividends **(g)** liability **(h)** public limited company **(i)** Registrar of Companies **(j)** creditors **(k)** ordinary **(l)** cumulative preference **(m)** ploughed-back profit **(n)** memorandum of association **(o)** articles of association **(p)** certificate of incorporation **(q)** trading certificate

Unit 19

1 **(a)** prospectus **(b)** issuing houses **(c)** underwriters **(d)** tender **(e)** rights **(f)** authorized **(g)** unquoted **(h)** second-hand **(i)** jobbers **(j)** broker **(k)** bargain **(l)** bear **(m)** market price **(n)** blue-chip **(o)** primary

Unit 20

1 **(a)** public **(b)** enterprise **(c)** nationalization **(d)** public corporations **(e)** day to day operation, policy decisions **(f)** Parliament **(g)** privatization **(h)** councillors

Unit 21

1 **(a)** net **(b)** superannuation **(c)** budget **(d)** liquid **(e)** gross **(f)** index-linked **(g)** premium bonds **(h)** gilt-edged **(i)** building societies **(j)** ordinary shares **(k)** endowment **(l)** inflation

Unit 22

1 **(a)** *(i)* £16 000 *(ii)* £5500 **(b)** *(i)* £3100 *(ii)* £930 **(c)** *(i)* £5000 *(ii)* £1500

2 **(a)** National Debt **(b)** Inland Revenue **(c)** basic **(d)** corporation **(e)** capital gains **(f)** HM Customs and Excise **(g)** ad valorem **(h)** VAT **(i)** excise duties **(j)** customs duties **(k)** indirect **(l)** progressive **(m)** increase **(n)** National Insurance Fund **(o)** budget **(p)** local authorities **(q)** rateable value **(r)** Rate Support Grant

Part IV

Hints on examination technique

Information about Examinations

There is a great deal of information you can obtain about an examination *before* you see the actual examination paper. Such information comes from three main sources:

1 the syllabus
2 past examination questions
3 the report prepared on each examination.

1 The **syllabus** gives details of:

(a) the **form** the examination will take e.g.
The examination will consist of two papers:
Paper 1 — Objective Test — 45 minutes — 30% of the total marks
Paper 2 — Essay Paper — 2 hours — 70% of the total marks

(b) the **topics** which could be tested e.g. (*AEB Commerce*)

1 The Structure of Industry and Commerce
The market and the mechanism of exchange.
Forms of production (primary, secondary and tertiary industries); the division of labour; the inter-relationship and relative importance of commerce, direct services and industry.

Candidates should understand the market as an economic concept and how exchange occurs via the medium of money (compared with bartering).

An appreciation of the specific benefits and disadvantages of the division of labour is required, as well as an awareness of its general relevance to productivity.

The branches of production should be understood in the broad context of the production process (chain of production), especially the rôle of the commercial services as a type of productive activity which provides the links throughout the process.

(*AEB Commerce — Section 1 of syllabus*)

The syllabus should be essential reading for all candidates taking the examination, and for the Chief Examiner setting the examination paper! The questions set must be based on the topics listed in the syllabus. Often specific words or phrases are taken straight from the syllabus and tested. Thus for Section 1 of the AEB syllabus referred to above a question could read:

What is meant by primary industry?

Such a question could easily be answered by those candidates who have worked through the syllabus learning definitions of the terms used.

A brief outline of the contents of Commerce syllabuses is given in Part 1 of this book (p. viii) but you should also obtain an *up to date* syllabus for the Commerce examination *which you are taking*. It is only by referring to this syllabus that you can find out the topics which you should cover. Your teacher or lecturer should be able to give you details of the syllabus or you can obtain a copy from your examination board (p. x).

2 Past examination questions are a very useful guide to the type of questions set by an examination board although, as syllabuses change, so do the types of questions set. You should, therefore, look at recent examination papers. Such papers are also useful for revision and in giving practice in answering questions. Past papers can be obtained from your school or college or from your examination board.

3 An **examiners' report** is written by the Chief Examiner responsible for an examination, and contains comments on the performances of candidates in the examination. The report is particularly useful because it gives reasons why candidates failed to score marks on certain questions and highlights the points examiners were looking for in answers. These reports can be obtained from your school or college or examination board.

Types of questions used in Commerce examinations

1 Multiple choice (objective) questions

For a multiple choice question you have to select the correct answer from a list of four or five possible answers lettered A to D or E.

Example:

The Bank of England is a
A clearing bank
B merchant bank
C central bank
D savings bank
E commercial bank

The correct answer is C and you must indicate this on the question paper itself or on a separate answer sheet.

A feature of such questions is that there is **only one correct answer.** If the correct answer is immediately obvious to you there is no problem! If you are unsure of the correct answer the best method to adopt is to eliminate those answers which are clearly wrong. If you then have to guess you stand more chance of guessing the correct answer.

For multiple choice questions it is important to attempt **all** questions—you lose nothing and you may gain some marks by guessing. This technique should, however, only be used as a last resort. If you have revised thoroughly you should be able to answer most questions without guessing.

The type of question shown above is called **simple completion** and it is the most common type of multiple choice question used in Commerce examinations. Other types of multiple choice question which you might have to answer are:

Multiple completion

Example:

A 1 only	B 3 only	C 1 and 2 only	D 2 and 3 only	E 1, 2 and 3

Table 1

Primary workers include
1 coalminers
2 steelworkers
3 shop assistants

The correct answer is A because, of the occupations quoted, only coalminers are included in primary industry. Steelworkers are part of secondary industry and shop assistants part of tertiary industry.

The table of combinations (Table 1) given for this question is used by some examination boards. Other boards may use slightly different tables. If such questions are used in the Commerce examination which you are taking, find out and understand the table of combinations which you will have to use **before** the examination.

Matching pairs

Examples:

For questions 1 to 3 choose the kind of insurance from the list A to E which matches the risk given. Each letter may be used once, more than once or not at all.

1 A shop window being broken.
2 A cashier stealing money.
3 An employee being injured at work.

The correct answers are 1C, 2B, 3A.

A Employers' liability
B Fidelity guarantee
C Plate glass
D Theft
E Public liability

Assertion-reason questions
Example:

	First statement	Second statement	
A	True	True	Second statement is a correct explanation of the first.
B	True	True	Second statement is **not** a correct explanation of the first.
C	True	False	
D	False	True	
E	False	False	

Table 2

First statement	**Second statement**
Crossed cheques are safer than open cheques.	Cheque books are issued to those with bank current accounts.

In assertion-reason questions the first step is to decide whether each statement is true or false. For the question above both statements are true so the answer, from Table 2, must be either A or B. The second statement, however, is **not** a reason for the truth of the first statement and the correct answer is, therefore, B.

2 Short-answer questions

As the name of this type of question suggests only the briefest of answers are required from candidates.

Examples:

1 Money which must be accepted in payment of a debt is called ....?

2 Name **one** public corporation.

The answer to question 1 is legal tender and this is the only answer possible. However, for question 2 more than one answer is possible—British Rail, British Steel, the National Coal Board are all acceptable answers.

3 Extended-answer questions

This type of question requires a much longer answer from candidates.

Examples:

1 What are the main factors which may contribute to the success of a firm operating a chain of supermarkets?

(*Cambridge June 1982*)

2 (a) Explain the following terms shown against certain items on a bank statement of accounts sent to a customer:

(*i*) Cash dispenser (*3 marks*)
(*ii*) Direct debit (*2 marks*)
(*iii*) Standing order (*3 marks*)

(b) How can the holder of a bank account pay several creditors with a single cheque? (*4 marks*)

(c) What is the purpose of a cheque card issued to the customer of a bank? (*4 marks*)

(*OLE June 1983*)

These two questions are both extended-answer questions but they are very different in the help they give candidates. Question 1 is the traditional **essay type** question in which candidates have to build their own framework for their answers. Such questions have become less popular with examination boards and, increasingly, **structured** questions like question 2 are set instead. This type of question is broken down into a number of parts and the number of marks available for each part is shown in the question.

When attempting any form of extended-answer question you should follow these points:

Before you write

(a) Read each question carefully more than once.

(b) Try to place yourself in the position of the examiner and assess what is expected from you.

(c) Try to relate each question or part of a question to a specific section of the syllabus or your notes. Remember that some questions cover more than one section.

(d) Where there is a choice tick those questions you think you can do and select from these.

When answering questions

(a) Make a **short** list of the points you wish to make. Are your points relevant? Are you answering the question which is set and not the question which you think should be set? Many marks are lost in examinations, not because candidates do not know the work, but because they are simply not answering the question.

(b) Pay particular attention to the words used in the question.

Example

Compare and contrast the work of Lloyd's brokers and Lloyd's underwriters.

The question does **not** ask for a description of the work of brokers followed by a description of the work of jobbers but asks for the ways in which their work is **similar** and **different.** Examiners know that a question phrased in this way is difficult and you will be rewarded for making an attempt to answer it properly.

(c) Many questions will probably use words or phrases which need to be **defined** although the question may not necessarily ask for a definition.

Example:

What contribution do invisibles make to the United Kingdom balance of payments?

Marks will be awarded for correct **definitions** of 'invisibles' and the 'balance of payments'. Such definitions are best included at the start of an answer.

(d) Most examination questions in Commerce now show the number of marks available for parts of a question. If part of a question is worth 2 marks do not write very much on that part and neglect a part which may be worth 8 marks. A useful guide is that 1 mark is gained for each correct and relevant point made. Look at the suggested answers to the examination questions given in Part V for examples of how much you should write.

(e) Do not repeat information.

(f) If you have to answer 5 questions in an examination do not spend all your time answering 4 questions and omitting the fifth. If you do this the maximum mark you score could be 80% rather than 100%; make sure, too, that you **spend enough time on each question.**

4 Data response questions

In Commerce examinations data response questions are being used increasingly. Information is presented in a variety of ways—graphs, business documents, newspaper articles and so on—and questions are based on the data given. Such questions are usually short-answer or extended-answer type questions.

Example:

	Western Bank, Medford	14.4.85
Pay	A. Thomas	OR ORDER
	Fifty Pounds only	£50.00
		D. Smith

1 Who is the payee? *(1 mark)*

2 Why is the cheque a safe method of payment? *(4 marks)*

When answering data response questions you should use the information given in the question.

For example:

The correct answer to question 1 is A. Thomas. An answer which simply refers to 'the person receiving the cheque' may be awarded no marks because no reference is made to the cheque shown in the data. A good answer to question 2 would contain a reference to:

(a) D. Smith has placed the word 'only' after 'fifty pounds' which makes the cheque more difficult to alter.

(b) The cheque at present is uncrossed. By crossing the cheque D. Smith would make it safer.

A brief guide to passing examinations

1 Obtain as much information as you can about the examination from the syllabus, past examination papers and examiners' reports.

2 Make a list of the terms used in the syllabus and write down and learn their definitions. It is surprising how many marks can be obtained by knowing definitions.

3 Plan a revision programme and stick to it. If you have twenty chapters to revise in ten weeks then make sure you revise two chapters each week.

4 After you have revised a chapter attempt questions based on that chapter. If you cannot do the questions, have you revised properly? Are your notes relevant and correct?

5 Get someone to test you on the work you have revised. It is often better to use a friend who is studying for the same examination so that both of you can benefit.

6 If there are points you do not understand ask your teacher or lecturer for help. Teachers and lecturers are only too willing to help those students who have taken the trouble to follow programmes of revision.

7 If you have revised properly there will be no need for last minute revision which, in most cases, does not help.

8 On the day of the examination, if you have studied past papers, you should not be surprised at the layout of the paper or the way it has to be answered.

9 When answering the questions on the paper:

(a) be relevant;
(b) include definitions;
(c) be guided by the number of marks available for questions or parts of questions;
(d) attempt all the questions you have to;
(e) make sure you spend enough time on each question.

Part V

Practice in answering examination questions

The questions in this section have been taken from a wide range of examination papers and have been selected so that they can be attempted by all candidates whether they are taking CSE, 16+ or GCE examinations in Commerce. The questions have been arranged in units which correspond to the core units of Part II. The relevant unit should be read before any attempt is made to answer an examination question.

The answers to most of these examination questions are given on pages 148 to 154. For some questions the answer given is the only one possible, while for others there may be a number of possible answers. For those questions requiring longer answers the ones given provide only an outline of what would be needed in an examination.

The examination boards accept no responsibility whatsoever for the accuracy or method of working in the answers given.

Unit 1 Production

1 Pick the odd one out and give reasons
farming; fishing; food processing; mining; quarrying.

(NIEC (CSE) 1982)

2 Carefully explain **five** of the following terms.
Barter
Money
Economic interdependence
Mass production
Standard of living
Specialization

(ALSEB 1980)

3 **(a)** Briefly describe the branches of production, giving **two** examples of each. *(8 marks)*
(b) In relation to manufactured products, explain in detail how all the branches are interdependent. *(12 marks)*

(AEB November 1983)

4 **(a)** Describe the main advantages of specialization of labour.
(b) What factors may limit this form of specialization?

(NIEC (GCE) June 1980)

Unit 2 Retailing

1 Each of the following definitions refers to a form or method of retailing. Write down the numbers *(i)* to *(x)* underneath each other and write opposite each the appropriate method or organization.

(i) An organization controlled by its members who are also its customers.
(ii) Stores whose chief aim is to sell their commodities, (e.g. furniture) at the lowest possible price.
(iii) A number of stalls, often in the open air, from which a large variety of goods is offered for sale.
(iv) An organization having 'many departments under the same roof.'
(v) A business owned and managed by one man.
(vi) One of a number of shops organized on a national scale which draws all its stock from a central warehouse.
(vii) The shop that goes to the customer.
(viii) A self-service store, several thousand square feet in area, selling a wide range of food and household goods.

(ix) The use of machines to sell goods when shops are closed.
(x) An organization using advertising and Post Office facilities to enable customers to shop in the comfort of their own homes.

(10 marks)
(YHREB (Syllabus A) 1983)

2 **(a)** Hypermarkets may sell the same products as department stores but their prices may be lower. Explain why this is so. *(10 marks)*

(b) In spite of competition from multiples and supermarkets, why do many small shops continue to survive? *(10 marks)*

(JMB June 1982)

3 **(a)** What are the advantages and disadvantages of self-service retailing?

(b) Why has self-service spread more rapidly in grocery than in fruit and vegetables?

(Cambridge November 1982)

Unit 3 Wholesaling

1 **(a)** Describe **three** ways in which a wholesaler helps in the distribution of goods.

(b) How can wholesalers help small independent retailers?

(c) How do large selling organizations manage to do without the services of the wholesaler?

(d) Explain briefly why the wholesaler will always be needed. (If you think the wholesaler will not, then explain that point of view.)

(LREB (Syllabus A) 1983)

2 **(a)** Define the term 'consumer goods'. *(2 marks)*

(b) Outline the channels (**not** forms of transport) used in the distribution of manufactured consumer goods. *(6 marks)*

(c) Contrast the retail and wholesale rôle in this distribution. *(12 marks)*

(AEB November 1983)

3 **(a)** Discuss the factors which have contributed to a decline in the importance of wholesalers in recent years. *(12 marks)*

(b) What steps should a wholesaler take in an attempt to secure his future? *(8 marks)*

(JMB June 1983)

Unit 4 Channels of distribution

1 State two types of business which are carried out at the Baltic Exchange.

(WMEB (16+) 1979)

2 Explain, and give the purpose of the following, in relation to organized commodity markets:
(a) auctions;
(b) grading;
(c) sampling;
(d) spot and future transactions.

(SUJB June 1982)

Unit 5 The middlemen of trade

1 Merchants, factors, brokers and forwarding agents are all middlemen engaged in foreign trade. Describe their functions in order to differentiate between them, and state how each is remunerated. *(18 marks)*

(WJEC (GCE) June 1980)

Unit 6 Foreign trade

1 Read the following extract from a newspaper and answer the questions relating to it.

'Britain earned a balance of payments surplus of £1000 million in 1978. There was a deficit of £1135 million on trade in goods offset by a big surplus on the invisible account. The biggest overseas earner was the services provided by the financial and other institutions of the City of London which had a surplus of £2307 million.'

(a) What is the meaning of each of the following?
(i) deficit
(ii) surplus

(b) What is the name generally given to trade in goods?

(c) Calculate the surplus on the invisible account.

(d) What types of service does the 'City' offer overseas countries?

(e) Name two other invisible items of trade.

(ALSEB 1980)

2 (a) What commercial benefits can a country derive from international trade? *(8 marks)*

(b) How does the United Kingdom government

(i) attempt to help international trade and *(6 marks)*

(ii) restrict international trade? *(6 marks)*

(AEB June 1983)

3 (a) Briefly explain the importance of warehousing. *(8 marks)*

(b) What are bonded warehouses? Under what circumstances and for what reasons would a trader use a bonded warehouse? *(12 marks)*

(WJEC (GCE) June 1983)

Unit 7 Business documents used in home trade

1 Study the following information and then answer the questions listed below.

Modern Fashions is the name of a small shop which buys all its goods from North West Suppliers. The invoice below gives details of one transaction between the two firms.

INVOICE NO. 426

NORTH WEST SUPPLIERS
MANCHESTER

MODERN FASHIONS
LIVERPOOL

10 JUNE 1982

			£
50 pairs	Jeans (No. 639)	£6.00 per pair	300.00
40	Sweaters (No. 48)	£5.00 each	200.00
			500.00
	LESS 20% Trade Discount		100.00
			400.00

Terms of Payment: 5% 14 days, 2% 1 month, net 2 months

(a) How do the numbers '639' and '48' help Modern Fashions when it orders goods? *(2 marks)*

(b) Give **two** reasons why Modern Fashions receives trade discount. *(2 marks)*

(c) If Modern Fashions pays by return of post, work out the amount which will be paid. (Show any calculations.) *(3 marks)*

(d) What is the meaning of the term 'net 2 months'? *(2 marks)*

(e) Modern Fashions now wishes to inform the public that these goods are in stock. Name **two** methods of advertising which can be used. Give reasons for your choices. *(4 marks)*

(f) Give **one** possible advantage and **one** possible disadvantage to Modern Fashions of buying all its goods from North West Suppliers. *(2 marks)*

(EMREB 1983)

2 (a) Explain the purpose of *(i)* an invoice, *(ii)* a credit note, *(iii)* a debit note and *(iv)* a statement of account.

(b) Name **two** other documents used in trading and state their purpose.

(c) From the statement of account given below, calculate the amount which should be paid if the account is settled within one week.

Statement of Account

Date	Item	Debit £	Credit £	Balance £
5 June	Invoice	100.00		
12 June	Credit note		20.00	
19 June	Invoice	160.00		
28 June	Debit Note	10.00		

Terms: 5% 2 weeks

(London January 1983)

Unit 8 Business documents used in foreign trade

1 'When goods are sent by sea a bill of lading is always required, a charter party is sometimes required, a consignment note is never required.' Explain why this is so, indicating the use and importance of these three documents.

(*Cambridge June 1983*)

2 (a) Explain fully the meaning of the term CIF. (*5 marks*)

(b) What document is used by a shipping line to set out the terms of the contract of carriage? (*2 marks*)

(c) How does the shipping line

(i) acknowledge receipt of goods for shipment

(ii) ensure that the goods are handed over to the right person at the port of destination? (*5 marks*)

(d) What is an *ad valorem* duty? (*4 marks*)

(*OLE June 1981*)

Unit 9 Banking: the commercial banks

1 Study the bank statement for Mr Small and answer the following questions.

(a) To which type of bank account does the statement refer? (*2 marks*)

(b) To what do the numbers 012621, 012622 etc in the 'Particulars' column refer? (*2 marks*)

(c) From what does Mr Small receive a dividend? (*2 marks*)

(d) What is a Standing Order? For what could the Standing Order for £7.50 be a payment? (*5 marks*)

(e) Mr Small receives his wages by Bank Giro Credit (or Credit Transfer.) Give **one** advantage of this form of payment in each case to

(i) Mr Small, (*2 marks*)

(ii) his employer, (*2 marks*)

(f) Mr Small has 'overdrawn' his account on 9 and 21 March. What is the difference between 'overdrawn' and having an 'overdraft'? (*5 marks*)

(g) On 24 March Mr Small pays his car repair bill of £66.50 using a cheque.

(i) In which column of the statement would £66.50 be entered? (*1 mark*)

(ii) What would Mr Small's balance be after this cheque had been cleared? (*1 mark*)

A MEMBER OF THE ROYAL BANK OF SCOTLAND GROUP

SPECIMEN
Mr. Small
1 You Place
Mytown
Homeshire

IN ACCOUNT WITH
WILLIAMS & GLYN'S BANK LIMITED

1234567890 ACCOUNT NO

7 PAGE

DATE	PARTICULARS	DEBITS	CREDITS	BALANCE
1983				
1 Mar	Balance Forward			250.00
7 Mar	012621	66.55		183.45
9 Mar	012622	200.00		16.55 DR
12 Mar	CC		300.00	283.45
15 Mar	7% Brit TPt DV		56.25	339.70
16 Mar	BG		60.00	399.70
17 Mar	012625	199.00		200.70
19 Mar	012623	90.20		110.50
20 Mar	DD	100.00		10.50
21 Mar	SO	7.50		3.00
21 Mar	CH	10.00		7.00 DR
23 Mar	BG		500.00	493.00

BG Bank Giro Credit
DD Direct Debit
CC Cash & or Chqs.
DV Dividend
CH Charges
IA Item Advised
DR Overdrawn Balance
SO Standing Order
TF Inter-Account Transfer

(h) Williams and Glyn's is known as a commercial bank. Name **three** other commercial banks. *(3 marks)*

(SWEB 1983)

2 (a) What are the safeguards which may be used when drawing a cheque?

(b) Why have cheques replaced cash as the most widespread means of settling debts?

(c) Describe **three** other methods of payment which are provided by the commercial banks.

(London January 1983)

3 (a) Distinguish between a bank overdraft and a bank loan. *(2 marks)*

(b) When might a bank manager recommend his customer to use one of these forms of finance rather than the other? *(8 marks)*

(WJEC (GCE) June 1983)

Unit 10 Other kinds of bank and methods of payment

1 Pair the most suitable method of payment provided by the Post Office for **each** of the following:

(a) Cash on Delivery	*(i)* A special offer by a cereal company for a toy priced 10p.
(b) Telegraphic Money Order	*(ii)* A firm wishes to supply £10 worth of goods to an individual of an unknown credit standing.
(c) Stamps	*(iii)* A person filling in a football pools coupon price 50p.
(d) Postal Order	*(iv)* A person wishing to send cash through the post.
(e) Registered Post	*(v)* Parents sending money urgently to a daughter who has lost her money while on holiday in Scotland.

(WJEC (CSE) 1982)

2 In what ways are the functions of the Bank of England different from those of a commercial bank? *(NIEC (GCE) June 1982)*

Unit 11 Buying and selling on credit

1 Look carefully at this price ticket for a TV set. Then answer the questions which follow.

> CASH PRICE: £200
>
> TERMS: deposit £30 and
> either £10 a month over 18 months
> or £8 a month over 2 years.

(a) How much does the TV set cost if it is paid for immediately?

(b) *(i)* What is the hire-purchase price over 18 months?

(ii) What is the hire-purchase over 2 years?

(c) Explain why there is a difference between the answer to **(a)** and the answers to **(b)**.

(WJEC (CSE) 1981)

2 (a) Distinguish between hire-purchase and credit sales. *(10 marks)*

(b) Briefly explain the role of the finance company in hire-purchase transactions. *(5 marks)*

(c) State, with your reasons, whether you consider hire-purchase to be advantageous to consumers. *(5 marks)*

(WJEC (GCE) June 1982)

3 Choose a suitable method for buying each of the following on credit:

(a) a car; **(b)** a house; **(c)** clothes; **(d)** a meal.

Select a different type of credit in each case and explain *(i)* its distinctive features and *(ii)* the reasons for your choice. *(London January 1982)*

Unit 12 Advertising and marketing

1 (a) Describe the work of advertising agencies. *(5 marks)*

(b) Explain **four** ways in which advertising benefits the consumer. *(4 marks)*

(c) How does the Advertising Standards Authority protect the consumer? *(3 marks)*

(YHREB (Syllabus B) 1982)

2 (a) Explain what is meant by the market for a product. *(4 marks)*

(b) Outline the possible marketing activities of a large manufacturing business. *(10 marks)*

(c) Show how any **one** of these marketing activities can contribute to the increased profitability of the business. *(6 marks)*

(AEB June 1983)

Unit 13 Consumer protection

1 Which of the Acts listed below is most appropriate in protecting the consumer from the following incidents?

1955 Food and Drugs Act	1971 Unsolicited Goods Act
1963 Weights and Measures Act	1974 Consumer Credit Act
1968 Trade Descriptions Act	

(a) Buying a bottle marked 'Pure Lemon Juice' containing artificial flavouring and colouring not included in the list of ingredients. *(1 mark)*

(b) Buying a coat described as 'waterproof' which does not keep the rain out. *(1 mark)*

(c) A firm sending goods to you which you have not ordered, then demanding that you pay for them. *(1 mark)*

(NWREB 1983)

2 (a) Describe the rôle of the Office of Fair Trading in providing consumer protection. *(8 marks)*

(b) How does

(i) the Trade Descriptions Act (1968) and *(6 marks)*

(ii) the Sale of Goods Act (1979) help to provide such protection? *(6 marks)*

(AEB June 1983)

3 (a) Why do consumers require protection? *(6 marks)*

(b) In what ways are consumers given such protection in the United Kingdom *(14 marks)*

(WJEC (GCE) June 1983)

Unit 14 Insurance

1 Show briefly the differences between **two** of the following pairs of terms used in insurance.

(a) premium and policy

(b) insurable risks and uninsurable risks

(c) indemnity and utmost good faith

(d) proposal and cover note *(10 marks)*

(YHREB (Syllabus A) 1982)

2 (a) What do you understand by the 'statistical basis' of insurance? *(8 marks)*

(b) 'A cannot insure B's premises against the risk of fire but that does not mean that B's premises are uninsurable.' Explain this statement. *(6 marks)*

(c) B insures his stock against the risk of fire for £8000. The stock however is only worth £6000. State, with your reasons, how much B will receive in the event of a total loss. *(6 marks)*

(WJEC (GCE) June 1983)

3 (a) With regard to insurance, describe the work of

(i) a broker,

(ii) an agent,

(iii) an actuary. *(10 marks)*

(b) Discuss the factors which an insurance company is likely to take into account when fixing its rates for motor car insurance. *(10 marks)*

(JMB June 1982)

Unit 15 Transport

1 (a) Give **four** reasons for transporting goods by road rather than by rail. *(4 marks)*

(b) What are the basic differences between a tramp steamer and a cargo liner? *(4 marks)*

(c) In connection with rail transport explain the terms APT and Inter-City. *(4 marks)*

(d) *(i)* State the word that correctly fits the following description:
'A portable structure filled with goods which can be moved with its contents by road, rail, sea or air.'

(ii) What is described by the following statement?
'A fixed and permanent installation which conveys gas, oil or water over or under land and sea.' *(2½ marks)*

(e) Write an account of the transport of electronic goods from Switzerland to London, including all the following terms in the correct context:
Less handling; containerization; roll-on/roll-off; speed; safety; cost; pilferage; TIR *(8 marks)*

(SEREB 1982)

2 Explain **with examples** why the means of transport chosen for a consignment of goods will depend on:

(a) the bulkiness and weight of goods (*4 marks*)
(b) the distance involved (*4 marks*)
(c) the value of the goods in relation to their weight (*4 marks*)
(d) the urgency of delivery (*4 marks*)

(You should assume that rail, road, sea (or waterway) and air transport are available.)

(*OLE June 1982*)

Unit 16 Communications

1 Describe **each** of the following Post Office services outlining the service they offer. Explain carefully how they might be useful to a mail order company.

(a) Registered letter post
(b) COD
(c) Freepost
(d) Certificate of Posting

(*LREB (Syllabus A) 1983*)

2 Describe **three** different ways in which British Telecom facilities can be used to send business information from one firm to another.

(*SUJB 1982*)

Unit 17 Business accounts

1 In 1982 a trader's net purchases were £85 000 and net sales amounted to £125 000. The trader paid £12 000 in wages to staff, £2000 for heating and lighting, £1000 for postage and telephone.

(a) Calculate the trader's gross profit.
(b) Calculate his business expenses.
(c) Calculate his net profit.
(d) Name **one** other business expense the trader may have to pay.

(*WJEC (CSE) 1983*)

2

Balance Sheet of A. Public Co. Ltd.

	£		£
Capital A	40 000	Premises	50000
B	30 000	Equipment	10000
C	10 000	Stock of goods	25000
Creditors	20 000	Debtors	9000
		Cash/bank	6000
	£100 000		£100 000

(a) Define *(i)* fixed capital and *(ii)* working capital.

(b) Using the balance sheet above, calculate *(i)* fixed capital and *(ii)* working capital for A. Public Co. Ltd.

(c) Describe **three** possible sources of capital as indicated in the balance sheet by the letters A, B and C.

(d) How could leasing help this company to increase its stock of fixed capital?

(*London June 1982*)

Unit 18 Private sector firms

1 (a) From which sources does a sole trader obtain his capital? (*3 marks*)

(b) Which type of shareholder takes the most risk in a business, but may also gain a larger share of the profits? What is the minimum and maximum number of shareholders in a public limited company? (*3 marks*)

(c) A public company may issue new shares; one type free of charge and one type at a reduced price. What are the names given to these two types of share issues? (*4 marks*)

(d) The Chairman reported to the shareholders that the company had made a very small profit during the year and that consequently dividends would be low. Additionally, turnover was down by £3 million.

Write the word or words from the passage above that match each of the definitions below:

(i) Funds remaining after all expenses have been met.
(ii) Reward for investing in the company.

(iii) Persons who provide capital but do not take part in management.
(iv) Net sales of the company *(6 marks)*
(e) What are the benefits of a cumulative preference share? *(2½ marks)*
(f) Explain the differences between limited liability and unlimited liability. *(4 marks)*
(SEREB 1982)

2

CO OP

Anderson Strathclyde PLC

PROVINCIAL BUILDING SOCIETY

BRITISH GAS

The symbols shown above represent some of the different forms of public and private ownership to be found in the United Kingdom economy.

(a) What is the name given to this type of economy? *1*
(b) Which of the above organizations are registered as friendly societies? *2*
(c) *(i)* Which **one** must prepare a memorandum of association? *1*
(ii) Explain the purpose of this document *2*
(d) *(i)* Which **one** is known, in the United Kingdom, as a public corporation? *1*
(ii) Outline the main arguments for and against the state ownership of a public utility. *6*
(e) A public company may raise capital by issuing different types of shares and other securities.
(i) Describe **two** such shares or securities and indicate any ways in which they are different from each other. *4*
(ii) Mention **two** ways in which the Stock Exchange assists in the buying and selling of such shares. *4*
(f) List **four** ways in which a share in a retail co-operative society is different from an ordinary share in a public limited company. *4*

Approximate marks 25

(WMEB (16+) 1983)

3 *X* has £5000 invested in a business in which he is a partner.
Y holds shares of £1 each in a limited company.
Z holds secured debentures to the extent of £5000 in a limited company.
All three businesses fail because they are unable to pay debts extending to £100 000.
How will *X, Y* and *Z* each be affected? *(6, 6, 4 marks)*
(OLE June 1982)

4 Consider a business owned by a single proprietor and a business owned by a public limited company.
(a) How might **each** business obtain the necessary capital?
(b) How is each business managed?
(c) What happens in **each** case to any profits which are made?
(d) The single proprietor may decide to form a private company to run his business. Give reasons why he might do so.
(NIEC (GCE) June 1982)

Unit 19 The issue of shares and the Stock Exchange

1 Miss Anna Buyer has bought 500 ordinary shares, at a cost of £1.50 per share, in Arc Production P.L.C. which, until recently, traded as a private limited company.
(a) What is the name given to the above document? *1*
(b) What is the nominal value of Miss Buyer's investment? *2*
(c) Explain **two** possible disadvantages of Arc Production becoming a public limited company. *4*
(d) What information would you find in the memorandum of association? *5*

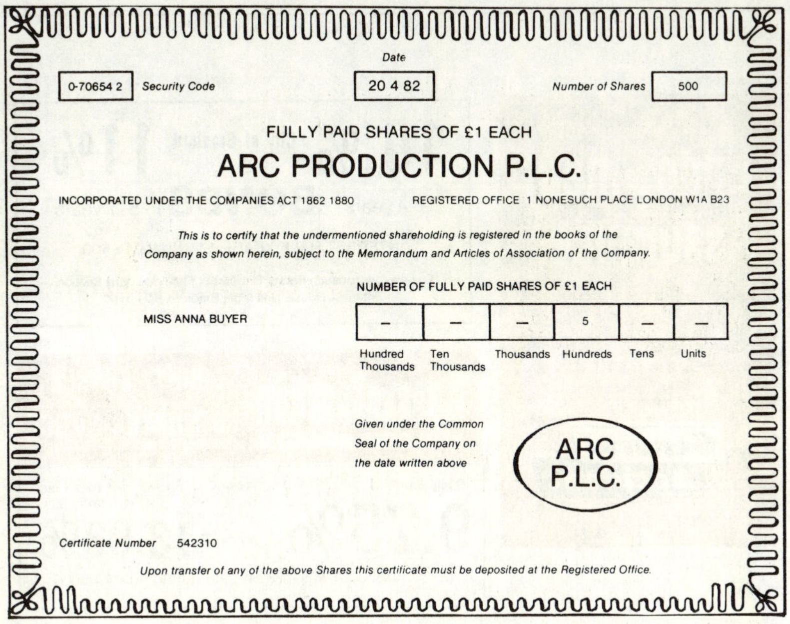
Date

0-70654 2 Security Code | 20 4 82 | Number of Shares 500

FULLY PAID SHARES OF £1 EACH

ARC PRODUCTION P.L.C.

INCORPORATED UNDER THE COMPANIES ACT 1862 1880 REGISTERED OFFICE 1 NONESUCH PLACE LONDON W1A B23

This is to certify that the undermentioned shareholding is registered in the books of the Company as shown herein, subject to the Memorandum and Articles of Association of the Company.

NUMBER OF FULLY PAID SHARES OF £1 EACH

MISS ANNA BUYER

Hundred Thousands	Ten Thousands	Thousands	Hundreds	Tens	Units
–	–	–	5	–	–

Given under the Common Seal of the Company on the date written above

ARC P.L.C.

Certificate Number 542310

Upon transfer of any of the above Shares this certificate must be deposited at the Registered Office.

(e) What assistance might Arc Production have had from a merchant bank in their change to a public company? *3*

(f) Describe the process by which these shares could have been bought on the London Stock Exchange. *6*

(g) Give **three** reasons why the London Stock Exchange is of great benefit to investors. *3*

24 marks

(WMEB (16+) 1982)

2 The function of the Stock Exchange is to act as market for securities.

(a) Why is this function important? *(5 marks)*

(b) Briefly indicate the main types of securities referred to in the above statement *(5 marks)*

(c) Explain how the purchase and sale of securities takes place on the London Stock Exchange. *(10 marks)*

(WJEC (GCE) June 1982)

Unit 20 Public enterprise

1 Nationalized industries are often organized as public corporations.

(a) Name **two** nationalized industries. *(2 marks)*

(b) Describe **four** main features of a public corporation. *(4 marks)*

(c) Explain **three** ways in which a public limited company differs from a public corporation. *(3 marks)*

(d) What are the main purposes of the Annual General Meeting of a public limited company? *(3 marks)*

(YHREB (Syllabus B) 1982)

2 (a) What are the main features which distinguish public sector enterprises from private sector enterprises? *(4 marks)*

(b) By what methods does the central government control and finance public enterprises? *(12 marks)*

(c) How do these methods differ with regard to the public enterprises operated by local authorities? *(4 marks)*

(AEB November 1983)

Unit 21 Income and saving

1 Read the following carefully. Then answer **all** the questions which follow.
Suppose that in your first year at work you earn £2600. Your employer deducts £200 from your wages for National Insurance contributions and £400 for Income Tax.

(a) Calculate your annual 'take-home pay'.

(b) Name the type of Income Tax which is deducted regularly from your wage packet.

(c) Name **two** benefits available from National Insurance contributions. *(WJEC (CSE) 1983)*

2 Shown above are five different ways in which people can invest their savings.

(a) Select **three** of these methods and for each **one** explain a particular advantage which it has over the others. *6*

(b) *(i)* Explain the ways in which an endowment assurance is different from a whole life assurance. *3*

(ii) Name **one** principle of insurance which must be borne in mind when filling in a proposal form for endowment assurance. *1*

(c) Gilt edged securities are another form of investment. Explain the meaning of this term. 2

(d) *(i)* What tax is referred to by the Lambeth Building Society in the term 'Basic Tax Paid'? *2*

(ii) Is this a direct or an indirect tax? *1*

(iii) Name **two** other taxes levied by central government. *2*

(iv) Mention **two** main areas of central government expenditure. *2*

(e) Which method of saving shown above allows people to have a financial interest in many companies without directly owning shares in them? *1*

(f) Explain, briefly, how unit trusts operate. *3*

Approximate marks 23

(WMEB (16+) 1983)

Unit 22 Government spending and income

1 'I pay tax on my wages, on the tape recorder I have just bought and even on the house in which I live!'

(a) Name and describe the tax this person pays on each of the above three items. Give an example of a benefit he might receive for each of these three taxes. *(12 marks)*

(b) What other deduction might be made from this person's wage packet? *(2 marks)*

(c) What is the 'Budget' and who is responsible for it? *(4 marks)*

(d) What do you understand by 'National Income'? *(2 marks)*

(NWREB 1983)

2 Study the table below and answer the questions which follow.

Local Authority — Current Revenue (£ million)

	1969	1974	1979
Grants from central government	2099	4738	11415
Rates	1678	3089	6584
Other revenue	986	2020	3925
Total	4763	9847	21924

(i) Use the information in the table above to describe the main features of local authority revenue between 1969 and 1979. *(6 marks)*

(ii) Why has there been public criticism about the way in which local people contribute to the cost of local government services? *(6 marks)*

(iii) Give **two** arguments against replacing the revenue from domestic rates by extra central government grants. *(4 marks)*

(iv) Discuss **one** alternative to rates (other than extra grants) as a source of revenue for local authorities. *(4 marks)*

(JMB June 1983)

Answers to examination questions

Unit 1 Production

1 Food processing is manufacturing (secondary industry); the remainder are extractive (primary industry).

2 Barter: goods are exchanged but no money is involved.
Money: anything which is acceptable in the payment of a debt e.g. notes, coins, cheques, credit cards.
Economic interdependence: in a chain of production each specialist part of the chain relies on other parts for its own survival (see Q3 below).
Mass production: output takes place on a larger scale with the possibility of economies of scale.
Standard of living: a measure of the wealth of a country or individual e.g. the United Kingdom has a higher standard of living than India.
Specialization: when individuals, firms, regions and countries concentrate on the production of a narrow range of goods and services (see Fig. 1.4).

3 (a) production can be divided into:
extractive, manufacturing, constructive, commerce and direct services.
Extractive means taking goods from the land and sea e.g. farming, mining, fishing.
Manufacturing means . . .
An alternative approach is to divide production into primary, secondary and tertiary and then to describe each of these.

(b) Interdependence means that each branch of production relies on other branches for its own survival. If one branch is not functioning properly then other branches suffer. For example:
extractive industry needs machines from manufacturing industry, buildings from constructive industry, transport (commerce) for its raw materials and doctors (direct service) to keep its workforce healthy.
constructive industry needs sand from extractive industry, shovels from manufacturing industry, loans from banks (commerce) and the police (direct service) to regulate traffic near motorway repairs.
Use the same approach for the other branches of production.

4 (a) Define specialization or the division of labour and list its advantages (see Unit 1.7).

(b) Workers may get bored — lower output results. Occupational disease — e.g. continuous working with asbestos.
If products are non-standardized individual skill is needed.
Firm may be too small to allow specialization.

Unit 2 Retailing

1 *(i)* a co-operative *(ii)* discount stores *(iii)* a market *(iv)* a department store *(v)* a unit shop *(vi)* a chain store *(vii)* a mobile shop *(viii)* a supermarket or superstore *(ix)* automatic vending *(x)* mail order.

2 (a) See hypermarkets and department stores, Unit 2.3.

(b) See Unit 3.4.

3 See Unit 2.4.

Unit 3 Wholesaling

1 (a) The wholesaler:
buys finished goods in bulk from home and foreign manufacturers
finds a market for these goods and
then breaks bulk so that the retailer is able to buy them (or any of the other services to manufacturers and retailers, Unit 3.1).

(b) Small independent retailers could be corner shops dealing in groceries and other items and trying to compete with the lower prices charged by supermarkets. Wholesalers can help the small retailer by running voluntary chains or cash and carry warehouses (see Unit 3.4).

(c) Large selling organizations such as chain stores, manufacturers' own shops and mail order firms can buy in large bulk directly from manufacturers. Packaging, branding and widespread advertising have also encouraged this trend towards the elimination of the wholesaler.

(d) The important point is that the wholesaling functions cannot be eliminated and must be performed even if a wholesaler is not used (see Unit 3.3).

2 (a) Consumer goods are goods bought by final consumers (the public). Examples of such goods are televisions and cars.

(b) See Fig. 3.2.

(c) This part is concerned with the differences between the rôles of retailers and wholesalers. The wholesaler, for example,

buys from manufacturers— which small retailers are unable to do
buys in larger bulk than retailers— with the exception of chain stores
usually sells to retailers— retailers sell to the public
usually holds larger stocks than the retailer— the small retailer only buys in small quantities
does not carry out large-scale advertising— which large-scale retailers undertake
does not have to provide after-sales service— which retailers of, for example, electrical goods usually provide.

3 (a) See Unit 3.2.

(b) See Unit 3.4.

Unit 4 Channels of distribution

1 See Units 4.4 and 15.5.

2 (a) An auction is a method of selling where prospective purchasers bid for the commodity which is sold to the highest bidder. An auction is used for commodities which cannot be graded and have to be sold by sample (see **(c)**) on a spot basis (see **(d)**).

(b) Grading is a method of classifying a commodity so that the prospective purchaser knows precisely what he is purchasing without having to inspect the commodity. One classification of wheat, for example, is US dark northern spring No. 1 14%. If commodities can be graded they can be sold on a futures basis (see Unit 4.5).

(c) Sampling occurs for commodities which cannot be graded because consignments vary so much in quality. A prospective buyer, therefore, has to sample a small part of the consignment to find out the quality of the whole consignment. Commodities which have to be sampled include tea.

(d) A spot transaction is an agreement for the immediate delivery of a commodity at a fixed (spot) price. Such transactions can be made for all commodities. A futures transaction is an agreement for the future delivery of a commodity at a price agreed on the day on which the contract is signed. Such transactions can only be made for those commodities which can be accurately graded e.g. wheat, cocoa.

Unit 5 The middlemen of trade

1 A summary of the main points required is given in the following table; you should not, however, attempt to present your answer in this form.

	Agent (A) Principal (P)	*Possesses goods*	*Type of trade*	*Buys and/or sells*	*Reward*
Merchant	P	yes	buying and selling	in own name	profit
Factor	A	yes	selling only	in own name	commission
Broker	A	no	buying and selling	in principal's name	commission
Forwarding agent	A	yes	not a trader – arranges transport	—	fee

Unit 6 Foreign trade

1 (a) *(i)* When the value of exports is less than the value of imports, e.g. in 1978 goods imported exceeded goods exported by £1135m.

(ii) When the value of exports is greater than the value of imports, e.g. in 1978 goods and

services exported exceeded goods and services imported by £1000m.

(b) Visible trade.

(c) £2135m (+£1000m = −£1135m + £2135m).

(d) Banking and insurance.

(e) Tourism, shipping.

2 (a) See Unit 6.3.

(b) *(i)* The United Kingdom government helps international trade: through the BOTB and the ECGD – by providing trade information from embassies abroad – through its membership of GATT (see Units 6.8 and 6.13).

(ii) The United Kingdom government restricts international trade by:
imposing tariffs, quotas, embargoes and by subsidizing United Kingdom industry (see Unit 6.13).

3 (a) Warehousing is the storing of goods until they are required and is carried out at all stages in the chain of production.
Warehousing is important because:
finished goods have to be stored until they are required by consumers,
this particularly applies to seasonal goods e.g. Christmas cards,
consumers can obtain their requirements on demand because shops hold stocks of goods,
it allows mass production, and production lines can be quickly cleared,
goods in seasonal supply can be stored e.g. apples.

(b) Emphasize that bonded warehouses exist in home trade and foreign trade (see Unit 6.11).

Unit 7 Business documents used in home trade

1 (a) The numbers are catalogue numbers — goods do not have to be described in detail.

(b) Modern Fashions is a trader — trade discount allows a profit to be made.

(c) Cash discount of 5% of £400 = £20
Amount paid = £380.

(d) Payment is expected at the latest by 10 August 1982 when no cash discount is given.

(e) Local newspapers — customers come from a small geographical area; pamphlets through doors — cheap form of advertising.

(f) Advantage: paperwork is reduced because only one supplier is dealt with.
Disadvantage: goods could be cheaper elsewhere.

2 (a) and **(b)** See Units 7. to 7.9.

(c) Amount owing £250
Cash discount of 5% of £250 = £12.50
Amount paid = £237.50.

Unit 8 Business documents used in foreign trade

1 Bill of lading, charter party, consignment note (see Units 7.5, 8.2 and 15.5).

2 (a) CIF stands for cost, insurance and freight and is a price quotation used in international trade. A price of £1000 CIF includes the cost of the goods plus insurance and transport charges to the port of destination. An importer would have to pay additional charges for transport and insurance from the port to his factory.

(b) A bill of lading.

(c) *(i)* A mate's receipt or bill of lading are receipts to show that goods have been received on board ship.

(ii) The bill of lading is a document of title and is sent to the importer. When the goods reach the port of destination the importer can present the bill of lading and claim his goods. Before handing over the goods the chief officer of the ship will check the importer's bill of lading against a copy of the bill of lading kept on board ship.

(d) An *ad valorem* duty is a percentage tax based on the value of a good. Thus an import duty of 10% would raise £100 in tax on imports with a value of £1000.

Unit 9 Banking: the commercial banks

1 (a) Current account.

(b) Cheque numbers.

(c) Gilt-edged stock.

(d) A hire purchase payment (see Unit 9.7).

(e) *(i)* Safer than being paid by cash.

(ii) Less cash on the employer's premises results in lower insurance premiums.

(f) An overdraft allows a current account holder to write cheques in excess of the balance in the account, up to an agreed maximum e.g. Mr. Small may be allowed an overdraft limit of £100. The amount of the overdraft that he actually uses is the amount overdrawn which is likely to vary in amount and in time e.g. £16.55 for 3 days and then £7.00 for 2 days.

(g) *(i)* Debit column.

(ii) £493.00 – £66.50 = £426.50.

(h) Barclays, Midland and Lloyds.

2 (a) To prevent the cheque being altered the drawer should write the amount in words and figures. If the cheque is for £10, the amounts should be written as—*Ten pounds only*—and shown in figures as *£10-00*. The cheque should also be crossed (Fig. 9.4).

(b) Cheques are safer than cash; cheques are easier to carry than cash; cheques are now widely accepted in shops because of cheque guarantee cards; many employees are paid by bank giro credit into bank current accounts which use cheques (see Unit 9.8).

(c) Standing order; direct debit; bank giro credit (see Unit 9.7 and 9.8).

3 (a) This part of the question does not ask for a description of a loan and an overdraft but asks for the differences between them. For example, a loan is a fixed amount and an overdraft is a variable amount, etc (see Unit 9.10).

(b) See Unit 9.10.

Unit 10 Other kinds of bank and methods of payment

1 (a) *(ii)*; **(b)** *(v)*; **(c)** *(i)*; **(d)** *(iii)*; **(e)** *(iv)*.

2 This question does not ask for a description of the functions of each type of bank but asks for the differences between the banks.

For example, the Bank of England:

issues notes in England and Wales— the commercial banks do not,

acts as a banker to the Government and to some banks— the commercial banks act as bankers to individuals and firms,

enforces Government economic policy— the commercial banks do not although they have to follow instructions given to them by the Bank of England,

manages the National Debt by paying interest to those who hold Government stock— commercial banks could fulfil a similar rôle by making interest and dividend payments on behalf of companies,

is owned by the Government and is non-profit making— commercial banks are organized as public limited companies with the aim of making profits.

Unit 11 Buying and selling on credit

1 (a) £200.

(b) *(i)* £30 + £180 = £210.

(ii) £30 + £192 = £222.

(c) An extra £12 has to be paid because of the longer period of credit.

2 (a) The question asks for the differences between the two forms of credits.

For example:

under HP the consumer is not the owner until payment of the final instalment— under credit sale the consumer is the owner after paying the deposit.

For further differences see Unit 11.2.

(b) See Fig. 11.3.

(c) The question asks for the advantages and disadvantages of hire purchase. For example: expensive goods can be used immediately but ownership does not pass to the consumer until the final instalment is paid.

For further advantages and disadvantages see Units 11.2 and 11.7.

3 (a) Hire purchase *(i)* See Unit 11.2 *(ii)* HP is suitable for buying a car because a car is expensive, has a long life and a good re-sale value (see Unit 11.2).

(b) A mortgage *(i)* See Unit 11.5 *(ii)* A mortgage is used because the house can be given as security for the long-term loan.

(c) Credit sale *(i)* See Unit 11.2 *(ii)* Clothes are suitable for one person only and have a poor re-sale value.

(d) Credit card *(i)* See Unit 9.10 *(ii)* Meals are not expensive and a short-term method of credit is needed. The restaurant also needs a guarantee of payment.

Unit 12 Advertising and marketing

1 (a) See Unit 12.4.
(b) See Unit 12.6.
(c) See Unit 12.5.

2 (a) The market is the geographical area over which buyers and sellers are in contact with each other e.g. the United Kingdom market for cars. Buyers and sellers could be in immediate contact with each other, as on the Baltic Exchange, or on a world-wide basis via communication links, as in the foreign exchange market.

(b) A number of activities are possible e.g. advertising, sales promotion (which itself covers many activities), market research, franchising.

(c) The link between increased advertising, for example, and increased profits should be clearly made as should the distinction between gross and net profits (see Unit 17.4).

Unit 13 Consumer protection

1 (a) Food and Drugs Act **(b)** Trade Descriptions Act
(c) Unsolicited Goods Act.

2 (a) See Unit 13.4.
(b) *(i)* The Act is enforced by Trading Standards Officers (see Unit 13.3).
(ii) The Act is enforced by the consumer (see Unit 13.2).

3 (a) See Unit 13.1.
(b) A wide range of answers is possible. A very good answer should contain information about help from Government, trade associations and independent organizations.

Unit 14 Insurance

1 (a) A premium is a regular payment by the insured to the insurance company to cover a particular risk. A policy is the contract of insurance between the insured and insurance company (see Unit 14.7).

(b) Insurable risks are risks which can be insured e.g. fire, theft because reliable statistics exist which allow premiums to be calculated. Uninsurable risks cannot be insured by anyone because no reliable statistics exist e.g. the risk of making a loss due to bad management (see Unit 14.13).

(c) Indemnity (see Unit 14.9). Utmost good faith (see Unit 14.6).

(d) A proposal is an application to take out insurance. The cover note is proof of insurance while the policy is being prepared (see Units 14.5 and 14.7).

2 (a) Risks can only be insured if there are reliable statistics which can be used to calculate premiums. Further details are given in Unit 14.13.

(b) A cannot insure B's premises because A has no insurable interest in those premises. B can, however, insure the premises (see Unit 14.6).

(c) B has over-insured the premises and will only receive £6000 because of indemnity (see Unit 14.11).

3 (a) *(i)* See Unit 14.3.
(ii) See Unit 14.3.
(iii) See Unit 14.13.
(b) See Units 14.12 and 14.13.

Unit 15 Transport

1 (a) Road is quicker than rail over short distances. Road is cheaper than rail over short distances. Road is more flexible — rail runs to a timetable. Road involves less handling of goods — with rail more than one form of transport is usually needed.

(b) Cargo liners run to a fixed timetable — tramps do not.
Cargo liners run on fixed routes — tramps do not.
The freight charges for liners are set by shipping conferences — the charges for tramps are set on freight markets e.g. the Baltic Exchange.
Cargo liners usually carry mixed cargoes — tramps carry one type of cargo.

(c) APT is the Advanced Passenger Train which is capable of high speeds.
Inter-City refers to passenger trains operating between the major cities e.g. London to Birmingham.

(d) *(i)* A container.
(ii) A pipeline.

(e) The Transport Internationale Routier (TIR) *containerization* system is less *costly* than using rail or air. In Switzerland a container is filled with electronic goods and the container is transferred to a lorry. The lorry is able to pass through W Germany and Belgium at *speed* because customs authorities check only that the seals on the container have not been broken. When the lorry reaches the channel port it is driven on to a *roll-on-roll-off* ferry but the container is not unloaded. This results in *less handling,* increased *safety* and less *pilferage.* The lorry is driven off the ferry at the United Kingdom port and continues to London where the container is unloaded.

2 Many answers are possible. All should refer to the four forms of transport named in the question. For example:

A bulky machine which is difficult to transport is carried by road, particularly over short distances. Loading and unloading is difficult if more than one form of transport is used. For longer distances rail is often used, particularly if the goods are heavy, e.g. coal. Expensive watches are sent by air from Switzerland to London because the watches can bear the high costs of air transport. Watches are also low-weight goods which are relatively cheap to transport by air. Food and medicines needed for an emergency are transported by air rather than by sea. Sea is cheaper but the goods have to be delivered urgently.

Unit 16 Communications

1 **(a)** Used by customers sending cash payments to the mail order company (see Unit 16.2).

(b) See Unit 16.2.

(c) Used by the mail order company to encourage customers to send for catalogues (see Unit 16.2).

(d) Used by mail order agents to provide proof that, for example, orders have been sent to the mail order company (see Unit 16.2).

2 The question asks for descriptions of British Telecom and not Post Office facilities. Answers include telex, the telephone, Prestel (see Unit 16.3).

Unit 17 Business accounts

1 **(a)** £125 000 – £85 000 = £40 000.

(b) £15 000.

(c) £40 000 – £15 000 = £25 000.

(d) Rates.

2 **(a)** *(i)* Fixed capital is the same as fixed assets (see Unit 17.2).

(ii) See Unit 17.2.

(b) *(i)* £60 000.

(ii) £40 000 – £20 000 = £20 000.

(c) Ordinary shares, preference shares, cumulative preference shares.

(d) See Unit 11.4.

Unit 18 Private sector firms

1 **(a)** See Unit 18.3.

(b) Ordinary shareholder. Minimum of two with no maximum.

(c) Free of charge — scrip; at a reduced price — rights.

(d) *(i)* profit *(ii)* dividend *(iii)* shareholders *(iv)* turnover.

(e) Dividends partly paid or not paid are owed to the shareholder who will be paid when the company has made sufficient profit.

(f) See Unit 18.3 and 18.6.

2 Answers not given.

3 X loses £5000. If he is an ordinary partner his personal assets can be claimed by creditors. If he is a limited partner then he has limited liability and can only lose £5000.

Y loses 5000 shares. The value of his loss depends on the price he paid for them. If they cost £3.00 each his loss is £15 000.

Z is a secured creditor of the company which means he has a claim on part of the assets of the company if the company is unable to repay what it owes him. These assets are sold and the proceeds used to pay £5000 to Z, who loses nothing.

4 **(a)** Sources of capital for single proprietor and plc (see Units 18.3 and 18.6).

(b) Business owned by a single proprietor is managed by the owner. Plc is run by managers and directors — the directors are elected by the shareholders.

(c) Single proprietor's profits kept by him or ploughed back into the business. Plc's profits distributed to shareholders by way of dividends or ploughed back into the business.

(d) The main reason is to obtain limited liability. Other reasons are:
to establish a separate legal existence for the firm, which will still exist if one shareholder dies; there is more opportunity to raise capital because the number of shareholders is unlimited (note that it is a private company and shares cannot be sold on a stock exchange).

Unit 19 The issue of shares and the Stock Exchange

1 Answers not given.

2 (a) See Unit 19.8.

(b) Gilt-edged stock — loans issued by the United Kingdom Government. Ordinary shares (equity) — of public limited companies plus debentures (loan stock), cumulative preference shares, preference shares etc of public limited companies.

(c) See Fig. 19.4. Explanations of broker, jobber, stock exchange account and settlement day are needed.

Unit 20 Public enterprise

1 (a) The National Coal Board, British Rail.

(b) See Unit 20.2.

(c)

Plc	*Public corporation*
owned by individuals and firms acting as shareholders	owned by the state
financed by shareholders	financed by the state
the major motive is to make profit	may have other motives as well as profits e.g. providing employment

(d) To allow shareholders to:
question the directors on the running of the company; approve the company's annual accounts; elect directors; approve the dividend to be paid to shareholders.

2 (a) See Fig. 20.1.

(b) The Government controls a public enterprise by:
setting up the enterprise as a public corporation by Act of Parliament
a Government Minister appointing a board of directors to run the enterprise
allowing MPs to ask questions in Parliament on the running of the enterprise
setting financial targets for each industry e.g. a profit target. For the finance of a public corporation see Unit 20.2.

(c) Local authority enterprises are local bus services, swimming baths etc.
They are:
subject to the control of elected councillors; run by council employees; financed from rates and the Rate Support Grant.

Unit 21 Income and saving

1 (a) £2600 − £600 = £2000.

(b) PAYE is the method of deducting income tax.

(c) Unemployment benefit, state pension.

2 Answers not given.

Unit 22 Government spending and income

1 (a) Wages — income tax (see Unit 22.2). Tape recorder — VAT (see Unit 22.3). House-rates (see Unit 22.10).
Income tax and VAT are part of central government revenue used to pay for social security, Defence, the Health Service.
Rates are part of local government expenditure used to pay, for example, for education.

(b) National Insurance.

(c) See Unit 22.8.

(d) A measure of total earnings in the United Kingdom.

2 Answers not given.

Index

Bold type indicates whole sections.